THE OPULENT INTERIORS OF THE GILDED AGE

ALL 203 PHOTOGRAPHS FROM "ARTISTIC HOUSES"

With New Text by
Arnold Lewis, James Turner
and Steven McQuillin

DOVER PUBLICATIONS, INC.
New York

ACKNOWLEDGMENTS

Several friends have given us invaluable assistance, and we are indebted to them for their specific contributions and general support. We thank Miriam Stewart for her research on Boston families and houses, Lynne Marthey, Phyllis Clark, Catherine Fruhan and Charles Jeffrey for their observant comments on the photographs, Tracy Robinson for raising pertinent questions at the beginning of this study, Lynn Maston for her photographs of Boston exteriors and Mike Hubartt for his archival efforts.

We are also grateful to owners and managers of properties who provided us with condition reports of extant houses: Sister Helen Loretta, Alice Wadsworth Strong, Larry Nemer, Marylouise Lynch, Peter Woodbury, Anne T. Holmes and Walter Weller.

The assistance of many individuals who work for libraries, museums, educational institutions, local historical societies, city governments, landmark agencies and historical commissions enabled us to enrich the text and captions with useful contemporary information. We thank Jefferson Moak, Philadelphia Historical Commission; William McKenzie Woodward, Rhode Island Preservation Commission; Esley Hamilton, St. Louis County Department of Parks and Recreation; Helen Login, Public Library, Millburn, New Jersey; Janice Stanland, Pennsylvania Academy of the Fine Arts; Lewis Gould, University of Texas; Jeanne Henderson, Public Library, Watertown, Massachusetts; Cynthia Howk, Landmark Society of Western New York; Maizy Wedderburn, Newark Public Library; Greer Hardwicke, Brookline Historical Commission; Elizabeth Roland, Sawyer Library, Gloucester Massachusetts; Robert Starkey, East Orange Public Library; Lola Dudley, Mamaroneck Free Library; Valerie Gores, Yonkers Public Library; Ruth Hagstrom, Gloucester, Massachusetts; Mara Kerr, Oswego County Historical Society; William Presson, Cape Ann Historical Association; Herbert Bengtson, Manchester Historical Society; Patricia Schaap, Historian, Livingston County, New York; Thomas Hoctor, City Historian, New Rochelle, New York; Martha Oaks, Cape Ann Historical Association; Margaret Cushing, West Orange Public Library; Gladys O'Neil, Bar Harbor Historical Society; Paul Glassman, Art Institute of Chicago; Deanna Kersnick, Luddington Library, Bryn Mawr, Pennsylvania; William Lane, State University of New York at Geneseo; Sandra Roff, New-York Historical Society; Edith McGandy, Hingham, Massachusetts; and Carolyn Durham, College of Wooster.

Finally, we are grateful to the College of Wooster, which has encouraged this project through its faculty-development program and a grant from The Henry Luce III Fund for Distinguished Scholarship. The research and writing of this project was also supported by the exceptionally generous leave program of the college.

This book is dedicated to one of its authors, James Turner (1937–1986)— teacher, scholar, friend.

Published in Canada by General Publishing Company, Ltd., 30 Lesmill Road, Don Mills, Toronto, Ontario.
Published in the United Kingdom by Constable and Company, Ltd.

The Opulent Interiors of the Gilded Age: All 203 Photographs from "Artistic Houses" with New Text is a new work, first published by Dover Publications, Inc., in 1987. The components of the present edition are described in the Preface.

Book design by Carol Belanger Grafton
Manufactured in the United States of America
Dover Publications, Inc., 31 East 2nd Street, Mineola, N.Y. 11501

Library of Congress Cataloging-in-Publication Data

The opulent interiors of the Gilded Age.

"Artistic houses," a work ascribed to G.W. Sheldon, was originally published: New York : D. Appleton, 1883–1884.
    1. Architecture, Domestic—United States. 2. Interior architecture—United States. 3. Interior decoration—United States—History—19th century.
I. Lewis, Arnold. II. Turner, James, 1937–1986. III. McQuillin, Steven. IV. Sheldon, George William, 1843–1914. V. Artistic houses.
NA7207.06 1987   728.3'7'0973   86-19816
ISBN 0-486-25250-7

PREFACE

Artistic Houses was published in 1883–84 by D. Appleton and Company of New York. It was subtitled *Being a Series of Interior Views of a number of the Most Beautiful and Celebrated Homes in the United States with A Description of the Art Treasures contained therein*. The first volume, consisting of two parts, appeared in 1883, and the second, also in two parts, appeared in 1884. However, these four parts were not equal in length or in the number of plates and houses included. In the first volume, part one contained 86 pages and 49 plates of 14 different houses and part two 98 pages and 51 plates of 19 different buildings. In the volume published the following year, part one consisted of 107 pages and 50 plates of 29 houses and part two 91 pages and 53 plates of 35 separate structures. In all, there were 203 photographs taken from the interiors of 97 buildings, all but two of them houses.

As the publisher had done so successfully with *Picturesque America*, *Artistic Houses* was sold only through subscription, the plate and text becoming the exclusive property of its 500 subscribers. The book was distributed over the two-year period in ten sections, each containing from 19 to 22 photographs. Printed in imperial folio size on thick, white woven matt paper and containing clear phototypes processed by the highly respected Gutekunst Company of Philadelphia, *Artistic Houses* represented a level of publishing lavishness appropriate for the houses it featured. Each photograph, approximately 7″ × 9″, was printed on light board measuring about 14″ × 20″. In a note accompanying the tenth and final section, the writer explained that the publication had been much more expensive and time-consuming than had been anticipated, citing as causes painstaking care, repeated takes of the photographer, owners who complained of poor angles from which their rooms had been shot and glass plates broken in transit. "Sometimes it has seemed as if the Fates themselves were in league against the appearance of a dilatory section." Despite such proclamations of conscientious preparation, the majority of photographs were printed reversed, printed from the wrong side of the negative. An error of this magnitude is incomprehensible, particularly when we know that the plates were distributed in ten parts over a two-year period. It seems reasonable to assume that some of the owners whose houses were included in the first set of plates, for example, former President U. S. Grant and his wife, or Mrs. A. T. Stewart, widow of New York's most influential dry-goods merchant, would have complained to the publisher that some of their rooms had been inaccurately publicized. There is no discernible pattern to the reversed photographs, though a higher percentage was printed correctly in the first volume than in the second. Only two of the 22 photographs in the last section have been identified as being correctly printed. The steps taken to determine whether a photograph in *Artistic Houses* was correctly printed will be discussed in the paragraphs explaining the differences between *The Opulent Interiors of the Gilded Age* and *Artistic Houses*.

The text was flattering, complimenting owners, architects and decorators for their roles in rescuing American rooms from the pre-Centennial dark ages of interior decoration and creating living environments reflecting the rising taste and artistic sensitivity of post-Centennial America. "The domestic architec-ture of no nation in the world can show trophies more original, affluent, or admirable." Usually, the text addressed the rooms photographed, calling attention to the woodwork, the wall coverings, the materials used for the floors and ceilings, the hangings and the color scheme. It also contained references to specific paintings and sculptures within a room but did not identify carefully objets d'art which had been collected by the owners. This text paid less attention to furniture, rugs, ceramics, the plan of the house and its exterior style and appearance. The author referred to decorators and architects occasionally, but did not elaborate and wrote virtually nothing about the families who inhabited these interiors. As the series progressed, the descriptions became shorter, suggesting that the initial enthusiasm of both author and publisher was not sustained throughout the two-year period.

Today historians regard *Artistic Houses* as the best source of information and illustrations for the private town house in the major Eastern cities of the United States in the early 1880s. Published references to it in the nineteenth century, however, were rare. The major periodicals and art journals of the day did not review it, a failure which may be explained partly by the reaction of *Art Age* in May 1883. This journal published a facsimile of one of the pages from *Artistic Houses* describing rooms in the William H. Vanderbilt house in New York and commended Appleton and Company for the elegance of the typeface and layout. Referring to Appleton's subscription scheme, the journal noted:

> Their method of selling such works, however, prevents any but a very few privileged persons from becoming acquainted with them, and were it not for special concessions, the plates from their last work, *Artistic Houses* of this country, would not be given here, owing to the sedulous care with which any information concerning the work is kept from all but the canvasser in charge of its sale.

Since Appleton printed only 500 copies which were distributed to presecured subscribers, the firm did not need reviews for additional profits, and it may have even discouraged reviews to protect the privacy of the families living in these houses.

There was no author listed on the title page of *Artistic Houses*, and in the twentieth century the book has been identified by its title and publisher. Although we do not have absolute proof, we are quite sure that its author or principal author was George William Sheldon (January 28, 1843–January 28, 1914) and, consequently, will refer to him in our text as the author.

Sheldon graduated from Princeton in 1863 and served the following year as a medic in Grant's army. From 1865 to 1870 he was a tutor in Latin and belles lettres at Princeton before moving to Union Theological Seminary in New York to teach Oriental languages. He evidently spent two years in England before returning to the United States to become the art critic of the New York *Evening Post*, a position he held from 1876 until 1882. Sheldon worked from 1884 to 1886 as drama critic and city editor of the New York *Commercial Advertiser* and from 1890 until 1900 in London as the literary adviser of D. Appleton and Company. Beginning in 1879 he published prolifically for the next decade, producing *American Painters* (1879), *Hours with Art and Artists* (1882), *Selections in Modern Art* (1885–86),

Artistic Country-Seats (1886–87), *Recent Ideals of American Art* (1888), *Ideals of Life in France* (1890) and *Woman in French Art* (1890). All of these were published by D. Appleton and Company. He died at the age of 71 at his residence in Summit, New Jersey.

Varied evidence supports the conclusion that Sheldon wrote or was responsible for *Artistic Houses*. In *Appleton's Cyclopaedia of American Biography* (1888), the *Dictionary of Authors* (1892), the *American Art Annual* (1914) and the *New York Times* obituary (January 30, 1914), he is cited as the author of the books listed above as well as *Artistic Homes*, which was dated 1882. Though the title and date are incorrect in these four biographical sketches, this would appear to be an error of transcription rather than of attribution. The text format of *Artistic Houses* is identical to that of *Artistic Country-Seats*, which Sheldon wrote three years later. Furthermore, the writing styles in both are similar, and the later publication, which includes several houses published in the earlier work, contains phrases and even paragraphs found in *Artistic Houses*.

The Opulent Interiors of the Gilded Age retains all of the photographs published in *Artistic Houses* but not the original text. The text of the present edition contains an introductory essay concerned with those who lived in these houses, their wealth and their interest in art, written by James Turner and Arnold Lewis, and captions for each of the illustrations, written by Lewis and Steven McQuillin. The captions include most of the valuable information in Sheldon's descriptions plus biographical comments on the house owners and their families, references to the houses published in the late nineteenth century, further comments on the paintings and sculptures displayed, the present condition of the houses and, where possible, specific locations. The new text contains short histories of several of the more significant or unusual houses. Although Sheldon did not include illustrations of exteriors of the residences in *Artistic Houses*, in this new edition photographs or drawings of numerous exteriors illustrate both the introductory text and the caption section.

In order to utilize this format effectively, the arrangement of the photographs in the original has been changed. However, the alphabetical list of illustrations includes the order of photographs in the original work. As mentioned, many of the plates in *Artistic Houses* were printed in reverse. Only 62 appear to be correct while 107 appear to be reversed; 34 of the photographs remain undetermined. The primary clues within the photograph verifying the correct or reversed condition were clocks, pianos, works of art and lettering on inscriptions and titles on book-bindings. External evidence has been found through careful reading of the original descriptions, from plans and illustrations of the rooms published elsewhere and from owners currently living in the houses.

The following illustrations, printed reversed in the original edition, are here reproduced correctly: 8–12, 27–37, 39, 41, 44, 47–49, 52, 55–57, 59, 63, 64, 66, 67, 71–74, 81–83, 94–96, 98, 99, 101–104, 109, 111–113, 119–121, 126, 128, 130, 131, 133, 137, 138, 143, 147, 148, 153–164, 166–174, 176–178, 180, 181, 183–189, 191–197, 199, 200, 203. The proper orientation for the following photographs has not been determined: 6, 20, 38, 46, 53, 54, 65, 68, 69, 75, 78–80, 86–93, 97, 100, 110, 127, 129, 132, 134, 135, 142, 182, 190, 198.

PHOTOGRAPHIC CREDITS

Bibliographic information is provided only for those works not included in the Selected Bibliography (p. 179).

Introduction. Fig. 1: Arnold Lewis, *American Country Houses of the Gilded Age.* Fig. 2: *History of Essex and Hudson Counties.* Fig. 3: Lynn Maston. Fig. 4: R. J. Smith. Fig. 5: James Spero and Edmund V. Gillon, Jr., *The Great Sights of New York*, New York, 1979 (Dover 23870-9). Fig. 6: Boston Public Library, *Houses of Boston's Back Bay.* Fig. 7: Mary Black, *Old New York in Early Photographs*, New York, 1973 (Dover 22907-6). Fig. 8: Arnold Lewis and Keith Morgan, *American Victorian Architecture*, New York, 1975 (Dover 23177-1). Fig. 9: Robert F. Looney, *Old Philadelphia in Early Photographs: 1839–1914*, New York, 1976 (Dover 23345-6). Fig. 10: *American Victorian Architecture.* Fig. 11: The Art Institute of Chicago. Fig. 12: Lynn Maston. Fig. 13: Lynn Maston. Fig. 14: *American Victorian Architecture.* Fig. 15: Steven McQuillin. Fig. 16: *American Country Houses of the Gilded Age.* Fig. 17: Museum of the City of New York. Fig. 18: *American Country Houses of the Gilded Age.* Fig. 19: Lynn Maston.

Text. Page 33: *Old New York in Early Photographs.* Page 56: Lynn Maston. Page 64 (top): *American Victorian Architecture.* Page 74 (bottom): *Harper's New Monthly Magazine*, September 1883. Page 92: *American Country Houses of the Gilded Age.* Page 106: American College of Surgeons. Page 114: *American Victorian Architecture.* Page 136: Mariana Griswold Van Rensselaer, *Henry Hobson Richardson and His Works.* Page 144: *King's Views of New York*, 1912. Page 154: The Society for the Preservation of New England Antiquities. Page 164: Steven McQuillin.

CONTENTS

ALPHABETICAL LIST OF ILLUSTRATIONS
ix

INTRODUCTION
1

ILLUSTRATIONS AND CAPTIONS
33

SELECTED BIBLIOGRAPHY
179

ALPHABETICAL LIST OF ILLUSTRATIONS

This list provides the illustration number of each item in the present edition. The parentheses contain the volume and page number of the plates as listed in the original Contents and List of Plates of *Artistic Houses*.

JAMES W. ALEXANDER HOUSE, New York, New York,
166 (II, 109)

OLIVER AMES HOUSE, Boston, Massachusetts,
33–37 (II, 117)

NICHOLAS L. ANDERSON HOUSE, Washington, D.C.,
144–146 (II, 127)

HERMAN O. ARMOUR HOUSE, New York, New York,
134 & 135 (II, 115)

GEORGE F. BAKER HOUSE, New York, New York,
125 & 126 (I, 35)

HENRY BELDEN HOUSE, New York, New York,
94 (II, 193)

G. B. BOWLER HOUSE, Bar Harbor, Maine,
44 (II, 129)

JOSEPH G. CHAPMAN HOUSE, St. Louis, Missouri,
98 (II, 171)

EDWARD E. CHASE HOUSE, New York, New York,
191 (II, 79)

KNIGHT D. CHENEY HOUSE, South Manchester, Connecticut,
66 (II, 181)

GEORGE W. CHILDS HOUSE, Philadelphia, Pennsylvania,
200 (I, 157)

GEORGE W. CHILDS HOUSE, Bryn Mawr, Pennsylvania,
201 & 202 (I, 157)

JAMES L. CLAGHORN HOUSE, Philadelphia, Pennsylvania,
9 (I, 175)

CLARENCE H. CLARK HOUSE, Philadelphia, Pennsylvania,
19 & 20 (I, 167)

WILLIAM CLARK HOUSE, Newark, New Jersey,
194–196 (I, 145)

SAMUEL COLMAN HOUSE, Newport, Rhode Island,
29 (II, 71)

SWITS CONDÉ HOUSE, Oswego, New York,
137 (II, 183)

JOSEPH S. DECKER HOUSE, New York, New York,
152 (II, 145)

WILLIAM H. DE FOREST HOUSE, New York, New York,
105–108 (I, 97)

EDWARD N. DICKERSON HOUSE, New York, New York,
75–77 (I, 81)

JOHN W. DOANE HOUSE, Chicago, Illinois,
180 & 181 (II, 55)

WILLIAM G. DOMINICK HOUSE, New York, New York,
175 (I, 71)

J. COLEMAN DRAYTON HOUSE, New York, New York,
197 (II, 41)

DAVID L. EINSTEIN HOUSE, New York, New York,
86–91 (I, 25)

RUDOLPH ELLIS HOUSE, Philadelphia, Pennsylvania,
38 (I, 165)

MARSHALL FIELD HOUSE, Chicago, Illinois,
55 & 56 (II, 43)

HAMILTON FISH HOUSE, New York, New York,
52 (II, 95)

HENRY M. FLAGLER HOUSE, Mamaroneck, New York,
39 (II, 191)

FRANK FURNESS HOUSE, Philadelphia, Pennsylvania,
97 (II, 169)

JOHN L. GARDNER HOUSE, Boston, Massachusetts,
138 (II, 185)

HENRY C. GIBSON HOUSE, Philadelphia, Pennsylvania,
46–49 (I, 149)

WILLIAM GODDARD HOUSE, Providence, Rhode Island,
161 & 162 (II, 133)

ROBERT GOELET HOUSE, Newport, Rhode Island,
27 & 28 (II, 81)

ULYSSES S. GRANT HOUSE, New York, New York,
31 & 32 (I, 19)

WILLIAM A. HAMMOND HOUSE, New York, New York,
131–133 (I, 87)

JULIA T. HARPER HOUSE, New York, New York,
40 (I, 179)

WILLIAM F. HAVEMEYER HOUSE, East Orange, New Jersey,
65 (II, 197)

HENRY C. HAVEN HOUSE, Boston, Massachusetts,
80 (II, 135)

HENRY HILTON HOUSE, New York, New York,
78 & 79 (I, 39)

SAMUEL P. HINCKLEY HOUSE, Lawrence, New York,
167 (II, 91)

HENRY S. HOVEY HOUSE, Gloucester, Massachusetts,
102 (II, 167)

WILLIAM S. HOYT HOUSE, Pelham, New York,
136 (II, 143)

HOLLIS HUNNEWELL HOUSE, Boston, Massachusetts,
11 & 12 (II, 29)

WALTER HUNNEWELL HOUSE, Boston, Massachusetts,
147 & 148 (II, 9)

SARAH IVES HURTT HOUSE, Yonkers, New York,
95 & 96 (I, 57)

C. OLIVER ISELIN HOUSE, Hunter's Island, New York,
182 (II, 189)

JOHN TAYLOR JOHNSTON HOUSE, New York, New York,
198 (II, 151)

CHARLES H. JOY HOUSE, Boston, Massachusetts,
30 (II, 25)

GEORGE KEMP HOUSE, New York, New York,
139–142 (I, 53)

WILLIAM S. KIMBALL HOUSE, Rochester, New York,
67 & 68 (II, 159)

WILLIAM T. LUSK HOUSE, New York, New York,
18 (II, 153)

HENRY G. MARQUAND HOUSE, Newport, Rhode Island,
92 & 93 (II, 85)

BRADLEY MARTIN HOUSE, New York, New York,
69–71 (II, 3)

JOHN T. MARTIN HOUSE, Brooklyn, New York,
149–151 (I, 139)

CLARA JESSUP MOORE HOUSE, Philadelphia, Pennsylvania,
41–43 (I, 153)

J. PIERPONT MORGAN HOUSE, New York, New York,
155–159 (I, 75)

E. ROLLINS MORSE HOUSE, Boston, Massachusetts,
10 (II, 19)

O. D. MUNN HOUSE, West Orange, New Jersey,
130 (II, 75)

H. VICTOR NEWCOMB HOUSE, New York, New York,
81–83 (I, 181)

H. VICTOR NEWCOMB HOUSE, Elberon, New Jersey,
84 & 85 (II, 1)

SAMUEL M. NICKERSON HOUSE, Chicago, Illinois,
103 & 104 (II, 49)

MARIANA ARNOT OGDEN HOUSE, New York, New York,
64 (II, 173)

OSWALD OTTENDORFER PAVILION, New York, New York,
72 (I, 67)

ROBERT TREAT PAINE, JR., HOUSE, Boston, Massachusetts,
73 (II, 21)

GILBERT R. PAYSON HOUSE, Watertown, Massachusetts,
173 (II, 155)

JOHN CHARLES PHILLIPS HOUSE, Boston, Massachusetts,
163–165 (II, 13)

ASA P. POTTER HOUSE, Nantasket Beach, Massachusetts,
57 (II, 111)

JACOB RUPPERT HOUSE, New York, New York,
128 & 129 (II, 101)

WILLIAM I. RUSSELL HOUSE, Short Hills, New Jersey,
74 (II, 77)

JOHN H. SHOENBERGER HOUSE, New York, New York,
109 & 110 (II, 105)

WILLIAM M. SINGERLY OFFICE, Philadelphia, Pennsylvania,
203 (I, 173)

CHARLES S. SMITH HOUSE, New York, New York,
50 & 51 (I, 129)

ELIZABETH E. SPOONER HOUSE, Boston, Massachusetts,
177–179 (II, 31)

FREDERIC W. STEVENS HOUSE, New York, New York,
21–23 (I, 101)

CORNELIA M. STEWART HOUSE, New York, New York,
1–8 (I, 7)

MARY STUART HOUSE, New York, New York,
99–101 (II, 87)

FREDERICK F. THOMPSON HOUSE, New York, New York,
58–63 (I, 47)

LOUIS C. TIFFANY APARTMENT, New York, New York,
13–16 (I, 1)

SAMUEL J. TILDEN HOUSE, New York, New York,
111 (II, 61)

SAMUEL J. TILDEN HOUSE, Yonkers, New York,
112 & 113 (II, 67)

FRANKLIN H. TINKER HOUSE, Short Hills, New Jersey,
143 (II, 187)

TRINITY CHURCH RECTORY, Boston, Massachusetts,
199 (II, 165)

WILLIAM H. VANDERBILT HOUSE, New York, New York,
114–124 (I, 111)

HENRY VILLARD HOUSE, New York, New York,
183–189 (II, 161)

JAMES W. WADSWORTH HOUSE, Geneseo, New York,
168 (II, 195)

GEORGE P. WETMORE HOUSE, Newport, Rhode Island,
192 & 193 (II, 83)

THE WHITE HOUSE, Washington, D.C.,
17 (II, 97)

JOSEPH H. WHITE HOUSE, Brookline, Massachusetts,
160 (II, 139)

R. H. WHITE AND COMPANY WAREHOUSE STORE PARLOR, Boston,
Massachusetts,
174 (II, 125)

CHARLES A. WHITTIER HOUSE, Boston, Massachusetts,
169–172 (II, 121)

EDWARD H. WILLIAMS HOUSE, Philadelphia, Pennsylvania,
45 (I, 169)

HENRY J. WILLING HOUSE, Chicago, Illinois,
153 & 154 (II, 35)

RICHARD T. WILSON HOUSE, New York, New York,
190 (II, 107)

EGERTON WINTHROP HOUSE, New York, New York,
53 & 54 (I, 135)

JOHN WOLFE HOUSE, New York, New York,
176 (II, 149)

JOHN A. ZEREGA HOUSE, New York, New York,
24–26 (I, 61)

UNIDENTIFIED DRAWING ROOM, New York, New York,
127 ((II, 198)

INTRODUCTION

HENRY VILLARD AND THE "GOLDEN MOMENT" OF AMERICAN WEALTH

In 1883, while George Sheldon was preparing his comments on the "magnificent and celebrated" Henry Villard house on Madison Avenue in New York, Villard himself rapidly reached the peak of his career as a railroad entrepreneur. In Sheldon's description, the house, whose "size is perhaps unequaled by that of any other similar edifice in the city," aptly matched Villard's grand-scale ambitions for the Pacific Northwest, which his completion of the Northern Pacific railroad was now opening to the world. Villard saw the Northwest as America's last productive frontier, able to bring prosperity to countless new farmers and other residents while pouring its grain out to the hungry of Europe. He in turn would be the great organizer of this bounty. Public acclaim was equal to Villard's expectations, for his efforts had brought success after several years of intermittent railroad construction and now, in September 1883, resulted in completion of the longest single railroad line in the world.

Villard celebrated appropriately, organizing a four-train expedition to open the road and pound the ceremonial last spike. Using the English and German financial connections that had made completion of the Northern Pacific possible, Villard filled the trains with the English, German and Austrian ministers to the United States, several heads of German banks and members of the British parliament, American cabinet members, "two earls and a couple of lords," and the ubiquitous former President Grant. The journey west from Chicago was an extended triumph. Financiers recognized Villard as the new peer of Jay Gould, William H. Vanderbilt and Collis Huntington, while crowd after crowd cheered the railroad builder and what he meant for their region. The *Daily Pioneer-Press* of St. Paul asserted that "but few men in the history of the country have ever been the recipients of such ovations as greet Mr. Villard and will continue to greet him as he moves westward."

Yet even while driving in the last spike on a September evening in western Montana, Villard knew that construction costs were at least tens of millions of dollars above both earlier estimates and his company's resources. By the end of the year, Villard found himself forced to resign several company presidencies and pledge his property to prevent complete collapse of his empire. Newspaper opinion now pilloried him as a typical example of the corporate looter, a view ironically corroborated by the Villard family's move at just that time into their new house, which Sheldon described as having "unusual significance" for both "its magnitude and costliness." The house became the symbol of Villard's supposed callous selfishness. He knew the move would only increase public hostility, but he had built the seeming palace, actually intended for six families, when his wealth warranted it and now he had no other city home, nor the funds to rent. Villard was never at ease in the house, as the sparsely furnished rooms in Sheldon's photographs (nos. 183–189) suggest, and in the spring of 1884 the family moved to a country home and soon left the United States for a two-year stay in Germany. As soon as he could, Villard sold the house to Whitelaw Reid, then editor of the *New York Tribune*. Although Villard had lived in the house less than six months and owned it for little over three years, he gave his name to the group of "Villard houses" that Sheldon recognized would become a landmark, although at the time his reference to their "chaste simplicity" might well have met with jeers from the public that now condemned Villard's lavish celebrations.

While few of Sheldon's 92 owners of the "Artistic Houses" experienced such a dramatic rise and fall as did Villard, particularly just as their houses were being publicized, Villard's career showed elements common to the lives of many of Sheldon's subjects. Several did indeed rise in fortune dramatically, only to drop as far. H. Victor Newcomb's rising to "boy president" of the Louisville and Nashville and plummeting into drug addiction and commitment to a mental institution was the most melodramatic of all, but far from unique in its pattern. For many of these men and for others among the house owners whose material fortunes remained stable, the rapid reversal of public attitude was a common phenomenon. Many entered the 1880s almost universally acclaimed as great builders of both their own often immense fortunes and of the country's material progress, only to find by the end of the decade that the same activities were now condemned as exploitive and parasitic. George Sheldon presented *Artistic Houses* to the public at what proved to be a key moment in shifting public opinion, marking years in which general fascination at ostentatious display turned to an increasing disgust. While most men of wealth found themselves still admired for their success by the end of the 1880s, it became increasingly necessary to fend off particular attacks and to justify certain of their activities.

Villard further typified many of Sheldon's house owners in the particular form of his economic success, the consolidation of several separate, often faltering enterprises into one smoothly organized and stable corporate empire. In Villard's case, although he failed dramatically for a time, the Northern Pacific survived in the hands of others as a solid, major element of corporate America. Virtually all the other great fortunes Sheldon found manifested in the houses stemmed from this same determination to bring order and stability to fragmented enterprises, whether in meat packing, oil refining, retail trade, insurance or any of several other areas. This process of large-scale organization, just like the personal reputations of the organizers, was commonly subject to a sharp change in public attitudes. While many of the "Artistic Houses" were going up physically, the creation of corporate empires was usually hailed as evidence of a distinctive American combination of efficiency and grandeur. Within a very few years in many cases, these same enterprises had become trusts and were being condemned for their rapacious determination to prevent any new competition.

Villard, like many of Sheldon's men and women of wealth, searched for the right combination of activities and characteristics, both to satisfy his own sense of how a man of wealth ought to behave and to respond to public attitudes. How ought a person of wealth to live and what did such a person owe to society? These were questions much on the mind of many Americans as Sheldon displayed some of the fruits of wealth in such detail. Direct public service by holding elected or appointed office was characteristic principally of Sheldon's older house owners, such as Presidential candidate Samuel Tilden, Secretary of State Hamilton Fish or New York Mayor James Harper, all born before 1815. Villard's own way of fulfilling a sense of obligation was less direct but common to his generation. In Villard's case it took the form of purchasing the *New York Evening Post* in 1881, in order to save one of America's most respected newspapers from possible extinction. Villard kept at a distance from daily management, naming three trustees to conduct the business financially and hiring a trio of editors unexcelled in distinction in American journalism: Carl Schurz, Horace White and E. L. Godkin. Many others among the owners of "Artistic Houses" found similar ways to serve, and perhaps elevate, public taste and opinion. The accumulation of art, which the public might view on occasion, and the organization of museums were the most common expressions of a sense of public responsibility, but in other areas George W. Childs secured a reputation as an unusually philanthropic employer, while Robert Paine worked to organize and expand charity and social service in a municipality. Some of Sheldon's subjects showed an intriguing beginning of the apparent loss of any sense of public obligation, as many of his younger house owners were already gaining reputations as "sportsmen" and "gentlemen of leisure." For C. Oliver Iselin, sailing became the central preoccupation of his life, while for Bradley and Cornelia Martin, entertainment was their hallmark.

SOURCES OF WEALTH

Who were the owners of the "Artistic Houses"? George Sheldon himself says little about the people who owned the homes he describes, providing only scattered information about individuals, nothing at all about the owners as a group, and occasionally even using only a last name. Nevertheless, it is possible to discover significant information about the great majority of Sheldon's house owners. Of the 84 men listed by Sheldon as house owners, only two, Henry Belden and F. W. Hurtt, remain too obscure for us to be sure of anything about their lives. Hurtt, in fact, may not have been living when *Artistic Houses* was published. Because of this possibility his house has been listed under the name of his wife, Sarah Ives Hurtt. Sheldon also referred to "Mrs. John A. Zerega's House" (nos. 24–26), but we have listed the residence under her husband's name because he was living in 1883–84. Five of the eight women owners were well known in their own time, either because of their own work, as in the case of Clara Jessup Moore, a successful writer, or as widows of prominent men, as was true of Julia T. (Mrs. James) Harper and Cornelia M. (Mrs. Alexander T.) Stewart. Yet three women owners are uncertain figures, and we know little or nothing about them.

Not surprisingly, Sheldon found most of the people whose homes he wanted to present along the Eastern seaboard. His own career had developed in New York and Americans assumed that the most up-to-date taste moved from East to West. Accordingly, 40 of Sheldon's 92 owners were studied with respect to homes they owned in New York, while ten more persons lived in "Artistic Houses" in the New York suburban area, stretching from Henry M. Flagler in Mamaroneck, New York, and Samuel P. Hinckley in Lawrence, Long Island, to William I. Russell, Franklin H. Tinker and O. D. Munn in the newer, planned New Jersey suburbs of Short Hills and Llewellyn Park. Three other men commonly lived in New York, but Sheldon preferred to describe the Newport homes of Samuel Colman, Robert Goelet and Henry G. Marquand.

Fig. 1. Samuel P. Hinckley house, Lawrence, New York.

Boston provided Sheldon with his next-largest concentration of homes, with 13 of his houses in Boston itself and four others in outlying towns, owned by men who earned their livings in Boston. Next came Philadelphia, providing ten homes that Sheldon described, including two of publisher George W. Childs's houses, one in the city and one in Bryn Mawr. After Philadelphia, only Chicago provided a cluster of house owners for Sheldon, giving him four. Although Newport also yielded four houses for Sheldon's study, only George P. Wetmore considered the town his principal residence.

Sheldon found eight more men and women who owned "Artistic Houses" scattered as far west as St. Louis, where lumber merchant Joseph G. Chapman's home was known "even in the East" for its "artistic treasures." The southern boundary to Sheldon's interest was Washington, D.C., where General Nicholas Longworth Anderson's new home, designed by H. H. Richardson, was "easily the most interesting private residence in the capital." In upstate New York Sheldon found three homes to include, those of woolen-mill owner Swits Condé in Oswego, tobacco manufacturer William S. Kimball in Rochester and the Geneseo home of gentleman farmer James W. Wadsworth. In New England, aside from Boston and Newport, Sheldon described three more homes. The new Bar Harbor home of Mrs. G. B. Bowler was being studied at the same time in a series of *Century* articles on contemporary architecture. Sheldon also included the home of silk-mill owner Knight D. Cheney in South Manchester, Connecticut, and the Providence, Rhode Island, home of another textile magnate, William Goddard. The inclusion of houses in such varied locations gave Sheldon's work a semblance of comprehensive coverage, but over four-fifths of his examples were from his three main metropolitan areas.

Sheldon's house owners were quite varied in occupation, representing most of the major sources of substantial wealth in the late nineteenth century. Yet the newer types of industrial activity were underrepresented. In the 1880s, railroads and iron and steel manufacturing were still the most fruitful newer sources of fortunes, joining the somewhat older textile mills as the principal foundations for industrial wealth. Only the relatively little-known John H. Shoenberger, who had recently retired from business and moved from Pittsburgh to New York, represented the substantial iron and steel industry. Railroads played a larger part in the wealth of Sheldon's subjects, but a proportionally small one considering their importance in the national economy. William H. Vanderbilt was one of Sheldon's best-known house owners, a man whose control of the New

York Central and other lines had made him a principal public symbol of railroad wealth. Also well known when Sheldon was writing was Henry Villard, as mentioned, a principal figure in the Northern Pacific. Two other men had made their initial fortunes in railroads but were not actively involved when Sheldon described their homes: John Taylor Johnston had been president of the Central Railroad of New Jersey for 30 years, until the depression of the 1870s led to a reorganization of the line; H. Victor Newcomb became president of the Louisville and Nashville Railroad following his father, but resigned the position in 1880, as his interest turned more toward New York banking. Two other men also represented the newer forms of industrial activity. Henry M. Flagler possessed "one of the great fortunes of the United States" as a result of his partnership with John D. Rockefeller in the Standard Oil Company, while Edward H. Williams rested his wealth on his partnership in Philadelphia's Baldwin Locomotive Works.

The older industrial activity of cloth and clothing manufacture was an important source of wealth in Sheldon's group, accounting for eight of his home owners. Henry S. Hovey and William Goddard owned cotton mills, Swits Condé and David L. Einstein woolen mills and Knight D. Cheney and William De Forest silk mills. William Clark was well on the way to becoming one of America's major producers of cotton thread while John T. Martin had made a fortune in clothing production during the Civil War, after which he diversified into banking and real-estate investment. Martin's pattern was common to many of Sheldon's subjects, who achieved substantial wealth in one field, but then increased it by activity in two or three others.

Fig. 2. William Clark house, Newark, New Jersey.

As with cloth and clothing, older types of raw-material processing were the foundation of the wealth of several of Sheldon's house owners. Like Standard Oil's Flagler, Herman O. Armour, one of four brothers in the meat-packing business, represented one of the better-known new fortunes of the post–Civil War era. William F. Havemeyer and Robert Stuart in sugar refining, Henry C. Gibson the Philadelphia distiller and Jacob Ruppert the New York brewer, Joseph G. Chapman in lumber milling and William S. Kimball the tobacco processor, rounded out this source of wealth among Sheldon's people.

Trade was another important activity for Sheldon's subjects. The most common figure was the dry-goods merchant, often a man who built up a substantial general hard-goods trade. Both A. T. Stewart and Marshall Field were preeminent in the developing department store, while Chicago's Henry J. Willing had accumulated his fortune with Field before retiring to travel. Ralph H. White built up a major retail dry-goods firm in Boston and Charles Stewart Smith secured his wealth from the wholesale dry-goods business in New York. Also prominent in New York merchandising were George Kemp in drugs and toiletries

and John Wolfe, who inherited his hardware business from his father. The sale of coffee, tea and groceries provided the origin of Chicagoan John W. Doane's millions, while the general import-export trade with China and the Philippines occupied John Charles Phillips in Boston. The China trade had also been the principal source of John L. Gardner's inherited wealth, but Gardner himself put the money into railroads, mining and other investments. Also in Boston, Gilbert R. Payson and Joseph H. White were partners in a firm marketing textiles for major New England mills.

Banking was the principal occupation of almost a dozen of Sheldon's owners and a major activity that many others took up after they had accumulated a fortune in some other field. Among Sheldon's bankers, J. Pierpont Morgan had already established a solid reputation in railroad financing. Morgan's conspicuous investment activity, accompanied by growing public attention, was almost the opposite of the quiet "bankers' bank" business of George F. Baker, who with Morgan would soon become one of the country's most powerful financiers. Sheldon found bankers prominent among his house owners in all his major cities, with the Hunnewells and Asa P. Potter representing Boston and Samuel M. Nickerson prominent in Chicago. In Philadelphia, Clarence H. Clark of the First National Bank was reputed to be one of the city's richest citizens. Rounding out Sheldon's group of bankers were several New Yorkers, including Joseph S. Decker, Frederic W. Stevens, Frederick F. Thompson and Richard T. Wilson, whose banking was much less well known than the socially advantageous marriages of his children.

The related fields of brokerage and insurance accounted for several other house owners, including James W. Alexander, first vice president of the Equitable Life Assurance Society, one of the largest firms in the field. Edward Eddy Chase, William G. Dominick, Rudolph Ellis and E. Rollins Morse all participated in stockbrokerage firms, while William I. Russell handled investments in metals.

Fig. 3. E. Rollins Morse house, Boston, Massachusetts.

Along with banking, real-estate investment was an activity that provided the central wealth of several house owners and a secondary activity for numerous others. Robert Goelet was heir, with his brother, to one of New York's major real-estate fortunes, begun in the early nineteenth century. Goelet needed to involve himself little in active management of the investments, as their value steadily increased with the growth of New York. Similarly, Nicholas Longworth Anderson in Washington lived a life of leisure on income from Cincinnati real estate developed by his grandfather Nicholas Longworth, the "first millionaire of the West." Samuel P. Hinckley took a more active role as a real-estate dealer on Long Island, while James W. Wadsworth managed the landholdings his father had put together in upstate

New York. The income of these four was most clearly tied to land, as was the inherited wealth of Mariana Arnot Ogden, widow of one of Chicago's earliest major landowners, William Ogden.

Real estate and banking also provided significant second careers for many of Sheldon's men of wealth, so that to some extent categories break down. John T. Martin, for instance, made enough money in a St. Louis clothing firm to retire before he was 40, in 1855. He then moved East and soon made a substantial fortune by means of uniform contracts during the Civil War. "Retiring" again, he concentrated on developing his increasingly significant collection of sculpture and paintings, but also served as a director of a half-dozen banks and trust companies and managed his large tracts of Brooklyn waterfront land. Many others, including William Goddard, George Kemp and Henry G. Marquand, followed similar paths, so that when Sheldon described their houses in the mid-1880s, they were as much or more involved in banking and real estate as in their original occupations.

Fig. 5. Julia T. Harper house, New York, New York.

Fig. 4. John T. Martin house, Brooklyn, New York.

One other business, publishing, was a significant occupation of Sheldon's house owners. George W. Childs, owner of the Philadelphia *Public Ledger*, was one of the best-known newspaper publishers of his generation. The *Ledger*'s "exceptionally high tone," which put it on "the right side of every question," had made it both eminently respectable and financially rewarding. This success and Childs's active philanthropy made him one of Philadelphia's most eminent citizens, a fitting host for President Grant and the Emperor of Brazil when they arrived in Philadelphia to open the Centennial Exhibition in 1876. One of Childs's competitors, William M. Singerly, who published the Philadelphia *Record*, was responsible for the only "artistic office" in Sheldon's collection. Sheldon's only other newspaper publisher was Oswald Ottendorfer, owner of one of the country's most important foreign-language papers, the New York *Staats-Zeitung*. Ottendorfer had married the woman principally responsible for the paper's early success, Anna Behr Uhl, who died as pictures of the couple's "Beautiful pavilion on . . . the North River" were being published. Sheldon included two magazine publishers, the young Franklin H. Tinker, whose firm published several trade journals, and O. D. Munn, whose *Scientific American* had been an important periodical since the 1840s. Another of Sheldon's house owners, Julia Thorne Harper, owed her inherited wealth principally to publishing, but she took no active role in Harper and Brothers, the firm that her husband James had helped to found.

Among the professions, law provided Sheldon with several house owners. Both Hamilton Fish and Samuel J. Tilden had legal practice at the center of their careers, but both had expanded their incomes with real estate and corporate investments and both had devoted much of their energy to political life. Fish capped his career with service as Secretary of State throughout the Grant administration, while Tilden went from the governorship of New York to an unsuccessful campaign as the Democratic nominee for President in 1876. When Sheldon described their houses, both were elder statesmen of their respective parties, each living "the private life of a gentleman of ample means and cultivated tastes." Owing his reputation more clearly to his legal practice was Edward N. Dickerson, one of the country's ablest patent lawyers, whose cases had included tests of Colt firearms and Goodyear rubber patents. In Boston, Robert Treat Paine, Jr., was a lawyer whose practice enabled him to find the profitable railroad and mining investments which, in turn, allowed him to retire to public service and philanthropy in 1870, at the age of 35. Several more of Sheldon's subjects trained in the law and were members of the bar, including J. Coleman Drayton, Judge Henry Hilton and Bradley Martin, but legal practice was not a significant source of their income.

Medicine contributed two of Sheldon's more accomplished house owners and one of his obscure ones. Dr. William A. Hammond had been Surgeon-General of the United States Army during part of the Civil War, but his "masterful personality" clashed with the "autocratic spirit" of Secretary of War Edwin Stanton and he was dismissed in 1864. While spending 15 years winning reversal of his court-martial verdict, Hammond also became an authority on nervous diseases and "one of the pioneer neurologists of the United States." Dr. William T. Lusk, by the mid-1870s "the fashionable obstetrician of the day" in New York, marked the opening of the 1880s with publication of his *Art and Science of Midwifery*, the most learned textbook on the subject at the time. Dr. Henry C. Haven, the third of Sheldon's physicians, practiced in Boston, where he specialized in the diseases of infants and helped found several medical institutions for children.

Three of Sheldon's owners made their livings in the arts, helping to create and decorate just the kind of homes Sheldon wanted to present as models for up-to-date taste. In the mid-1880s, Philadelphia's Frank Furness was just reaching the apex of his career as an architect. Having already designed several important public buildings in his hometown, he was now being called on by the city's banking and railroad magnates for both office buildings and suburban homes. Samuel Colman, a Newport painter who had begun to receive recognition during the Civil War years, also created during the 1880s designs for fabrics and wallpapers and experimented with interior wood stains. Similar experimentalism characterized the third of the professionals in the arts, Louis C. Tiffany, who had studied painting under Colman before turning toward more varied decorative arts, especially the many uses of stained glass.

Another of Sheldon's owners, Clara Jessup Moore, was a prolific author, but did not think of herself as a professional. While her husband lived, Moore published social advice, poetry and short prose under pseudonyms for about 20 years. By the late 1870s, living on the fortune from her late husband's paper-manufacturing business and donating to charity the proceeds of her writing, Moore published more frequently under her own name and became a popular writer of novels and children's stories.

Two of society's traditionally honorable professions, the clergy and the military, were also represented among Sheldon's people. Phillips Brooks, in the 1880s still the minister of Boston's Trinity Episcopal Church, was among the country's most widely known clergymen. He had turned down academic offers from Harvard and the University of Pennsylvania in order to remain in the church, a commitment rewarded a few years later when he was chosen Bishop of Massachusetts. Sheldon's military figures included Nicholas L. Anderson, Charles A. Whittier and Ulysses S. Grant. Grant, who had commanded the victorious Northern forces in the Civil War and then served two terms as President of the United States, was in these years facing the last of many low points in his life. His investment firm failed in 1884 and in the same year he discovered the cancer that soon killed him, but not before Grant's characteristic determination had enabled him to complete his *Memoirs*.

Fig. 6. Trinity Church rectory, Boston, Massachusetts.

While their professions provided the shape and focus of the lives of most of Sheldon's house owners, a sizable group found earning an income of no particular significance. Inherited wealth was not the defining characteristic of these house owners, for others among Sheldon's subjects had fallen heir to fortunes but had devoted their efforts to active management of inherited businesses. The single wealthiest owner in Sheldon's array, William H. Vanderbilt, was also well known for his constant attention to his railroad empire. Others, such as Samuel J. Tilden and Hamilton Fish, gave a large part of their lives to public service, but only after strenuous effort in accumulating the fortunes that made such service possible. Unlike these men were the house owners who spent all their lives as men of leisure or the few who did engage in cultural or political activity made possible by wealth they had done little to develop.

Assignment of some men to such a category represents a judgment not strictly factual and objective. Robert Goelet, for instance, was seen as "uncommonly sagacious" in augmenting the immense New York real-estate fortune left to him and his brother by his father and uncle, but such activity seems never to have provided the focus to his life, which he devoted to music, sport, club life and travel. The Metropolitan Opera and his

magnificent steam yacht represented his paramount concerns. A more clear-cut example of the man of leisure was Bradley Martin, a man who "began at college the social career in which he subsequently attained such a conspicuous place as a leader of society both in America and Europe." When Martin married Cornelia Sherman in 1869, he married the fortune that launched them both on an increasingly lavish series of balls and enabled them to spend the last portion of their life in Britain, after public reaction to their depression-era ball of 1897 made life in America too unpleasant. Skill at leisure activity was seen as most noteworthy in such others as New York banker's son C. Oliver Iselin, "whose love of sports and his prowess in coaching, polo, hunting, quail and pigeon shooting, made him a notable and colorful figure." Iselin, from one of the country's wealthiest families at the time, was especially well known as a yachtsman and defended the America's Cup in three famous races.

If Iselin used wealth to cultivate a firm mastery of recreational skills, other house owners demonstrated a talent for scandal and defeat. When Sheldon was describing his home, J. Coleman Drayton was coasting smoothly through an active social life that rested on the fortune of his wife, Charlotte Astor, whose family combined wealth and social distinction as few others did in the 1880s. By the end of the decade the Draytons were headed toward the separation and subsequent divorce that became the "most conspicuous society scandal of the generation." Less explosively dramatic but equally precarious in his good fortune was Henry Hilton, early in his career an inconsequential municipal judge in New York. Hilton's wife was a cousin of the wife of department-store millionaire A. T. Stewart, a connection the Hiltons carefully cultivated. The matter-of-fact Stewart made Hilton his social master of ceremonies and friend, coming to treat him as a son and leaving in Hilton's hands management of the fortune he left his widow upon his death in 1876. As custodian of Stewart's millions, Hilton lived lavishly, bought a luxurious house, donated freely to charity, but so mishandled Stewart's business, especially after Mrs. Stewart's death in 1886, that he rapidly ran through and dissipated the huge fortune ($20 to $40 million) that observers estimated he began with.

More productive in their use of inherited wealth were John L. Gardner of Boston and George Peabody Wetmore of Newport. Neither had much involvement in the businesses their merchant fathers created and both initially used their wealth for extended and frequent tours of Europe. Gardner, and particularly his wife, the former Isabella Stewart, soon became increasingly committed to sponsorship of the arts in Boston, while Wetmore entered Rhode Island politics in the mid-1880s, starting at the top with election as governor in 1884.

A quieter life, free from both great scandal and notable achievement, characterized Sheldon's remaining families of leisure. Representative of several was the amalgamation John Hay saw when he ushered at the wedding of William Sprague Hoyt and Janet Chase in 1871: "He is a very nice fellow—and no end of cash. She is a very nice girl—and no end of talent." Although Hoyt's cash had its ups and downs depending on the fortunes of his cousins' cotton firm, and although Mrs. Hoyt's connections with national and Rhode Island politics (through her father and brother-in-law) sometimes presented problems, the marriage included European and Caribbean travel, a comfortable home the couple designed for themselves on an island near Pelham, New York, and enough jewelry to warrant newspaper coverage of its theft, with time for Janet Chase Hoyt to gain a reputation as a writer and illustrator of children's books. Apparently similar was the life of Charles A. Whittier and his wife Lillie, who divided their time between homes in Boston, Buzzard's Bay and New York; traveled frequently to Europe; and married one daughter to a wealthy Iselin and the other to a Russian prince.

Such families devoted themselves chiefly to private pleasures, often centered in the homes Sheldon presented. For some, personal enjoyment and their home became a preoccupation equivalent to a business career for others. Sheldon notes that Egerton Winthrop imported from France every article of furniture in his New York apartment (nos. 53 & 54), including papier-mâché ornamentation. Winthrop had spent much of his early married life in France, where his second son was born, and he became a pioneer in the use of antique French furniture in America. His concern with taste in art led novelist Edith Wharton to find in Winthrop her first real adult friend, the first to provide her with "intellectual companionship." As Winthrop turned more and more toward devotion to such amenities as the perfection of his dinners, Wharton described him in a way that suits many of Sheldon's men of leisure: "Never, I believe, have an intelligence so distinguished and a character so admirable been combined with interests for the most part so trivial." For Winthrop, the rooms themselves that Sheldon portrayed, and the activities he orchestrated in them, became essentially the entire content of his life.

Defining an American Elite

Fortunately for later researchers, the contemporaries of Sheldon's house owners were becoming increasingly interested in establishing and defining categories of elite status in America. Wealth and social prestige had long fascinated Americans, in part because possession of either could change so rapidly, in part because great wealth and high status paradoxically both affirmed and denied American tenets of social mobility, individual ambition and egalitarian democracy. As a result of this American fascination with wealth and status, there had always been impressionistic identification of the richest or most well-born Americans. In the 1880s, both outside observers of the wealthy and those who saw themselves as inside guardians of "society" began to be more systematic and explicit in their defining of categories, producing extensive lists of families and individuals. The lists, among their other functions, help to define Sheldon's house owners.

Among the first to attempt a comprehensive identification of men of great wealth was Thomas G. Shearman, who intended his series of articles for The Forum in 1889 and 1891 as an alarm signal calling attention to the growing concentration of wealth in the United States. In an effort to prove that the "wealthiest class in the United States is vastly richer than the wealthiest class in Great Britain," which Americans were used to thinking of as an aristocratic society, in 1889 Sherman published a list of all those Americans easily identifiable as having at least $20 million in individual wealth. His 67 people and estates were those commonly accepted as the very top level of wealth in America. Although his list was current for the late 1880s, and thus came after the death of some of Sheldon's house owners, eight of them figured in Shearman's list in some way. Henry M. Flagler, J. Pierpont Morgan and Marshall Field were counted as individuals; William H. Vanderbilt's spirit was present through the listing of several of his heirs; and inheritance or other family connections gave Herman O. Armour, Robert Goelet, William F. Havemeyer and Cornelia M. Stewart either a place on, or a link with, Shearman's list.

Shearman's efforts, as well as a rising public concern with concentrated wealth, led to an even more careful study by the New York Tribune in 1892. The Tribune's interest was prompted by arguments that recently raised protective tariffs were responsible for unjust concentrations of wealth. The protariff Tribune hoped to show that most Americans who possessed great wealth gained it in fields that received no advantage from the tariff, but overall it also devoted great time and effort to accumulating the most accurate list of all Americans who were worth $1 million or more. After much correspondence and cross-checking, the Tribune's researchers discovered and listed 4047 millionaires from all over the country, about .0001 percent of the adult population.

As with Shearman's list, the Tribune's came too late to include those of Sheldon's owners who had died in the 1880s. Thirteen of the owners of "Artistic Houses" had died by the time of the Tribune's list, yet even so five of them were represented. Three men whose houses Sheldon described (Anderson, Shoenberger and Vanderbilt) had passed on sufficient wealth so that their widows merited inclusion on the list of millionaires, while two (Gibson and Phillips) had their estates listed. Mrs. James Harper, a widow, was not listed, but all of her brothers-in-law were, while the fathers of three other house owners (Hovey, Walter Hunnewell and Tiffany) were included by the Tribune, though the sons were not. The Tribune listed the wives of four men whom Sheldon considered the owners of houses (Drayton, Iselin, Bradley Martin and Wadsworth) as millionaires by inheritance, but not the husbands. Fully 44 more of Sheldon's subjects, almost half his group, made it onto the Tribune list in their own right. Twenty-two of the house owners who were still alive in 1892 had not accumulated enough wealth to merit inclusion, while in the case of five it is not known if they were still alive or where they were living.

According to the Tribune's systematic assessment, one major characteristic Sheldon's house owners had in common was great wealth, for almost two-thirds of his subjects, either personally or by family association, rated inclusion in the category of millionaire, the pinnacle of the pyramid of wealth in America. Even among the 22 men still living in 1892 but not ranked as millionaires or represented by a relative, many had accumulated substantial wealth. James W. Alexander was vice president of the Equitable Life Assurance Society, one of the country's major insurance companies. Knight D. Cheney was moving up toward the presidency of his family's silk mills, the largest in the country. Although neither Frederic W. Stevens nor Frederick F. Thompson, had amassed a million dollars, each was director of a half-dozen significant New York banks, insurance companies and other financial institutions. Still others, who lacked a million of their own, constantly rubbed shoulders with the very rich, either as their pastor (the Reverend Phillips Brooks), their decorator (Samuel Colman) or their architect (Frank Furness). Among those dead by 1892, the year of the Tribune's list, and not represented by heirs, Cornelia M. Stewart had briefly enjoyed one of the country's great fortunes and several others, such as James L. Claghorn, Edward N. Dickerson and Samuel J. Tilden, had been men of substantial wealth.

Thus, the homes Sheldon presented were owned almost entirely by men and women of unusual wealth. In a few cases, notably those of Marshall Field, Henry M. Flagler, Robert Goelet, J. Pierpont Morgan, Cornelia M. Stewart and William H. Vanderbilt, Sheldon was discussing homes owned by people of legendary wealth, the sort of immense fortune that made the family name a household word throughout America.

In dozens of other cases, Sheldon's subjects constituted what English observer James Bryce identified as one of "the most remarkable phenomena" of the late nineteenth century, the rapidly growing class of "millionaires of the second order, men with fortunes ranging from $5,000,000 to $15,000,000." The prosperity of the 1880s was creating a great surge of such wealth, a development that fascinated the general public, alarmed reformers and perplexed Society itself.

With the great rise of new fortunes, various leaders of Society decided it was necessary to define the boundaries of acceptability. Of course, there had always been social definition, but it had been largely informal and simply in the minds of those who belonged. As late as the 1870s, according to such old-family representatives as Edith Wharton and Mrs. John King Van Rensselaer, it had still been possible for "New York Society" to be "a representative, exclusive body of all that was best in the city," on a basis of mutual recognition and privately agreed-upon invitation lists. Then, according to Wharton, "the first change came in the 'eighties, with the earliest detachment of big money-makers from the West." Just as the great increase in "millionaires of the second order" had led journalists to develop their explicit, categorized lists of the wealthy, so too the influx of new families led to a formalization of membership in Society, most clearly exemplified by the *Social Register*.

The *Social Register* was another new phenomenon of the 1880s, designed to end confusion as to who truly belonged in Society. American journalists had been attempting to define Society, looking for "Class Distinctions in the United States" or "Caste in American Society," but they found themselves puzzled. One writer, Kate Gannett Wells, reported that she had been to eight society functions in a week and had not seen one person twice. "Where is society?" she asked. "At each door there were carriages, and each house was well appointed. Some would fold their napkins; others would throw them crumpled on the table. Some would have wine, others water." She could find no certain key to Society behavior and membership. The *Social Register* sorted this out, both recording and in a sense creating in print the formal Society that the 1880s called into being. Published by the Social Register Association, the first volume of the *Register* appeared in 1887 and naturally devoted itself to New York. Listing fewer than 2000 families, the *Register* included Dutch and English families from the colonial era, families who had made fortunes and gained status in the early nineteenth century and some of the more recent arrivals.

Forty-nine of Sheldon's house owners were still alive in 1887 and in the New York area. Of them, 28 merited inclusion in the first *Social Register*, a slightly lower proportion than earned their place on the *Tribune*'s list of millionaires. Among Sheldon's members of Society were several whose families had been prominent for several generations, such as the Fishes, the Goelets, the Iselins and the Winthrops. Early-nineteenth-century wealth was represented by such men and women as Julia T. Harper and William F. Havemeyer. Some of Wharton's "money-makers from the West" (and others from the South) won a listing as well, among them H. Victor Newcomb, born in Kentucky and at the beginning of the decade the youngest president of a major railroad, the Louisville and Nashville. Another post–Civil War arrival in New York Society was Richard T. Wilson, a Georgia native who settled in New York in the 1860s with money gained marketing Confederate cotton in England. Still others of Sheldon's owners gained a presence in Society primarily through professional contacts. Two of his physicians, William A. Hammond and William T. Lusk, acquired only moderate wealth but were well known as society doctors.

Doctors Hammond and Lusk, in their *Social Register* inclusion but absence from the *Tribune*'s list of millionaires, represented six other New York–area owners of "Artistic Houses." James W. Alexander and William Sprague Hoyt were others who had inherited or married social connections, but failed to achieve great wealth. Among Sheldon's New Yorkers, the largest single group consisted of those 19 house owners who were both socially prominent and wealthy. All of the wealthy owners noted above were in the group, as were bankers George F. Baker and J. Pierpont Morgan; such substantial merchants as George Kemp, Henry G. Marquand and John Wolfe; and John T. Johnston, a railroad investor. Edith Wharton might have been pleased to note that there were a dozen house owners with enough wealth for the *Tribune* who had not been accepted into Society and that such Western millionaires as Herman O. Armour, Henry M. Flagler and John H. Shoenberger were prominent in the excluded group. They were joined by Sheldon's one Jewish house owner—David L. Einstein—and several millionaires of German immigrant background, such as Oswald Ottendorfer, Jacob Ruppert and Henry Villard. Eight of Sheldon's New York–area owners were not distinguished for either wealth or social prestige in the 1880s.

Fig. 7. Jacob Ruppert house, New York, New York.

The Social Register Association followed its New York debut with volumes for Boston and Philadelphia in 1890. The first Philadelphia *Social Register* was much smaller than New York's—one-tenth the names for a city about half the size of New York. Of Sheldon's Philadelphians, only James L. Claghorn had died by 1890. Among the others, George W. Childs, Frank Furness, Henry C. Gibson and Clara Jessup Moore had earned state or national recognition for their achievements or philanthropy and, except for Furness, they owned at least the $1 million that the *Tribune* looked for, as did three others of Sheldon's group, but neither wealth nor achievement won them or any other owner inclusion in Philadelphia Society, a group noted in the late nineteenth century for its high degree of exclusiveness.

Fig. 8. Joseph H. White house, Brookline, Massachusetts.

Boston Society, on the other hand, was more inclusive or else Sheldon had selected his Boston owners in a different way, for, of 16 families who owned houses in Boston itself or in nearby towns, 12 merited inclusion in early *Social Registers*. An additional person, Phillips Brooks, died too early for listing in the extant *Registers* but surely would have been included. Of Sheldon's owners, only two Boston merchants, Joseph H. and Ralph H. White, banker Asa P. Potter and Elizabeth E. Spooner failed to be listed. In Boston, then, Sheldon had a group with an unusually high proportion of membership in the social elite. The other house owners lived in cities which produced *Social Registers* only in the 1890s or never, but there is no question that men like Joseph G. Chapman, trustee and benefactor of Washington University and the St. Louis Museum of Fine Arts; John W. Doane, who presided over one of Chicago's banquets for Ulysses S. Grant after completion of his world tour in 1879; or William S. Kimball, one of Rochester's foremost businessmen and philanthropists, were considered among the elite of their communities. Overall, Sheldon assembled a group that enjoyed not only great wealth but high social status.

The Upper Class Organizes Culture, Leisure, Education and Manners

The *Social Register* was simply one way in which the American upper class attempted to define itself and achieve what proved to be an elusive stability and organization. In the 1880s, such an achievement of order still seemed possible and Sheldon's owners played an active role in most of the activities designed to bring it about. To some extent, the efforts of the 1880s built upon, yet in a way opposed, earlier work by an upper class that thought of itself as more exclusive. This earlier elite included some of Sheldon's older house owners, among them Hamilton and Julia Kean Fish, pillars second to none in New York's Knickerbocker aristocracy. The home itself was central to social organization, for Mrs. Fish's invitations were crucial in defining who belonged and who did not. While she (no. 52) or such a friend as Elizabeth Marquand (nos. 92 & 93) hosted a "limited but exceedingly brilliant gathering of society people" in their homes, Hamilton Fish took his turn presiding over the older cultural institutions, such as the Academy of Music and the New-York Historical Society, that helped define his generation's elite. According to longtime New York diarist George Templeton Strong, what he and Fish and several others had been trying to do was to "take charge of polite society, regulate its institutions, keep it pure, and decide who shall be admitted . . . ."

Such efforts proved unable to cope with the surge of new wealth during and after the Civil War, so that the 1880s became the crucial period for the establishment of a sufficiently inclusive yet durable upper class. Local cultural institutions played a notable part, as they had earlier, with such newer organizations as the Metropolitan Opera and the Metropolitan Museum of Art expressing the energies of the newer upper class. Among Sheldon's owners, A. T. Stewart was one of the biggest early donors to the Metropolitan Museum, sugar refiner Robert Stuart was active on the organizing committee and railroad president John Taylor Johnston became the museum's first president. The Metropolitan Opera provided an even greater opportunity for new families to shine, for box ownership gave conspicuous places to such new arrivals in New York as H. Victor and Florence Newcomb and Richard T. and Melissa Wilson and to other rapid risers in society, such as George and Juliet Kemp and Bradley and Cornelia Martin.

Parallels were to be found in such other cities as, for instance, Philadelphia, where banker James L. Claghorn, retired from active business since the outbreak of the Civil War, took over leadership of the Pennsylvania Academy of the Fine Arts. The Pennsylvania Academy, Philadelphia's preeminent art museum since soon after its founding in 1807, moved into its new home, designed by Frank Furness, a few years after Claghorn became its president in 1872. Claghorn, one of America's foremost collectors of etchings and engravings, worked on the Academy's board with another Sheldon subject, distiller and wine importer Henry C. Gibson, and the two made substantial donations to the collections. Rising to challenge the eminence of the Academy was the Pennsylvania Museum of Art, begun only in the late 1870s as a result of the great Centennial Exhibition. Gentlemen such as Claghorn and Gibson kept the museum at arm's length, but it received a solid foundation in the fine arts from the mid-1880s gifts made by still another Sheldon owner, Clara Jessup Moore.

In Chicago too, men of newer wealth built up a new museum to help symbolize their own economic and cultural achievements. For Chicago, the Great Fire of 1871 gave particular impetus to new beginnings and the Board of Trustees that set out to reestablish the Academy of Design soon founded instead a new Academy of Fine Arts, which in 1882 became The Art Institute of Chicago. Active on the Board in all these stages was Samuel M. Nickerson. Born in Massachusetts, and later clerking in his brother's store in a Florida town in the early 1850s, Nickerson had moved to Chicago in 1857 and by the time of the fire was president of both the First National Bank and the Union Stockyards National Bank. By the time Sheldon presented his home (nos. 103 & 104), Nickerson's art collection was considered one of the largest in the West, a collection he ultimately donated to the Art Institute.

Art, both in the home and in museums, had long been a way for an upper class to combine personal pleasure with a declaration of social status. To this and other traditional expressions of rank, the newly enlarged upper class of the 1880s brought several innovations intended to make clear lines of social distinction and establish homogeneity. Residential patterns, for instance, took on a new significance as the 1880s brought the rise of the upper-class suburb, a planned community with firm restrictions on who could buy and build. In *Artistic Houses*, Sheldon limited himself primarily to distinctly urban homes, but Short Hills, New Jersey, the home of William I. Russell and Franklin H. Tinker, typified the new suburban pattern. As Sheldon noted, "six years ago the place was a wilderness of forest-growth," while when he visited it contained three dozen attractive year-round homes and all the amenities of "a beautiful village, without the nuisances of a village." In other words, it had music hall, church, club, stables and greenhouses but "no stores, no unsightly sheds, no country 'bar.' " Russell, a broker in metals who late in life wrote an autobiography, moved into his new home, "Redstone" (no. 74), in 1882, soon made friends with Tinker, a fellow book collector, and found life in the small, self-contained suburb "all that we would have it—peaceful, happy, contented." Given the small size and homogeneous character of the community, social activity involving all the residents soon became a hallmark of Short Hills life. Russell found that "the frequent pleasant little dinner-parties of four to six couples, where bright and entertaining conversation was general," made his new home the key to "serenity and delight." Bringing together the whole little community were "enjoyable amateur dramatic performances, followed by light refreshment and a couple of hours' dancing." Now and again there would be a special community event, as when Russell hosted a ball to open his new carriage house and stable. The stable itself was transformed into a ballroom, with floral horseshoes, a bronze jockey and coaching pictures for decorations, the orchestra upstairs around the open hay doors, and guests receiving with their dance cards "a sterling silver pencil representing the foreleg of a horse in action, the shoe being of gold."

A complementary innovation, drawing the well-to-do out of the city in an organized and exclusive way, was the country club, also a new phenomenon of the 1880s. Such clubs, springing up on the outskirts of most Eastern cities in the decade, brought together the rising interest in sport, such as riding, coaching and tennis, with the growing concern for social exclusiveness. The Country Club, founded in Brookline, Massachusetts, in 1882 is commonly considered the first of its kind, and one of Sheldon's Boston couples, John L. and Isabella Stewart Gardner, were active members. Coaching with two, three or four horses and a variety of conveyances became a particular interest of the Gardners; leading a line of coaches from Boston out to The Country Club gave Isabella Gardner an opportunity to cultivate and display flamboyance. Similarly, in Washington, Nicholas Longworth Anderson was writing to his son in the 1880s that he and his wife were helping to establish a similar country club, perhaps inspired in part by Gardner, "one of my most intimate friends." The Andersons found their new club a welcome opportunity for recreation and a new vehicle for the social life that included frequent entertainment of American political leaders and European diplomats.

Club and suburb were important not only for who was included and accepted, but for who was excluded. In many cases no doubt a man of wealth found himself left out because others did not care for his personal habits, his business practices or his family. One type of exclusion by group identity was becoming more pronounced and formal in the 1880s— anti-Semitism. Institutionalized anti-Semitism was relatively easy to bring about when one was forming a new club or residential area, but the practice received its most well-publicized beginning in a long-established place of public accommodation. In the late 1870s, one of Sheldon's owners, Judge Henry Hilton, had recently begun effective management of the A. T. Stewart millions and one of his responsibilities was the Grand Union Hotel in Saratoga, New York, a summer retreat popular with the wealthy. When Hilton, in 1877, refused rooms to Joseph Seligman, a prominent New York Jewish banker, he incurred a flurry of denunciation, but Hilton's anti-Semitic policies soon caught on and set the pattern for an increasing number of upper-class institutions in the 1880s.

While the exclusive suburb and the country club offered upper-class definition to separate local groups, the prestigious boarding schools begun in the 1880s were designed in part to cultivate links between elites in different cities, to help bring about a self-conscious national upper class. A few of what became socially selective boarding schools had been founded earlier, notably Phillips Exeter, Phillips Andover and St. Paul's. They had been day schools, educating a local clientele at a time when many wealthy families hired tutors to educate their children at home. The shift of the older schools toward boarding students drawn from throughout the Northeast mirrored the character of the new schools founded in the 1880s expressly to educate a national elite. Foremost among the new schools was Groton, founded in 1884 by Endicott Peabody to help train gentlemen. Learning was important, but it was also essential "to have good manners and be decent and live up to standards." On his first small Board of Trustees, Peabody enlisted the vital support of two of Sheldon's householders, Trinity Church's pastor Phillips Brooks and prominent Episcopal layman and banker J. Pierpont Morgan. As one of his first two teachers, Peabody hired William A. Gardner, nephew of John L. Gardner and raised in the Gardner home.

Such formal institutions were important ways of organizing society, but the home itself remained the key to definition and cultivation of a recognizable and responsible upper class. Clubs and schools affected people only at a particular time in their lives or through a specialized interest, and for the most part their activities included only men. Invitation into the home was the one act that could touch all aspirants to inclusion in Society. Such an invitation was first an opportunity and a testing and later a confirmation that one belonged.

Proper behavior in the home was not something that could be taken for granted, for the rapid increase in the number of wealthy Americans meant that there were many men and women who believed they ought to be invited into upper-class homes but who were unsure how to behave once they got there. They solved the problem with a book. The fictional Silas Lapham, for instance, as soon as his family had been invited to dinner by the long-established Coreys, immediately bought an etiquette book to save himself from obvious blunders.

Lapham had innumerable real parallels, as the great popularity of such books in the 1870s and 1880s demonstrated. Of these the most widely read was *Sensible Etiquette of the Best Society* by one of Sheldon's Philadelphia house owners, Clara Jessup Moore. Moore first published the book under a pseudo-

nym in 1878, and it soon went through 20 editions. Having inherited some $5 million on her husband's death in the same year, Moore had a solid place among the wealthy in Philadelphia, but her father had suffered business failure when she was young and wealth had come only in the 1850s, as a result of a partnership between her father and her husband in paper manufacturing. Moore was perfectly aware of at least a part of her market, giving the name "Madame Newrich" to one of the recipients of instruction in her book. Moore assured her readers, however, that they need worry about no inherent inferiority in manners. No one had natural or inborn manners, which were "only acquired by education and observation, followed up by habitual practice at home and in society." So there was no reason for men or women to fear betraying their origins, as long as they applied themselves to learn the intricate and rigid code Moore described.

Fig. 9. Clara Jessup Moore house, Philadelphia, Pennsylvania.

As in the other efforts to define a stable upper class, etiquette too required fixed order. Moore recognized that mobility and economic growth made a fixed code of manners difficult to achieve, but American heterogeneity made such a code all the more necessary because friction and conflict could be avoided only as a result of "our obedience to the laws of that etiquette which governs the whole machinery, and keeps every cog and wheel in place, and at its own work." People had to know what to expect of each other and only agreed-upon manners could prevent serious misunderstandings or "rudenesses suspected where none are intended." Writing after the upheavals of the Civil War and of the depression of the 1870s, Moore hoped that America had settled into a pattern that would make possible fixed manners. Otherwise, if "the first principles of social intercourse" are "violated at the foundations, the entire structure of society becomes insecure."

Quite apart from such goals of national stability, Moore also knew that people going through her own earlier experiences would feel more comfortable in the homes of the Claghorns and Gibsons and the like if they knew just what to do. She would tell them, in chapter after chapter of specific instruction. Suppose a reader found him- or herself in one of the dining rooms Sheldon pictured, exactly the kind of situation Silas Lapham worried about:

> As soon as seated, remove your gloves, place your table-napkin partly opened across your lap, your gloves under it, and your roll on the left side of your plate. If raw oysters are already served, you at once begin to eat; to wait for others to commence is old-fashioned. Take soup from the side of the spoon, and avoid making any sound in drawing it up or swallowing it. Vegetables are eaten with a fork. Asparagus can be taken up with the fingers, if so preferred. Olives and artichokes are always so eaten.

To master such rules and go on to host such social events was no trivial accomplishment, Moore and other etiquette authorities argued. The person who could "make her parlor a rallying-point for nice people is doing a great public service," according to M. E. W. Sherwood, author of *Manners and Social Usages.* She and Moore agreed that a society leader was a power for good, by refining and elevating standards of behavior, checking the pretensions of the vulgar and the immoral, and raising to influence those with genuine merit in a country where all sorts of people were mixed together. The home in this way was the key to decency, honesty and stability in society.

Moreover, the home gave women in particular an influence otherwise difficult to exercise. Women of wealth recognized that the lack of household work gave them no practical importance in the home. As adults in the 1880s, most such women had not enjoyed a substantial formal education and they did not expect important roles in the public institutions of their lives, such as the church. They faced a dilemma well described by a fictional young woman in a popular novel of the decade, Ruth Cheever in Edgar Fawcett's *A Gentleman of Leisure.* As Cheever explained to the novel's hero, "A woman gets no satisfaction, in this age, out of the most legitimate discontentments. She has a choice between two extremes, and that is all. She must either consign herself to frivolities, or else be satirized as a prig, a person 'with views.' And in either case she is satirized, I find, all the same." Moore and Sherwood offered women a way out. They could transform those social activities that others might label frivolous and infuse them with moral purpose. "What do women want with votes," Moore asked, "when they hold the sceptre of influence?" This influence, she made clear, was not just that traditional influence of moral motherhood, for it did require rigorous formal education, but it was a use of domestic position well beyond the benefit of one's own family to achieve goals that men alone could not. By setting a standard in society and organizing it so as to make social distinction both clear and desirable, women could see to it that members of the American upper class "really fulfill certain important functions, that they really offer a higher standard of elegance and culture, that they really encourage an improvement in manners, and stimulate the growth and spread of refined taste."

The ordinary dinner party or tea naturally offered opportunities for working toward Moore's ends, but what most caught the public's eye was the much more conspicuous effort to organize one unified upper class, as seen in the great balls of the 1880s. Probably the single most important event of this sort took place not in one of the homes that Sheldon described, but in that of Mr. and Mrs. W. K. Vanderbilt, son and daughter-in-law of Sheldon's William H. Vanderbilt. The younger Mrs. Vanderbilt's ball to open her new Fifth Avenue home on March 26, 1883, marked the at least limited acceptance of the newer aristocracy by the older, symbolized by Mrs. William Astor's attendance. The desire of Mrs. Astor's daughter Caroline to be invited to the ball had supposedly been the principal reason for the mother's social acceptance of the younger Mrs. Vanderbilt. The amalgamation of older and newer aristocracy would soon be made more vivid by Caroline's marriage to another ball guest, Orme Wilson, son of the Richard T. Wilsons who had been making such a social splash in New York since their arrival from Georgia after the Civil War.

A more substantive indication that old differences could be overcome in the interest of upper-class unity was the presence at the same ball of two other Sheldon house owners, Mrs. Hamilton Fish and Mrs. William H. Vanderbilt. To her own generation, Julia Kean Fish, even more than Mrs. Astor, represented the most rigorous exclusiveness of the old Knickerbocker elite. Edith Wharton and M. E. W. Sherwood, for instance, both singled her out as an example of the high moral tone and seriousness of the old-school social leader. Her ability to live up to expectations had been amply demonstrated when she set the social standard for the Grant administration, in which her husband was Secretary of State. Maria Louisa Kissam, on the other hand, had been socially unacceptable even to the self-made Cornelius Vanderbilt when his son married her at the age of 19. The senior Vanderbilt virtually exiled William H. and Maria to a farm on Staten Island, and Mrs. Vanderbilt never felt comfortable with the position in New York society to which her wealth and home entitled her. That she and Mrs. Fish could converse readily at her daughter-in-law's ball indicated a coming together of the urban upper class such as the new boarding schools, for instance, were trying to achieve or that Boston minister Phillips Brooks was working for in his church.

The junior Mrs. Vanderbilt's guest list included a variety of representatives of the older and newer upper classes. Among other Sheldon home owners were former President and Mrs. Grant, friends of both the Fishes and the senior Vanderbilts, and J. Coleman and Charlotte Drayton, she the daughter of Mrs. Astor. Bradley and Cornelia Martin no doubt surveyed the ball for usable ideas in their own beginning social campaigns. Others participating in the lavishly costumed quadrilles or observing included Mr. and Mrs. Robert Goelet, who enjoyed one of New York's older real-estate fortunes, and Mr. and Mrs. John T. Johnston. Frederic W. Stevens, on the board of a half-dozen banks and insurance companies and another half-dozen museums and libraries, was present with his wife. From out of town came Mr. and Mrs. George P. Wetmore, owners of a Newport "Artistic House," but thoroughly at home in New York social and cultural activity.

The Vanderbilt ball, which according to the *New York Tribune* "equalled, if it did not excell, any similar entertainment ever given in this city," marked the beginning of a decade of flamboyant entertainment. Grand costume balls became a standard method either of claiming or of consolidating social position and the most elaborate were noted as the pinnacle of social activity for decades before and after in their respective cities. Such, for instance, was the "Mikado Ball," hosted in 1886 in Chicago by another of Sheldon's home owners, Marshall Field (nos. 55 & 56). Some 500 guests attended in oriental costume and the reputed $75,000 expense helped make the Field ball a landmark event in late nineteenth-century Chicago.

The great balls, with their published guest lists, together with the appearance of the *Social Register* late in the 1880s, might be thought to have achieved the goal of a fixed, defined Society. In New York at least, such methods of selection still produced too large a group, so further refinement seemed necessary, and in 1888 society organizer Ward McAllister first used the term "the Four Hundred" to describe the core group, the most elect. The term supposedly derived from the number of guests who could be entertained comfortably in the ballroom of Mrs. William Astor, foremost of the three principal society hostesses in New York. The other two, Mrs. William K. Vanderbilt and Mrs. Stuyvesant Fish, were daughters-in-law of Sheldon householders.

Not until 1892, when McAllister agreed to an interview with the *New York Times*, did the public get a reliable list of the Four Hundred by name, and then it included fewer than 300 individuals. The list showed that the core of Society was much as the interested public had come to think, a group of men and women who devoted their lives primarily to entertainment of themselves and each other. Few of the men had an active occupation, but had lived on family income for most of their lives, and most had used their leisure in club life, yachting and the like rather than in museum trusteeships or some other form of public service. Among Sheldon's house owners, McAllister's list did include former Rhode Island Governor George P. Wetmore and his wife, long mainstays of New York society. Egerton Winthrop was more representative. Mr. and Mrs. Robert Goelet, owners of one of the most magnificent steam yachts afloat, were included, as were those constant party givers, Bradley and Cornelia Martin. The Richard T. Wilsons were by now well established at the center of New York society through their son's and daughters' marriages into the Astor, Goelet and Vanderbilt families. By the end of the 1880s, then, Society leaders had accomplished what they set out to do: make clear the composition of the accepted American upper class.

THE EFFORT TO ACHIEVE LASTING ORDER IN AMERICAN SOCIETY

The Four Hundred made up one small but well-publicized segment of wealthy America. The ever more lavish entertainments sponsored by Vanderbilt and Fish heirs and others increasingly captured public attention by the end of the 1880s and gave a false sense of frivolity to upper-class activity. In one respect, however, the Four Hundred did show a pervasive current in upper-class concern—the determination to create a lasting order, to impose unity where there had been fragmentation. The decade of the 1880s saw the ripening of a generation of wealthy men and women who seized the opportunity to gain firm control over the American economy in order to make permanent what they saw as the necessary conditions for continued prosperity and social stability and, based on those two factors, the flourishing of American culture.

At the opening of the decade, such men and women looked back on a period marked by upheaval, disorder and tension in many areas of life. Political life had been tarred by corruption and scandal in the Grant administration, although the President himself escaped with his reputation for personal honesty intact. The panic of 1873 and subsequent depression had revealed instability in economic expansion. A by-product of the depression had been bitter conflict between workers and employers, most vividly seen in the great railway strikes of 1877. Continued dissent over race relations and the federal government's responsibility for civil order in the South remained a source of friction through much of the decade. Corporations seemed plagued by guerrilla warfare waged against each other, as in the railroad skirmishes launched by the Erie Railroad, or by internal weakness that brought bankruptcy after the 1873 panic. In all of these areas and others, those men who survived the 1870s with wealth and power intact saw patterns of instability and disorder that they were determined to correct. They would impose their control in crucial areas and launch a period of calm which would not only profit themselves but make possible widespread prosperity and cultural advance. For a time they succeeded, and the 1880s proved to be the last period in which men of wealth enjoyed not only such relatively unchallenged power in America but also so much public acclaim. In most of these achievements, Sheldon's householders were at the forefront.

For many of Sheldon's owners, men who were in the midst of creating their own fortunes, business success was, of course, the focus of their lives and their activities give little sign of larger social concerns. For some, such as silk manufacturer Knight D. Cheney, woolen maker Swits Condé, or another wool manufacturer, David L. Einstein, concentration was on rescuing and strengthening a family business. Each of these men found himself fully busy in the 1880s saving and expanding a business, founded by father or uncles, that had slipped in the depression of the 1870s and now needed a newer, firmer hand. Sheldon's group also included several who had started their own business, devoted their lives to them, and saw the prosperity of the 1880s essentially as a chance for personal gain. Irish immigrant George Kemp, who had arrived in New York in 1834 at the age of eight and gradually built up a major drug- and perfume-manufacturing and wholesaling firm, and metals broker William I. Russell, who had started with one clerk and a tiny office in 1871, concentrated on making the most of the expanding economy. For Russell, increased prosperity meant opportunities to get rid of small customers and concentrate on large ones. The resulting satisfaction and continued focus on one's own business, with recognition simply among one's business associates and friends, was characteristic of many of Sheldon's owners.

While men like Kemp and Russell remained inconspicuous, strict devotion to one's own business became part of Marshall Field's increasing reputation. If men of wealth had any obligation to society, Field saw that responsibility as pure and simple efficiency in business. Find products that people needed and sell them at a uniform, moderate price; the man who could do that well had fulfilled his most important social role, in Field's view. Starting in retail trade in Chicago in the mid-1850s, Field had already gone through several partners by the mid-1880s and was well known for taking no active part in Chicago politics and giving little attention to any charitable activities. Field was becoming a recognized model for the strict, no-frills businessman who never borrowed or speculated, who kept all transactions on a cash basis, who held all his associates to a strict meeting of obligations, and who spared no energy from the affairs of his own firm. In this light Field embodied the virtues that men of wealth respected, but he was an inadequate model for an upper class that welcomed wider responsibilities.

Similar to Field in some respects, seeing his business itself as his main form of public service for a time, was John Taylor Johnston. Johnston entered railroading by means of the practice of law and helped consolidate several New Jersey lines into the Central Railroad of New Jersey, of which he became president in 1848. Like Field, Johnston saw economical provision of an essential service as his main contribution to society, but he expanded that idea somewhat to a hope that his railroad could be a particularly safe and attractive example. Accordingly, Johnston used his control to eliminate grade crossings wherever possible, to erect well-designed stations and to surround his stations with landscaped parks. Though focusing clearly on the railroad business, Johnston accepted responsibilities other than efficient service.

If running one's own store or railroad well was the focus for some of Sheldon's owners, others were gaining a reputation for attempts to dominate a whole segment of the economy. To such men, the lesson of the 1870s had been that economic instability resulted from fragmented industries in which too many firms lacked the resources to survive temporary setbacks. The solution was consolidation, with major firms buying out and absorbing competitors while at the same time gaining control over the suppliers and distributors of their product. For Americans at the time the greatest and most controversial example of this effort to impose order and stability was the Standard Oil Company and, except for its principal founder John D. Rockefeller, no person had played so large a part in Standard Oil's success as one of Sheldon's house owners, Henry M. Flagler.

Flagler, in Bellevue, Ohio, had dealt with Rockefeller in Cleveland as early as 1850, when both were buying and selling grain. After an unsuccessful venture in salt in Michigan, Flagler moved to Cleveland and, in 1867, entered into a partnership with Rockefeller and others in oil refining. At the time, the petroleum industry was made up of innumerable small, independent drillers, refiners, tank-car companies, retailers and the like. Flagler and Rockefeller set out to bring order to what they saw as chaos. They concluded that they could enlarge the market and lower the price of petroleum products, ensure stability of supply and make fortunes for themselves if they eliminated the waste and duplication of competition, so for some 15 years they persistently extended their control and discipline over the industry until, by the time they formed the final Standard Oil Trust in 1882, they controlled at least 90 percent of American refining.

Flagler's work in Standard Oil was probably the best example among Sheldon's group of the characteristic determination to impose order and set a pattern expected to last, but other house owners were equally active in other areas of the economy, if not as successful as Flagler. In meat packing, Herman O. Armour worked with several brothers in Armour and Company to consolidate an activity earlier characterized by many small packers. Another food-processing field, sugar refining, experienced the very successful amalgamating efforts of the American Sugar Refining Company, in which the Havemeyer family, represented in Sheldon's collection by William F. Havemeyer, played a significant role. Railroading was one of the country's most active fields of consolidation and two of the most well-publicized entrepreneurs of the 1880s, Henry Villard of the Northern Pacific and William H. Vanderbilt of the New York Central system, were among Sheldon's owners.

While some consolidators were able to rely largely on their own resources, banking houses were heavily involved in much of what went on. If the achievement of order and stability through the elimination of competition and the strengthening of dominant firms was a hallmark of the 1880s, then already playing a leading role was another Sheldon figure, investment broker J. Pierpont Morgan. From the late 1860s on, Morgan had built a career on the identification of his own fortunes with the elimination of weak or erratic firms in major industries, especially railroading. Morgan sought to put out of business those he saw as working only for short-term gains and to put industrial activity into the hands of those who would ride out economic fluctuation. In 1879 Morgan helped William H. Vanderbilt maintain the value of New York Central stock by placing a large block of shares directly with English investors, an act that particularly solidified his reputation as a man of both great ability and great concern for stable control.

If the foremost public responsibility of the man of wealth was capable management of his own firm, then charitable giving was expected to follow soon after. Many of the rich certainly accepted the obligation, thinking, with John T. Johnston, that "I consider it just as much my duty to give to benevolent institutions as to pay my butcher's bill." Often the giving was to local charities and, as was said of Boston merchant John C. Phillips, done in a "quiet and unostentatious manner."

Charitable donations, however, were also one of the few areas in which wealthy women could be active in public ways without being unladylike. Among Sheldon's home owners, several women gained reputations for philanthropy as their expression of upper-class involvement for social good. Best known in the 1880s was probably Cornelia M. Stewart, widow of department-store millionaire Alexander T. Stewart. The Stewarts had no children and Mrs. Stewart received what she thought of as an overwhelming number of requests for charity when her husband died. While denying most requests, Mrs. Stewart made major gifts to a residence for working women and to a school for boys, and a particularly impressive donation to construct a cathedral in Garden City on Long Island.

Another widow who carried on her husband's giving, but more fully and with more continuing personal interest, was Mary McCrea Stuart, whose husband Robert had made his fortune first in candy manufacture and then in sugar refining. When Robert Stuart died in 1882 he left his wife about $5 million, much of which for the rest of the decade she distributed in gifts. Princeton was her main interest, but she also made substantial donations to the New-York Historical Society, to boards for foreign and domestic missions and to establish residences for newsboys and orphans, frequently with the stipulation that she receive no public recognition. When Mrs. Stuart herself died at the end of 1891, newspaper attention was as substantial and appreciative as for any other woman in Sheldon's group.

A third woman for whom charitable work was important had done much to earn the family fortune herself. Anna Behr, born in Bavaria in 1815, arrived in the United States in 1837 and soon afterward married Jacob Uhl, with whom she published the New York *Staats-Zeitung,* soon the major American German-language daily. Jacob Uhl died in 1852 and his widow carried on the paper by herself, hiring Oswald Ottendorfer to help, and marrying him in 1859. The continued growth of the German community in America increased the newspaper's prosperity and Anna Ottendorfer turned more toward philanthropic activity. She concentrated on the welfare of German-Americans and contributed generously to hospitals, schools and homes for the elderly that served that group—activity for which, in 1883, shortly before her death, she received a medal from Empress Augusta of Germany.

Among philanthropic businessmen, the best-known of Sheldon's owners was surely George W. Childs, publisher of the Philadelphia *Public Ledger.* Born in Baltimore in 1829, his father never acknowledging his birth nor marrying his mother, Childs was an epitome of the self-made man. He spent his teens in naval service and as a store clerk, but soon opened his own bookstore, then began to publish and built a substantial reputation as a book publisher. Childs bought the *Ledger* in 1864 and made it the most profitable paper in Philadelphia. Almost as soon as he was making a large income, Childs began to build lavishly and to donate money to worthy causes. His most conspicuous gifts honored literature, for he gave a stained-glass window to Westminster Abbey to honor William Cowper and George Herbert, raised funds to mark the grave of Leigh Hunt, built another monument for the grave of Edgar Allan Poe, and subscribed generously to a memorial window for Thomas Moore.

In Philadelphia he created a printer's cemetery and endowed a maintenance fund, and engaged in such intermittent public charities as paying admission fees for some 2000 deaf and dumb or homeless children to the Centennial Exhibition. Far from "quiet and unostentatious," Childs in the 1880s was widely admired as the model employer and generous citizen, "the living illustration of that noble characteristic so rare among men of influence—the accumulation of riches, not for himself alone, but to make others happy during and after his life." Indicating a similar uneasiness about the accumulation and use of wealth, observers also commonly remarked that Childs had made his fortune in a way that injured no other person, seemingly an unusual characteristic.

Childs's lavish giving had certain common strands, honoring Anglo-American literature and aiding the poor and printing workers locally, but it lacked the system and order increasingly thought essential in charity. Just as business had to be consolidated and made efficient, benevolence too required control and discipline if it was to have maximum effect. This antipathy to individual, idiosyncratic giving and to the prevalent form of poor-relief that simply gave money to the poor, was best expressed in the Charity Organization movement, a self-styled scientific approach to charity that took form simultaneously in several Eastern cities in the 1870s and developed into the National Conference on Charities and Corrections by the end of that decade. The coordination of all charity by one local organization, the resulting elimination of waste, the differentiation between the "worthy" and the "unworthy" poor, and the substitution of advice and good management for money charity were central characteristics of the movement, with clear parallels to trust building in the corporate area. What the Charity Organization movement also made possible, as corporations sometimes did not, was a place for "men of leisure with the tradition of public service," in the words of one early leader.

No one better represented the upper class's turn to organized charity than one of Sheldon's Boston householders, Robert Treat Paine, Jr. Paine's direct ancestors included a signer of the Declaration of Independence and a governor of Connecticut. After practicing law in Boston for about ten years, Paine was able to retire in 1870, at the age of 35, to devote his time to charitable work. By that time Paine had combined inherited wealth, his wife's property and his own investment skills to create a reliable and substantial income. As Paine described the shift in his interests, "the conviction was forced upon my mind that we only have this life in this world once, and that I was not willing to devote it to business when noble uses of it could be found to make the world a bit happier around me."

In the early 1870s, Paine was particularly involved with the community work of Trinity Church and its pastor, his friend Phillips Brooks. When the church was destroyed by fire in 1872, Paine played a major role in raising funds for the new church and rectory, designed by H. H. Richardson. With his experience both in church-related benevolent work and in large-scale money raising, Paine came to see a need for efficient, coordinated charity and was one of the founders of the Associated Charities of Boston in 1878, becoming its first president, and from that base gaining a national reputation as an authority on scientific charity and a leader in the national Charity Organization movement. Paine hoped to see much charity made unnecessary as low-income workers were helped to live economically, save money and become property owners. Toward this end he organized the Wells Memorial Institute, a club for working men and women that included an industrial-trades school, a cooperative savings bank and a loan association for home building. He helped finance the construction of model tenements and helped establish the People's Institute, a meeting place frequently open to labor-union speakers.

In the mid-1880s, Paine, apparently deciding that direct private involvement was insufficient, entered politics and secured election to the Massachusetts legislature, where he chaired the committee on charitable institutions. In 1884 he ran for Congress as a Democrat but was unsuccessful, perhaps in part because of what others saw as his thoroughly patrician manner. In any case, Paine's Charity Organization work continued and he was able to help create in Boston a comprehensive network of institutions designed to help workers make intelligent use of their talents and resources, so as to minimize simple poor-relief. He did not expect any significant alteration of social structure but he did think that diligent workers deserved fair opportunities and he was particularly concerned that his own class open up those opportunities. As Paine put it, "the rich, the happy, the cultured, are put under a conscious moral servitude to every form of distress," a religious obligation that he learned in part from Brooks and then implemented with business efficiency in his Charity Organization work.

Elected public service, a brief interlude for Paine, was not something that many of Sheldon's owners tried, but the exceptions were conspicuous. Since most of the men had quite successful business careers, friends often thought of them for public office, but in most cases the house owners declined. Like Charles Stewart Smith, a New York dry-goods merchant offered the Republican nomination for mayor and several times spoken of for governor, they did not want the problems of an electoral campaign or the constant and varied demands of office. On the other hand, such men often had a definite sense of what was needed in public life. Smith was active in police-reform work in New York, served several years as president of the city's Chamber of Commerce and frequently wrote articles on political and social issues for the *North American Review*. He expected others to implement his ideas.

Among those of Sheldon's owners who held elected office, several were just embarking in the early 1880s on what would prove to be successful careers. In Massachusetts, Oliver Ames may have had a sense of general public responsibility but more particularly he was out to rehabilitate his family's reputation. His father, Oakes Ames, had been among the congressmen most tainted by corruption in construction contracts for the first transcontinental railroad. Oliver first built up the neglected

family farm-implement and shovel business; after putting the business on solid ground Ames secured election as a Republican to the Massachusetts Senate in 1880 and in 1882 began four terms as lieutenant governor. From that post Ames would go on to the governorship, holding office for three terms: in 1887, 1888 and 1889.

In Rhode Island, George Peabody Wetmore followed a similar pattern in the 1880s, though without a parental stigma to erase. Wetmore, who inherited several million dollars from his merchant father, was a member of both the New York and Rhode Island bars but never practiced. He married in 1869 and spent much of his time traveling in Europe. He entered Republican politics in 1880, when he served as a Presidential elector, a post he held again in 1884. In his substantial Newport home (nos. 192 & 193) he regularly entertained political leaders, including President Chester Arthur in 1882. In 1885 the party ran Wetmore for the governorship, a race he won and then won again for a second term. His third-term bid failed and he remained out of office for a time, but he would go on to the United States Senate, where he served from 1895 until 1913. In and out of office, Wetmore had a continuing interest in architecture, which showed not only in his alterations of the family home, but also in his service as an important member of commissions with responsibility for building the Rhode Island statehouse and the Metropolitan Opera House.

As Ames and Wetmore were beginning their elective careers, two other owners of "Artistic Houses" were enjoying the respectful afterglow of distinguished political service, each in "the private life of a gentleman of ample means and cultivated tastes." Near neighbors in their New York City homes, Samuel J. Tilden and Hamilton Fish had risen through the Democratic and Republican parties, respectively. Tilden had reached the New York governorship in 1874 on his record of cleaning up the political corruption associated with William "Boss" Tweed and was his party's candidate for President in 1876. Fish too had been governor of New York, a generation before Tilden, and then senator in the 1850s. Ulysses S. Grant brought Fish out of retirement to serve as his Secretary of State from 1869 through the end of Grant's term in 1877. In their political careers both Tilden and Fish had come to be seen as almost the epitome in their respective parties of the values of moderation, honest efficiency and businesslike organization. Particularly in the later stages of their political careers, each had worked to minimize the disruptions associated with Reconstruction to create the political conditions they saw as necessary for stable economic growth.

Fig. 10. Samuel J. Tilden house, New York, New York.

Both Tilden and Fish had a role in another significant aspect of public service by the wealthy, the creation or strengthening of cultural institutions. Tilden, virtually a recluse in his later years, acted through his will, leaving several millions to found a free library in New York. Fish served at different times as a trustee of the Astor Library (with which the Tilden funds later would be combined), chairman of the trustees of Columbia University and president of the New-York Historical Society, in mid-century the country's most significant art museum.

Except for success in their own business field and, by means of such success, organization of the American economy, Sheldon's home owners were most likely to see work for major cultural institutions as their most significant form of public service. Work for museums not only enabled members of the upper class to define Society, as described earlier, but was also their best opportunity to help shape a durable order and set of standards in American society. As was appropriate for owners of "Artistic Houses," more than a dozen of Sheldon's subjects were active, knowledgeable collectors, while three more, Samuel Colman, Frank Furness and Louis C. Tiffany, earned their livings in the arts. Among the wealthy collectors, about ten not only gathered paintings, drawings, sculpture and the like for their own enjoyment, but devoted a significant part of their energy to creating or managing major museums, one of the most visible examples in the 1870s and 1880s of a determination by the wealthy to create symbols of a new urban culture.

The creators of this culture were conscious of living in what they themselves called a Renaissance. As Mary Elizabeth Sherwood, a cultural commentator and society hostess, wrote in 1882, the term Renaissance might seem trite but no other would do to describe "our emergence into the full floodtide of modern art improvement and beauty." Americans, she continued, had "lived through a very dark night, to be rewarded with an exceedingly fresh and brilliant morning." Wealth was one of the primary factors making possible this triumph. Another critic, O. B. Frothingham, summarized a widespread view when he wrote in the same year: "Wealth in America is becoming firm, settled, established. The period of convulsion is over. Wealth is the precursor of fine art [because it] gives the opportunity, provides the motive, furnishes the attraction, directs mental force, stimulates talent, brings floating genius to a useful point." Encouragement of such an artistic flowering was not simply an end in itself, for by inculcating values of generosity and service, and standards of taste, men of wealth could moderate and direct social change. As Henry Lee Higginson, Boston banker and active philanthropist, put it at the end of the 1880s, "The gentlemen of this country" can "save ourselves and our families and our money from mobs" by leading "the new men, who are trying to become gentlemen." This was to be accomplished by setting an example of giving and by working in behalf of cultural institutions.

All of the major cities Sheldon drew on for his houses yielded examples of men and women acting as Higginson advised, although perhaps not necessarily for his reasons. In St. Louis, Joseph Gilbert Chapman's "artistic treasures" were "known throughout the West," according to Sheldon (no. 98), and Chapman's interest made him a prominent manager of the St. Louis Museum and School of Fine Arts in the 1880s. In Chicago, Sheldon found Samuel M. Nickerson, whose art collection (nos. 103 & 104) was perhaps "the largest in the West," and who was active in reestablishing the Academy of Design after the Great Fire of 1871 and then in creating The Art Institute of Chicago in 1882, a museum to which he later donated much of his collection. In Philadelphia, James L. Claghorn and Henry C. Gibson were among the most influential leaders of the old and prestigious Pennsylvania Academy of the Fine Arts, of which Claghorn was President from 1872 until his death in 1884. The two men were active private collectors, Claghorn of prints (no. 9) and Gibson of paintings (nos. 46–49), made extended collecting trips in Europe, and collaborated closely on construction of the Academy's new museum building in the mid-

1870s, a project that marked one of the first major commissions of another of Sheldon's home owners, architect Frank Furness.

In New York, several of Sheldon's subjects worked together to create one of the major new museums of the postwar period, the Metropolitan Museum of Art. When fund-raising began in the early 1870s, John Taylor Johnston and A. T. Stewart were among the biggest donors, with Henry G. Marquand and Robert Stuart also active in early leadership. By the early 1880s, both Stewart and Stuart were dead and their widows, owners of the houses that Sheldon described, did not keep up their husbands' involvement in art, but Johnston was serving as the Metropolitan Museum's first president, a position he held from 1870 until his retirement in 1889. In the 1870s, Johnston traveled in Europe and Egypt, assembling the core of the museum's first collection owned by itself and buying for himself a group of paintings which at the time was considered to have no parallel in America. When his Central Railroad of New Jersey collapsed in the depression of 1876–77, Johnston sold his collection at New York's first great art sale in an unsuccessful effort to strengthen the company's finances. When Johnston yielded the museum presidency, another Sheldon house owner followed him in the office. Henry G. Marquand's first artistic interests were in architecture; early in life he became the first honorary member of the American Institute of Architects. Later he became the Metropolitan's most substantial nineteenth-century donor, marking his election to the museum's presidency in 1889 with a gift of old masters still considered among the best works the museum owns. Marquand remained president until his death in 1902.

The last of Sheldon's great artistic organizers had not yet found her mission in the 1880s. Born in 1840, Isabella Stewart had been traveling in Europe since her late teens. After her marriage to John L. Gardner in 1860, she settled in Boston. After her son died in his second year and she suffered a miscarriage in 1865, Isabella and John L. Gardner turned more and more toward art collecting, beginning in 1867 what became regular trips to Europe and the Middle East. By 1883 their travels had expanded and in that year the couple sailed to Japan and China by way of India, Indochina and the Dutch East Indies. Their collection of painting and sculpture increased rapidly and, although John L. Gardner was a trustee and treasurer of the Boston Museum of Fine Arts, the couple began to think seriously of building a significant gallery of their own. Not until after John L. Gardner's death in 1898, however, did Isabella Gardner embark on creating the museum that would ensure her lasting reputation.

While the biggest single group of Sheldon's house owners saw art collecting and museum management as their vehicle for affecting public values and organizing a significant dimension of society, two were embarking on the realization of visions that would shape the development of entire states. For Henry Villard the 1880s brought both the rise and the collapse of his plans for the Pacific Northwest, while in the same years Henry M. Flagler began what would be decades of activity in Florida.

Flagler was able to do in Florida much of what Villard had projected for Oregon. In his case, the plan was almost a hobby, carried out in a more leisurely fashion than Villard's rapidly unfolding empire building. Like Villard, however, Flagler was attracted to the possibility of creating basic institutions and economic order in a relatively undeveloped state. Flagler first visited Florida for his wife's health, but her death in 1881 indirectly increased his interest further, for the death jarred him from his preoccupation with the Standard Oil Company, led him to devote more time to his children and opened his mind to new opportunities for social organization.

Flagler married again in 1883 and continued to visit Florida, becoming more and more impressed with its resort possibilities, if these were properly managed. Within a few more years he had begun to build substantial hotels and to consolidate small railroad companies into the Florida East Coast Railroad. In effect, Flagler started a whole new life for himself and found new springs of enthusiasm as he not only built several more hotels and gradually extended his railroad to Key West, but also began to found and donate money to schools, churches, hospitals and other local institutions. Flagler's more gradual involvement produced more enduring results than had been true of Villard. By the time of Flagler's death in 1913 he had done more than any other individual to shape the character of Florida's economic growth.

While Villard and Flagler set their sights on organizing a state, still another of Sheldon's house owners had his hand in organizing and consolidating virtually every significant dimension of national life. Although still new to power when *Artistic Houses* appeared, J. Pierpont Morgan was soon recognized as the most powerful individual in America, a man to whom even the federal government would turn in a financial crisis. Morgan epitomized his generation's preoccupation with consolidation, stability and order, gaining his first reputation by pursuing just those ends in the railroad wars of the late 1860s and the 1870s. Morgan thought it essential for economic growth that railroads be in the hands of men whose wealth would enable them to weather periodic crises and that competition be minimized, so that substantial profit would keep service reliable. In the 1880s, he put his greatest energy into railroad consolidation, particularly helping the Pennsylvania Railroad and William H. Vanderbilt's New York Central gain dominance over competing lines. While concerned primarily with railroads, Morgan was alert to other opportunities as well and provided, for example, important financial help for commercial development of Thomas Edison's electrical innovations. Morgan's home (nos. 155–159) was the first in New York to have electric lighting.

In addition to economic development, Morgan played an important role in other efforts to consolidate an upper-class role in American society and achieve widespread social order. As already noted, he was one of the founding trustees of Groton, and was one of the most active and influential laymen in the American Episcopal Church, seeing in it, too, a force for stability in society. By the late 1880s, Morgan and his wife were among the 50 patrons and patronesses of the principal subscription balls recognized by the Social Register and they were prominent among the box holders in the new Metropolitan Opera House. Morgan was also beginning the serious interest in art collecting that would take him to the presidency of the Metropolitan Museum of Art in 1904, the third of Sheldon's house owners to hold that position. When, in 1895, President Grover Cleveland found himself forced to rely on Morgan to market government bonds in Europe, in order to save the government's gold reserve, Morgan emerged as the very symbol of stability in America. The symbolic role would cause Morgan, and his class, great problems, but, for the moment, he and they appeared to have achieved the great end of using private wealth to impose order and control on all facets of American life.

ACCOMPLISHING AND OVERREACHING

As many of Sheldon's house owners discovered, Morgan's handling of the gold loan and other contemporaneous events proved to be the last time men of wealth realistically could expect such a direct measure of control over the economy. In retrospect, the owners of "Artistic Houses" often saw the 1880s, the decade in which their homes were opened photographically, as the peak of the era of stability and order they had hoped to sustain permanently. Although in some respects the achievements of the elite proved durable, others of their expectations collapsed. For the most part, the corporations and cultural institutions that Sheldon's owners helped to create survived their founders and became lasting monuments to the energy of men and women of wealth in the 1880s, but the hope of establishing an agreed-upon Society that would set a widely accepted standard proved vain. Where collapse occurred, it was commonly because Sheldon's owners and others overreached themselves.

At the personal level, the 1880s or early 1890s proved to be decisive years for several of the men and women celebrated in *Artistic Houses*. Henry Villard's rapid rise and sudden fall, the best-known example of that pattern, was not unique. Another railroad magnate, H. Victor Newcomb, experienced much the same reversal in the decade, but in an even more melodramatic way. Newcomb had taken over direction of the Louisville and Nashville Railroad soon after his father died in 1874, making Newcomb the youngest head of a major railroad. He extended its lines and built up its major terminal facilities, then in the early 1880s turned his attention to banking in New York. He established himself quickly, owning two of the houses Sheldon described (nos. 81–85). When the first *Social Register* appeared, Newcomb was included, and when the *Tribune* compiled its list of millionaires, Newcomb was among them. According to one of his obituary notices, overwork soon caused Newcomb to break down and to retire. The inactivity or some other cause led him to experiment with chloral hydrate, a narcotic, and by 1891 he was "enslaved to the habit," according to the *New York Times*. His wife soon had him committed to a sanatorium, where he remained for ten years. Upon his release he embarked upon a long court fight to regain control of his property and to separate from his wife; both efforts were successful, but Newcomb never regained his former wealth or position and died in 1911.

On a smaller scale, William I. Russell's success and subsequent personal disaster paralleled Newcomb's. Russell created his own fortune as a broker in metals and when his suburban New Jersey home (no. 74) appeared in *Artistic Houses*, the honor sealed his rise. "Oh, it was a great year!" Russell said of 1884 in his autobiography. His income of $30,000 was his largest yet and was "earned by my own efforts, out of a business that I alone had created . . . I wanted to succeed. I felt I had succeeded." The 1880s remained prosperous for Russell but financial panic in 1893 and new tariff legislation undermined his firm, so that in 1895 he could meet none of his major obligations and the firm failed. Russell tried to continue operating as a small independent broker but had difficulty earning enough to support his family. Farming in New Jersey helped somewhat, but Russell had fallen into near-poverty and an obscurity broken only when his suicide note and his brief jailing for debt brought him publicity in the first few years of the twentieth century. The suicide letter to an office clerk prompted a citywide search for Russell, who acted as if nothing unusual had happened. With that crisis passed, he lived on till 1925 and received a perfunctory obituary noting his former prominence.

Villard, Newcomb and Russell were the most dramatic in their fall from the eminence ratified in *Artistic Houses*, but others joined them. William H. De Forest, for example, after establishing a substantial fortune in silk importing and manufacturing, followed the pattern true for many wealthy Americans and shifted his attention to real estate. Concentrating on Manhattan, De Forest augmented his wealth but finally extended himself too far with his purchase of the former Alexander Hamilton "Grange" in the upper part of the island. Newspaper accounts in 1888, describing De Forest as "a speculator by habit and inclination," asserted that by holding out for more than double what he had recently paid for the property, De Forest forfeited solid opportunities to sell, soon found he could not meet his own debts and had to sell much of his property at a loss. Land may have been the basis for some of the greatest American fortunes, such as those of the Goelets and the Andersons, among Sheldon's owners, but it was likely to be a trap for those determined to rise quickly.

For some among Sheldon's house owners, the decade brought personal tragedy. Financial collapse for some has already been noted but, not surprisingly, death began to claim some owners or members of their families almost as soon as the houses were photographed. Robert Stuart had died in 1882, as Sheldon's project was under way, and others followed soon afterward, with James L. Claghorn, Hollis Hunnewell and Mary Goddard Tiffany, Louis C. Tiffany's first wife, all dying in 1884. The next year brought death to two of Sheldon's most famous owners. Ulysses S. Grant died after a painful and well-publicized struggle with cancer, while William H. Vanderbilt died more simply, not long after completion of the house to which Sheldon gave such ample attention (nos. 114–124). John Charles Phillips died the same year, as did Mrs. Henry Hilton, followed in 1886 by her cousin, Cornelia M. Stewart. Two prominent representatives of the older social order, Julia Kean Fish and Samuel J. Tilden, died in 1887. In many cases, Sheldon had presented the homes of men and women with long-established wealth so it was not unexpected that the group of owners would soon diminish.

For others in Sheldon's group, the 1880s produced significant moments of success, often leading on to productive careers. Dr. William A. Hammond, for instance, entered the decade with his Civil War court-martial sentence newly reversed and his rank of surgeon-general and brigadier general (retired) restored to him. Becoming one of the founders of the New York Post-Graduate Medical School in 1882, Hammond consolidated his reputation as one of the country's leading neurologists, extended his list of major medical publications, and published several popular novels in the middle years of the decade. The 1880s brought him cultural and social distinction as well, with M. E. W. Sherwood, in an 1882 *Harper's Monthly* article, citing his house (nos. 131–133) for "one of the first conspicuously artistic interiors in New York." An article on medical education in another issue of *Harper's* in the same year saw Hammond as the epitome of the successful professional. Watching Hammond address a medical class, the writer observed: "His private practice is enormous; he is called to testify as an expert in courts of law; and his reputation is so wide that patients come hundreds of miles to see him. [He is] a voluminous writer of books on his specialty, a famous entertainer, a frequent diner-out . . . . Very few men combine the successful pursuit of science and literature with the pleasures of society as Dr. Hammond does." With their daughter married to an Italian nobleman and themselves listed in the *Social Register,* William and Helen Hammond could see the 1880s as remarkably generous to them.

Many others found the years surrounding their homes' appearance in *Artistic Houses* particularly rewarding and productive. Continued business success was the common denominator for most. They had already built the fortunes that enabled them to own the homes Sheldon described and few of the men embarked on new career directions. Henry M. Flagler did shift his attention to Florida in the mid-1880s and George F. Baker began to assemble what would become the Southern Railway, but for the most part successful businessmen continued to expand along familiar lines.

Outside of business, the 1880s brought distinction to many of Sheldon's owners, as when Empress Augusta of Germany awarded Anna Ottendorfer a gold medal in 1883. The decade saw Oliver Ames, James W. Wadsworth and George P. Wetmore embark upon their long political careers and gave Robert Treat Paine, Jr. his term in the state legislature, before he decided his temperament fitted him more for charity organization. Recognition came also to Phillips Brooks in 1884, when he was chosen for the founding board of Groton; to Charles Stewart Smith in 1887, when he began nine years of service as president

of the New York Chamber of Commerce; and to William Goddard in 1888, when he was elected chancellor of Brown University. Varying forms of personal achievement were also enjoyed by Nicholas L. and Elizabeth Anderson, who moved into their home, designed by H. H. Richardson, in 1883; and by Dr. William T. Lusk in 1887, when he performed the second birth by caesarean section in the United States in which both mother and child survived. At the time, Lusk's *The Science and Art of Midwifery* was the standard textbook in its area and had been translated into Arabic and several European languages. Success of a more indirect sort came to Richard T. and Melissa Wilson in 1884, when their eldest son, Orme, married Caroline Astor, confirming the Wilsons' ties to the richest and most well-connected of New York families. For the Wilsons and for many other families, the 1880s were a key period, bringing recognition for past accomplishment or setting patterns of new ambition.

As the Wilsons consolidated their hard-won social position by means of marriages to a Goelet, an Astor and a Vanderbilt, Society itself was beginning to come apart. According to Clara Jessup Moore and other commentators on manners, a social elite justified itself by setting a moral and cultural standard, by behaving in ways that earned acceptance and respect from most of the thinking public. Moore's expectation had been reasonably well met during the decade of Sheldon's *Artistic Houses,* but the collapse of standards and a stable order was evident within only a few more years, as two of the house-owning families brought about a sustained public reexamination of the American upper class.

Fig. 11. J. Coleman Drayton house, New York, New York.

J. Coleman Drayton and his wife, the former Charlotte Astor, produced the first problem. When they married in 1879, Drayton brought to the match old South Carolina and Philadelphia ancestry, while Charlotte brought the usual Astor dowry of an income from about $500,000 and a Fifth Avenue house (no. 197). Charlotte also carried with her the power of her mother, "the" Mrs. Astor, who took seriously the responsibilities of a Society leader. These included a fierce moral rectitude applied to herself and her guests. In 1892, when newspapers first began to publish gossip-column items about her daughter's apparent affair with a New York insurance executive, Hallett Borrowe, cracks in the moral standard were evident. Charlotte left for Europe with Borrowe; Drayton followed and challenged Borrowe to a duel that never occurred. Drayton returned home and sued for divorce, keeping the couple's several children, and in 1896 Charlotte married, not Borrowe, but a Scot named George Haig. Through all of what became known as "the most conspicuous society scandal of the generation," Mrs. Astor remained loyal to her daughter. Charlotte was welcome beside her mother in a receiving line even while the divorce suit was being fought. The loyalty was impressive but American readers could also conclude that Society had no claim to moral leadership.

J. Coleman and Charlotte Drayton gave a blow to Society by pursuing individual emotional satisfaction, but Bradley and Cornelia Martin's cataclysmic error was the result of careful planning. The Martins were model social climbers, noted for practicing their skills even in their youth. Landmarks in their rise included the leasing of a large Scottish estate for hunting, beginning in 1881, and the marriage of their daughter Cornelia to the Earl of Craven in 1893. So far, the Martins' social activity had been noted largely for self-indulgence and perhaps that image bothered them. At any rate, in 1897, after several years of deep economic depression in the United States, the Martins decided to use their position to do some good for others. According to Bradley's brother Frederick, who tells the story in one of his autobiographical volumes, the idea occurred at breakfast one morning when Bradley said, "I think it would be a good thing if we got up something; there seems to be a great deal of depression in trade." Cornelia objected to his suggestion for a concert, arguing that the money would just go to foreign musicians. Instead she urged, "Let us give a costume ball at so short notice that our guests won't have time to get their dresses from Paris. That will give an impetus to trade that nothing else will." Frederick later concluded she had been perfectly correct in her expectations, for "many New York shops sold out brocades and silks which had been lying in their stockrooms for years."

Most observers did not draw the conclusion that Frederick Martin did. The ball, given in February 1897, excited the most vigorous criticism of any social event in the decade. Sermons denounced it, editorials criticized it, cartoons caricatured it— all, ironically, for its supposed insensitivity to the needs of the poor. That the rich could indulge themselves so ostentatiously while others starved had become unacceptable to many vocal Americans. Feeling themselves thoroughly misunderstood, the Martins soon found the criticism too overwhelming and left the country, living most of the rest of their lives in England.

Sheldon's house owners, struggling to define and maintain an upper-class order in American society, did much to undermine their goal. William H. Vanderbilt's earlier remark about his railroad's obligations to society—"the public be damned"— had caused a sensation at the time but had been an isolated example. In the 1890s, the Drayton divorce and the Bradley Martin ball produced a more lasting impression of the rich as merely self-indulgent. At the same time, J. Pierpont Morgan's handling of the government's gold borrowing became a symbol of great power unaccountable to the public. More and more the corporate empires once seen as marks of American greatness— Flagler's Standard Oil, Armour and Company, the Havemeyer family's sugar-refining company, the Clark Thread Company, Vanderbilt's New York Central, George F. Baker's First National Bank—were increasingly identified as irresponsible, rapacious trusts instead. To combat such perceived selfishness and greed, Samuel J. Tilden's great creation, the stable and orderly Democratic party, was first thrown into disarray and then taken over by outsiders. From a position of apparently solid power in the 1880s, the American upper class found itself in the 1890s undermined from within and attacked on several fronts. Although the dominant public image of men and women of wealth was influenced for generations primarily by the excesses of a few in the last decade of the nineteenth century, the years of the upper class's greatest influence and achievement left enduring monuments in the form of major corporations, eminent schools, great museums and other cultural institutions, and in many cases the family houses themselves.

A SPECIAL MOMENT IN AMERICAN ART

Occasionally in our study of the past we will find a quotation that seems so apropos, one that seems so timely, catches a particular viewpoint of its day, reveals assumptions and attitudes, and itemizes points that we would like to underscore. Such an observation, pertaining to the state of culture and art on the Eastern seaboard of the United States in the early 1880s, was written by Earl Shinn under the pseudonym of Edward Strahan and appeared in the introduction to his *Mr. Vanderbilt's House and Collection*, a multivolume study of the W. H. Vanderbilt house and its treasures, published in 1883–84. Many twentieth-century historians and art historians have also appreciated and cited this passage:

> In these volumes we are permitted to make a revelation of a private home which, better than any other possible selection, may stand as a representative of the new impulse now felt in the national life. Like a more perfect Pompeii, the work will be the vision and image of a typical American residence, seized at the moment when the nation began to have a taste of its own. . . . The country, at this moment, is just beginning to be astonishing. Re-cemented by the fortunate result of a civil war, endowed as with a diploma of rank by the promulgation of its centenary, it has begun to re-invent everything, and especially the house.

This quote reflected Sheldon's thinking, and its appearance coincided with the publication of *Artistic Houses*. It contains a number of statements, assumptions and implications that deserve closer examination to understand better the artistic climate of the time when *Artistic Houses* appeared. It can also serve as a springboard to comment on several general points before focusing on Sheldon's publication. These are: The years of the early 1880s were seen as a special moment in the evolution of American art and taste; this positive self-assessment was an Eastern phenomenon inspired by New York; many thought the best fruits of the heightened taste and the best efforts of contemporary American designers were to be seen in interior decoration; and, finally, the commentators of the period thought recent achievements were not temporary but permanent because they had been realized at the core of the nation— in its homes.

Shinn was referring to an important stage in American art when he observed that the country "is just beginning to be astonishing." One of the country's leading art authorities was stating, with an intriguing mixture of confidence and wonder, that those long-awaited signs of cultural and artistic maturity were now too numerous and reassuring to deny. This must have been a heady time for him and others, like Sheldon, who agreed with his conclusion. American art was growing up, leaving an adolescent stage and preparing to compete with the artists of the old nations of Europe. Generations of American intellectuals, poets and artists never doubted that the country would one day fulfill its artistic promise despite the persistence of European doubts, such as Prime Minister William E. Gladstone's contention that where the industrial spirit is strong beauty will suffer. For Shinn, the sober Vanderbilt house and its dazzling though newly acquired contents proved that, in New York at least, the rough ways had been made smooth. And the other mansions on Fifth Avenue, many too restrained by restrictive lots to convey adequately the enormous wealth behind them, represented a patronage that mocked the support art once received from fifteenth-century Italian princes.

A number of art commentators who wrote for metropolitan newspapers and the monthly journals of the East Coast also thought the country was coming of age artistically. Although they wrote about such indicators enthusiastically, they were unable or were not inclined to explain why the transformation was taking place. They mentioned reasons quickly—the reunification of the nation after the Civil War, an expanding economy and instant private fortunes, the cultural influence of the 1876 Centennial Exposition in Philadelphia, better education (especially for women), more leisure time, the popularity of foreign travel—but rarely tried to explain the causes carefully. On the other hand, some evidence of the growing importance of art could be cited easily. In the late 1870s and early 1880s new art journals, such as the *Art Review* and *The Art Amateur* (1878), appeared, articles on art and architecture were published in increasing numbers, such art organizations as the New York Etching Club (1878) and the Architectural League of New York (1881) were created, city art museums were strengthened or established, and annual salons received closer scrutiny. Shinn and Sheldon sensed the moment and documented it with impressive publications. In addition to his catalogue of the Vanderbilt collections and careful description of the interiors of the mansion, Shinn completed *The Art Treasures of America* (three volumes) in 1882, an attempt to describe and inventory the major private collections of the country. For *Artistic Houses* Sheldon probably visited the interiors of most of these 97 buildings in order to describe their appearance.

Shinn concluded that the country was just beginning to be astonishing because of what he had seen in New York, Boston and Philadelphia. When he wrote of the nation beginning "to have a taste of its own," he was not thinking of Cheyenne or Sacramento. If the United States was on the threshold of artistic maturity, most of the country was not aware of it, though cities and states outside of the Eastern corridor would soon be. *The American Architect and Building News* (August 9, 1884) acknowledged that "in these days of rapid transportation, and almost electric speed of ideas the fashions change almost simultaneously everywhere, so that the latest work in Chicago is not appreciably less advanced than the latest work in the East . . . ." However, this observation, in retrospect, is more accurate when applied to the end of the 1880s than to the beginning of that decade. Shinn and Sheldon were functioning in 1883–84 in a greenhouse art world dominated by the wealthy and pedigreed of New York City. Approximately 60 percent of the 93 private residences included in *Artistic Houses* were located in New York or its metropolitan area. Both men generalized about national achievements and prospects from evidence that was geographically and socially narrow. But filled with goodwill and confidence, they probably assumed that what was happening on Fifth Avenue could be repeated elsewhere and that people elsewhere would want to repeat it. It was Shinn's expansive, upbeat mood that inspired him to characterize the Vanderbilt house, built for approximately $1,759,000 and constructed by a regular staff of 600 laborers and 60 European sculptors and decorators, as "a typical American residence." Paradoxically, Shinn was expansive and parochial, assuming with no evil intent that as New York goes so goes the nation. Ironically, attempts to outdo the Europeans at their own game, so visible in the Vanderbilt interiors and also in many published by Sheldon, were not as astonishing ultimately as the changes taking place across much of the country in the freestanding suburban houses of the upper middle class.

When Shinn claimed the United States was reinventing "everything, and especially the house," he was not referring to spatial or technological but to decorative changes in recent domestic architecture. It was the decorative features of the rooms—the inlaid paneling, painted friezes, rosewood tables, porcelain vases, silver tea sets, brocaded walls, stained-glass windows and the paintings—that he concentrated on in his four volumes on the Vanderbilt house. This was understandable because the decorative-arts movement had captured New York interiors in the early 1880s. Writing in *Harper's Monthly* in October 1882, M. E. W. Sherwood noted, "There are, perhaps, no two words more frequently on the lips of the present generation than these two: 'Internal Decoration.' " "Nothing," she claimed,

"can be more beautiful, more orderly, more harmonious, than a modern New York house which has blossomed out in this fine summer of perfected art." M. G. Van Rensselaer (*Lippincott's Magazine*, February 1880) thought the recent advances in the expression of beauty had been most successful "along the line of decorative art . . . ." The demand for artistic houses had become so heavy, reported Sherwood, that many promising artists were giving up their canvases to work on plaster ceilings. The best example of such an artist was Tiffany, whose firm, Louis C. Tiffany and Company, Associated Artists, was swamped with commissions during its four-year existence (1879–83). Sheldon was pleased to see such artists as Tiffany, La Farge, Lathrop, Low and Saint-Gaudens accepting commissions to work on interiors, and predicted that "the time must come when our best artists generally will contribute the creations of their genius to the adornment of American homes in other shapes than in that of the oil-painting in a gilt frame." *Artistic Houses* was published during the heyday of the decorator. In the opinion of many contemporary authorities, the decorative arts, not painting or sculpture, were America's strongest suit.

Finally, Shinn makes the point in his quote that the private home is the best example by which to judge the "new impulse" in the country. Why the private house rather than the country's churches, municipal buildings or libraries? One answer would be that there were more houses than other types of architecture, providing judges with a surer sample. Furthermore, the house was an American phenomenon reflecting the structures of American society; no European nation rivaled the United States in these years in the percentage of its families living in separate houses. The house was also the environment that taught the young and sustained them in later years, a point clearly stated by Harriet Spofford in *Art Decoration Applied to Furniture*, 1878: "Its study is as important, in some respects, as the study of politics; for the private home is at the foundation of the public state, subtle and unimagined influences moulding the men who mould the state . . . ."

But the reason that is given or implied most frequently in the literature of the early 1880s is that the house reveals its owners. Spofford underscores the influence of the house on the family; the shepherds of the art scene of the early 1880s are more intrigued with its revelations to the public. "Just as there is no more certain means of gauging a man's social position than by discovering what manner of womankind belongs to him, so there is no better way of measuring his degree of intellectual or artistic culture than by examining his library, or the furnishings and arrangements of his house . . . " (*American Architecture and Building News*, August 9, 1884). Vanderbilt intended a public statement when he asked Shinn to inventory his rooms. And Sheldon consistently stresses the house as a revelation of character and not as a private educator. "The interior of the house of a professional man of scholarly pursuits, cultivated tastes, and wealth sufficient to gratify both, is at least the proximate expression of his experience and convictions . . . ." In Sheldon's view, cultural elites were essential to stimulate and direct the course of a nation's artistic development. That these American elites were responsible enough to demand good art for their houses was reassuring to him.

COLLECTING OBJETS D'ART

Sheldon probably visited most of the houses he included in his survey and walked through the rooms with their owners. They pointed out particular pieces they had collected, frequently explaining when, where or how the purchases had been made. Sheldon took these comments seriously, for he repeatedly accounted for the provenance of a vase or retold an anecdote associated with a given painting. This information could only have come from the collectors themselves, which makes his text valuable not only for its inventory of pieces and artists but also because it reveals why these owners prized certain works. On the other hand, comments in the text about quality or beauty could be Sheldon's judgments, not necessarily those of the collectors. Though we would assume that beauty or merit would be major reasons for adding a piece to a collection, the text is surprisingly uninformative on this issue. Granted, there are numerous references to quality in phrases like "some exquisite Sèvres porcelains glisten from a wall-cabinet" or "on the center-table is a superb Capo da Monte casket" or "the specimens of Rico, Delort, Meyer von Bremen, and Papperitz are excellent." Such evaluative but imprecise phrases abound. He tells us the works are beautiful but seldom why they are beautiful. Furthermore, the absence of any negative criticism of the art in the homes he visited suggests that his declarations of the exquisite or superb quality of a work may have had more to do with goodwill than discrimination.

If he slighted questions of artistic merit, Sheldon did not ignore the associative aspects of art, those extrinsic to the formal properties of the work itself. The text of *Artistic Houses* contains numerous lengthy passages in which the author relates "interesting" information associated with particular works of art. This kind of commentary occupies so much of the text and is written so earnestly that Sheldon and the owners seem to value the paintings and the bric-a-brac in these houses for what can be told about them—their age, who had owned them, where they came from, their rarity, their cost and their stories.

His hosts repeatedly stressed the age of their favorite pieces in order to convince Sheldon they had been responsible collectors. He accepted age as a prime factor of artistic importance, pointing out, among scores of examples, a Scandinavian silver loving cup dated 1763 in Judge Hilton's reception room, a Beauvais tapestry "perhaps two hundred years old" in Egerton Winthrop's reception room (no. 54), "an Eastern rug one hundred and fifty years old" in George Kemp's hall (no. 139), and "old oaken furniture" that seemed to have "come from the baronial halls of poesy" and cabinets, their age affirmed by worm-eaten backs, in Clara Jessup Moore's house. He liked David L. Einstein's house because it had "the soberness and seriousness of demeanor which belong to age." These comments provide insights into two characteristics of the families featured in these photographs. This group of art patrons did not brag about its bric-a-brac, furniture or tapestries which had been manufactured recently. If these collectors owned modern works (paintings and sculpture excluded), they did not call them to Sheldon's attention. Secondly, their reverence for the past encouraged them to make purchases in which age was often a distinguishing and conversational feature.

The provenance of a work was also mentioned frequently in the text. American collectors of the early 1880s were quick to explain that choice items in their houses had once been choice items in noted collections of the past. We can imagine the pride with which Edward N. Dickerson told Sheldon that his Bohemian blue-glass punch bowl had been bought in Paris by Thomas Jefferson himself. Dr. William A. Hammond explained that the candelabra in his dining room had been made for the King of Bavaria. Candelabra once owned by Napoleon stood in Henry C. Gibson's dining room (no. 48). If a work could not be assigned to the household of a figure of history, it was common to assign it to an acceptable class, as the Joys did when explaining that their bronze statues of Henry IV of France and his wife, Marie de Médicis, had been in the "possession of a noble French family until within a few years." Sheldon did not question the accuracy of these claims and did not ask for verification; the claim of distinguished previous ownership was enough. This is another illustration of the way in which talk becomes a substitution for the object so that what is said about a collection may be more impressive than the works on display.

A work was also singled out by reference to its place of origin. *Artistic Houses* contains numerous references to suites of furniture imported from Europe, and, in the case of the Stevens' ballroom (no. 21), an entire apartment from a palace in Belgium. Others searched beyond Europe to find furniture in Morocco, hangings in Turkey, bowls on the Mount of Olives and fans in Japan. Often the goal of artistic unity was superseded by a stronger desire to show proof of world travel. These acquisitive journeys were considered creative attempts to find the finest artifacts money could buy, not acts of international plundering. Sheldon was complimentary when he reported the Einsteins had "ransacked the ends of the earth for *objets d'art*" and that Bradley and Cornelia Martin had obtained their "rare and beautiful *objets d'art* from European palaces and treasurehouses." A work of art created in a foreign country, then, in addition to age and previous ownership, was another measurement of worth respected by the majority of these American collectors in the early 1880s.

These collectors assumed the singularity of many of the objects they showed Sheldon and made statements to this effect. They wanted him to know they owned not just representative, but exceptionally fine examples of a medium or type. Trusting their comments, Sheldon alerted his readers to the "rare and costly pieces of Dutch marquetry," doors "of rare East India wood," Limoges enamel of "extremely rare and exquisite workmanship," "Persian rugs of rare quality and color" and "rare old hangings of velours." If Sheldon did not designate a work as "rare," he might call it "genuine." If it were neither rare nor original, he would frequently reassure his audience that it was "an exact copy" of the prime version found in a given museum or private collection.

The cost of an object was another attribute cited by the author of *Artistic Houses*. He implied in his commentary a corresponding relationship between money paid and quality obtained. "Baron Rothschild, of Frankfurt-on-the-Main, is said to have paid two hundred and fifty thousand dollars last year for the original of an old silver goblet, of which Mr. Einstein owns an excellent copy. . . ." References to "costly Sèvres vases" and "the costliest and best mahogany" were typical of many comments about money scattered through the text. However, Sheldon may have underscored the price paid for an object more strongly than the patrons he interviewed. His information also could have come from the popular press, which routinely stressed the sums paid for works of art in these years. Wealthy patrons, on the other hand, discreet about the extent of their wealth, were more inclined to talk about the collections from which their vases and tables had come than to talk about the amount of money paid for them.

If the owners of these well-stocked rooms and galleries tried, through remarks about the age, provenance, source, uniqueness and cost of their prized pieces, to convince friends and the public of the quality of their domestic museums, they also romanticized particular objects by telling stories and anecdotes about their histories. This was another indication of the tendency of the relatively inexperienced American collector to resort to words as compensation, and even as substitution, for understanding and engagement. These stories focused on what had happened to the pieces over the decades and centuries and, like the remarks about age and ownership, were difficult to verify and easy to embellish. Again, Sheldon was empathetic to this kind of associative criticism, believing, as he put it in reference to Marshall Field's hall furniture (no. 56), that "every article . . . has its history" and that these histories were inseparable from the work and should be retold. His attitude was well expressed in a comment about some Japanese pieces in the collection of the Zerega family:

One of them is an immense Japanese fan, opened to its full extent and six feet wide, painted by hand, and imported in a case as big as a coffin; the other a Japanese bill of lading, covered with mysterious Japanese characters, and inviting the visitor to ask the hostess (who, by-the-way, saw it in some *débris* of a fancy-goods establishment, and carried the trophy off for its immediately discerned adaptability to its present use), "Won't you tell me the story about that?"

Often the story concerned the length of time taken by a noted artist to complete a distinguished piece of peculiar artistic or functional qualities. The Bradley Martins owned six Italian chairs, each carved from a single piece of wood. They had discovered them in Amsterdam where they had been sent as models for reproduction. William A. and Helen Hammond had found some white-oak chairs that would not break if thrown from a fourth-story window.

Fig. 12. Charles H. Joy house, Boston, Massachusetts.

Owners singled out certain pieces of furniture and hangings because they had played inanimate roles in the lives of history's personalities and in recorded moments from the past. The Hammonds owned two corner tables supported by gilt cupids that had been removed from the palace of the Duke of Parma when King Victor Emmanuel's troops were trying to unify Italy. Marshall Field claimed that Savonarola may have used one of his chairs. George W. Childs had a table made from ebony that had been brought to the United States from Africa by Paul du Chaillu. The Joys of Boston still had Gobelin tapestries that had been brought from France by his ancestors and had once been in Concert Hall in Boston when a reception for President Washington was held there.

Though these photographs of rooms crammed with materials collected from the "ends of the earth" document the phenomenon of bric-a-brac mania, they also describe interiors in which objets d'art were less noticeable. Also, Sheldon met collectors—James L. Claghorn, John Taylor Johnston, Henry G. Marquand, John Wolfe—whose long familiarity with art resulted in different conversations, discussions that revealed their knowledge or sensitivity rather than their self-consciousness, their desire to share delight rather than to impress. Regionally, those who lived in the impressive town houses of Boston and Philadelphia were less inclined to turn their houses into museums of the world's artifacts than were the New Yorkers included in this study. Compare, for example, the Boston apartments of E. Rollins Morse (no. 10), Robert Treat Paine, Jr. (no. 73) and Walter Hunnewell (nos. 147 & 148) with the New York rooms of H. Victor Newcomb (nos. 81–83), Robert Stuart (nos. 99–101) and John Wolfe (no. 176). There were exceptions, such as the quarters of Oliver Ames (nos. 33–37) in Boston, but New Yorkers entered the competition for international art objects and fashionable modern paintings more aggressively than did residents in this anthology who lived in other cities.

Fig. 13. Walter Hunnewell house, Boston, Massachusetts.

A number of these photographs depict country houses in which spatial interaction and casual comfort are more conspicuous than vases or portieres. Some rooms belonged to artists like Louis C. Tiffany (nos. 13–16) and Samuel Colman (no. 29), who, dedicated to revitalizing the present, not venerating the past, created new kinds of interior decor for such clients as William S. Kimball (nos. 67 & 68) and George Kemp (nos. 139–142).

Despite evidence to the contrary, the paragraphs and photographs of *Artistic Houses* document an economic, social and cultural phenomenon of the early 1880s—families, possessing extraordinary wealth (often freshly acquired), who used their money to purchase or build town houses on fine avenues in major cities and then transformed these houses into personal museums displaying art objects, paintings and sculpture from around the world. *Artistic Houses* regarded the men and women whose houses it featured as the enlightened agents of an American Renaissance.

Fig. 14. John Charles Phillips house, Boston, Massachusetts.

Some of these home owners had launched their collections before the Philadelphia Centennial Exposition of 1876, among them Claghorn, Johnston, Marquand, Wolfe, Hamilton Fish, A. T. Stewart, J. Pierpont Morgan and Joseph G. Chapman. A larger number, however, inspired by this infusion and display of international culture, became active collectors in the last half of the 1870s and the early 1880s. Samuel M. Nickerson and John W. Doane in Chicago, John Charles Phillips in Boston and William H. Vanderbilt in New York intensified their buying as their new houses were being finished between 1879 and 1883. Individuals who had been buying art prior to the centennial were not necessarily more sincere and informed than those who entered the market later. However, art collecting was more fashionable about 1880 than it had been earlier, and several of the later collectors appear to have become involved for social reasons.

In the 1980s it is impossible to separate cleanly those collectors of a hundred years ago who bought art primarily because they enjoyed it from those who bought art primarily because it was the thing to do. The motives of most collectors were probably mixed and in some cases these motives changed with time. J. Pierpont Morgan began as a fashionable collector but became increasingly absorbed and ultimately transformed by his contact with art. More research is needed on this question of motives spurring the large number of private collections in these years.

Directly and indirectly, Sheldon provides us with some sense of the seriousness or sophistication of the collectors he encountered. Occasionally, he referred to a collector as an authority—"Mr. Claghorn's extensive knowledge of the art and history of engraving . . ."—but these tributes were reserved almost exclusively for those who had been purchasing art for several decades. When discussing the rooms of those who had recently become involved with art, Sheldon can be indirectly informative in the amount of space he allots to associative commentary about provenance and anecdotes. The collectors most eager to tell him who had previously owned their works and to recount the silent roles these objects had played in great moments in history—Egerton Winthrop, H. Victor Newcomb and Bradley Martin, all of New York City—had put their collections together after 1876. Furthermore, they remained collectors whose lives were essentially unaffected by public commitments to art. If we lack sufficient evidence to make hard judgments about the relative integrity in the relationships between owners and their art, we can conclude that *Artistic Houses* argued that important people should own works of art and that the artistic content of their houses and the skill with which their art was displayed were signs of their good taste and cultural sophistication.

If Sheldon was aware of questionable motives and concerned about their possible negative consequences, he never mentioned them. His silence was not shared by all contemporary critics, particularly those who argued that money might buy art but not insure judgment or even encourage sensitivity. These critics questioned the wisdom of people with abundant and often new money but with little previous training acting as the country's arbiters of beauty. The following attack appeared in *Lippincott's Magazine*, February 1883:

> Let us contrast the qualities which go to make a genuine lover of beauty, with a delicate and accurate perception of it in all varied forms, and those which are essential to the composition of a capable and successful "bric-a-brac" collector . . . . First, the collector. Apart from any intrinsic quality of his own, he must belong to the well-to-do class, must have "money in bank" or in his pocket: this is evidently a requisite. But what must be in himself? Some uninitiated person cries out, "He must, above all, love beautiful things, and know them when he sees them." By no means. Nothing could be more detrimental to his success, should his love and perception of beauty be largely developed or allowed free action, for under their dominion he may be led into fatal and irretrievable errors. In order that his collection of "objects" may be admired and valuable, it must be composed primarily of "rarities" as nearly "unique" as possible, secondly, of "objects" possessing a certain money-value and a floating capacity of increasing value, so as to be put advantageously on the market when the owner wishes; for the salient mark of the "collector," by which he might readily be distinguished from the beauty-lover, is the love of variety and change . . . .

This spirited piece raises questions about the relationship between art and wealth that Sheldon did not understand or did not wish to publicize.

Individuals who wanted to live in artistic houses in which acceptable works of art were displayed in the mode of the day, but who lacked the experience, knowledge or confidence to achieve this goal, could rely on experts to help them. These experts were the architects who designed their houses, or the decorators who arranged and furnished their rooms, or the art agents who recommended and procured works of art. Much of the ceramics, glass, silver, tapestries and furniture visible in these photographs had been acquired by the owners themselves in antique shops, at auctions or on their tours of Europe, the Middle East, China and Japan. However, owners appeared to rely more heavily on agents when purchasing paintings and sculptures and when the costs of desired works were high. The agents would visit dealers and the studios of agreed-upon artists, represent the patron at auctions, act as consultants in shaping collections and as instructors in the history and appreciation of art.

As collectors became better informed and developed a clearer idea of the works they wished to purchase, their dependence on authorities might decrease. At first their agent might bargain with Goupil and Company in Paris or visit specific studios alone. Later the patron might travel with the agent on a trip to France and, finally, the patron might travel alone to renew friendships with painters whose works he or she had previously bought. Twentieth-century historians regularly mention William H. Vanderbilt's friendship with Jean-Louis-Ernest Meissonier and his meeting with Rosa Bonheur. John Wolfe claimed the *Wine Tasters* in his dining room (no. 176) had been given to him by the German painter J. P. Hasenclever. Henry C. Gibson bought heavily in 1879–80 when he toured Europe with his sister, son and granddaughter.

There were disadvantages to relying on agents. If a family had assembled a reputable collection, the family wanted the credit. Owners tended to employ art advisers discreetly in order to discourage the public from concluding they were possessors without understanding. William H. Vanderbilt was sensitive to gossip that he was really an artistic dolt incapable of a decision without the approval of Samuel P. Avery. Though evidence to the contrary exists, the image of him at the end of Avery's leash persisted. On several occasions Avery stated that his assistance was minimal, but he failed to change the mind of a public that wanted to think otherwise. He wrote the *New York Times*, March 10, 1882:

> In the account of Mr. Vanderbilt's collection of pictures in this morning's *Times* the writer gives me credit for what I am not entitled to, viz: that I "selected" them for him. Mr. Vanderbilt's collection is not a rapid accumulation. He has been a picture buyer for over 20 years and does not need the services of any person to "select" for him, willing as he may be to be advised by his friends.

The public should not have been surprised that capitalists turned to experts for assistance in developing their collections; before purchasing a mill or a railroad, the investor or the developer turned to those knowledgeable about the prospects for textiles or the likelihood of population shifts along certain routes. However, there was a qualitative difference between buying mills and buying art. A purchase of art was "successful" if an ineffable but transforming relationship between owner and work existed and grew. Purchasing art was risky because it was impossible to predict the evolving nature of this mysterious intercourse. The patron could not be a disinterested spectator or absentee owner; personal involvement was unavoidable. If owners permitted experts to determine their choice, they were substituting another's criteria of quality and taste for their own. The fact that this person was a professional in determining quality did not guarantee the integrity of the emerging relationship.

Agents may have contributed to this problem, but they were not the cause of it. Collectors, working independently of professional help, often overlooked personal criteria when judging collections—their own included—according to the names they contained, and when they engaged in "painted to order" transactions. Though Sheldon did not state flatly that good collections contained the names of certain artists and that collections in which these were missing were poor, he argued this implicitly throughout *Artistic Houses*. If patrons did not own a work of a painter in vogue, they often searched until one was found. Adding a name, then, could be more important than subject or quality. Names could be added by writing to the artist in Europe and requesting a painting of a given size and subject. In such instances the client would be expressing a personal preference, though not one that would insure enjoyment of the painting once it arrived. Probably less than ten percent of the individuals and families included in *Artistic Houses* engaged in this practice.

THE PAINTINGS IN THE DOMESTIC MUSEUM

Judging from these photographs, town houses from Boston to Washington and as far west as Chicago and St. Louis were repositories of various kinds of collections in the 1880s. Robert Stuart commissioned cabinetmakers to design ebonized oak cases to hold his rocks and to place them below the paintings in his gallery (no. 99). Sheldon included several homes that held impressive libraries: Franklin H. Tinker (no. 143) owned books autographed by Victor Hugo, Tennyson, Ruskin, Whittier and Holmes; Frederick F. Thompson (no. 60) claimed 3000 titles; Edward N. Dickerson (no. 76) possessed a very good collection of scientific literature; and Samuel J. Tilden's library, though not featured in this series, was one of the largest in New York City. By the 1880s the library had become an expected, if not obligatory, room in a well-appointed city residence, forcing those who did not enjoy reading to "stage" their literary enthusiasm. These photographs show several rooms in which even rows of printed leather, some covering boards, not pages, suggest symmetrical display rather than active use.

Fig. 15. Edward N. Dickerson house, New York, New York.

Works of art represented the most common type of collection. Most of these interiors displayed carefully chosen textiles, ceramics from Europe or the Orient, historical furniture or well-made revivals of earlier styles, and many a mantel showed off some of the most complicated marble or metal clocks in the history of artistic clock making. The then-current popularity of stained-glass windows can be measured in numerous interiors, for example, the library of the Clarence H. Clarks (no. 19), the Russells' hall (no. 74) and the dining room of the Armour residence (no. 135). We also see sculpture in these interiors, but with the exception of the collections of Stewart, Smith,

Singerly, Gibson and Hilton, these owners did not develop holdings in figurative, three-dimensional art. There were many watercolors, drawings and prints hung on these walls or kept in specially prepared print drawers, but the oils were the medium by which the press, the owners and even Sheldon judged the importance of an art collection.

Collections of oil paintings, varying in size from a few originals to more than 200 in the Stuart (no. 99) and Vanderbilt (nos. 119 & 120) houses, were common in this series. Approximately 60 percent of the houses contained works by known contemporary painters or, occasionally, a painting from the Renaissance or Baroque. Fifteen of these owners would have been considered in the early 1880s among the foremost collectors of fine art in the country. Sheldon's familiarity with the European-American art market partially explains why such a high percentage of houses with strong collections was chosen for *Artistic Houses*.

The author's comment, "Mr. Doane [nos. 180 & 181] has not yet had time to cover his walls with art-treasures—a process requiring care and time," provides us with several insights into contemporary attitudes toward the house as a museum. Sheldon assumed that walls of splendid houses would be hung with works of art. Walls not adorned by paintings could be embarrassing. As soon as new houses were completed, the "treasures" would be displayed. To qualify his implication of inevitability, Sheldon reminds us that decorating a house with paintings requires patience and skill.

As more paintings were purchased, opportunities to display them effectively decreased. The quantity of exhibition space was one factor convincing a number of these families to move to new quarters or to build new city residences in the late 1870s and early 1880s. In 1883 Samuel M. Nickerson, who eventually gave his paintings to The Art Institute of Chicago, moved into his new home where its gallery (no. 104) was equipped to handle paintings, prints and folios. "Mr. Nickerson's collection of art treasures is probably the largest in the West, and now that his beautiful gallery is completed, he will undoubtedly continue to add to its numbers." Robert Stuart died several months before his new residence at the corner of East 68th Street and Fifth Avenue in New York was completed in the spring of 1883. His widow arranged 66 paintings in the picture gallery (no. 99), along with his geological treasures, and scattered the remaining 174 oils throughout the principal rooms of the house. Objecting to leaving their house at 450 Fifth Avenue, in which she had raised eight children, Maria Louisa Vanderbilt tried unsuccessfully to convince her husband to add a wing if he needed more space to hang his pictures. Although his gallery at their new address, 640 Fifth Avenue, was the largest in New York when completed in 1882, he enlarged it the following year. Rarely were all the paintings of a collection housed within one space. Several of the better-known collectors, J. Pierpont Morgan and John Wolfe, for example, had no formal gallery room. One out of ten houses included in this publication contained a picture gallery.

Serious collectors assembled their collections of paintings and prints for their enjoyment and the enjoyment of their friends, and some invited the public to see their originals. After Sunday evening suppers, Cornelia and Alexander Stewart would take their guests into the art gallery (nos. 7 & 8), illuminated by gas jets, for conversation and coffee and cigars for the men. Stewart was less generous to the general public. Initially he permitted an authority or an artist to study his paintings but later discontinued this practice, a policy that was enforced from his death in 1876 until his wife's death ten years later. In the last years of Stewart's life, he spent much time alone in his gallery, smoking cigars and contemplating his masterpieces. On the other hand, community-minded John T. Martin of Brooklyn often displayed his paintings (nos. 149 & 150) for the benefit of a specific charity or deserving institution. Prior to the sale of his collection in December 1876, John Taylor Johnston opened his gallery once a week to the public and once a year to all the artists of New York City. James L. Claghorn in Philadelphia welcomed visitors from all over the United States to study his outstanding collection of prints.

Twentieth-century historians have depicted William H. Vanderbilt as the epitome of the rich but crass American who waved an infinite supply of dollars before mediocre French painters in order to obtain the "finest collection" in the New World. They have not given him credit for doing more than any other New Yorker included in this series to share his collection with the public. On Thursdays, from 11:00 A.M. to 4:00 P.M., by cards of invitation, individuals were admitted to his galleries through a specially constructed entrance on West 51st Street. His most expansive gesture occurred on December 20, 1883, when he invited 3000 business associates, out-of-town visitors and the bulk of the city's art community to an "art levee" at his house. More than 2500 responded, many of them dressed in "threadbare Prince Alberts." Full of pride and goodwill, he greeted them at the door and later joined the crowds inside to discuss the paintings. But many of the guests wanted to gawk rather than examine and discuss works of art; the *Times* reported they opened books in the library, handled expensive bric-a-brac and wandered into the elegantly furnished bedrooms. Offended, and perhaps even threatened by such etiquette, Vanderbilt reconsidered his role as public educator and sharply curtailed access to the gallery during the last year of his life.

Like Vanderbilt, most of these collectors purchased works for private enjoyment, not public instruction. Most were pleased to share their paintings and sculptures with authorities and with reputable artists. Some felt an obligation to make their holdings available to the public on special occasions, but unless these affairs could be carefully controlled, owners concluded the invasion of their privacy was not worth the effort. The majority considered that they had served their civic duty admirably by establishing a notable collection in their city, even if these works of art were rarely seen by local subsistence-level artists.

Private museums, more numerous and conspicuous in New York than in Boston, Philadelphia or Chicago, flourished during the 1870s and early 1880s. These were the same years in which the major museums of those cities were founded. The Metropolitan Museum of New York and the Boston Museum of Fine Arts were started in 1870, the predecessor of the present Philadelphia Museum of Art in 1876–77 and The Art Institute of Chicago between 1879 and 1882. While fledgling city museums struggled, searching for money, instructive and celebrated objects, adequate galleries, appropriate addresses, clearer missions and logical directions, private museums, supported by restless money, could be formed quickly and installed in instant galleries on prestigious avenues. These two kinds of art institutions competed with each other in the decade of the 1870s, but in the later years of the 1880s the competition became less intense. Private galleries and collections continued to be fashionable during the 1880s, but collectors were increasingly inclined to think of their prized objects as instruments of public education. They were far more willing to support the public museum through bequests in the mid- and later 1880s than they had been in the previous decade. To illustrate, A. T. Stewart purchased *Friedland, 1807* by Jean-Louis-Ernest Meissonier for approximately $60,000. In 1876 this painting and *The Horse Fair* by Rose Bonheur were probably the best-known pictures in his collection and regarded as among the most important examples of modern French art in the country. At the sale of the Stewart collection in March 1887, Judge Henry Hilton and his son bought *Friedland, 1807* for $66,000 and then gave it to the Metropolitan Museum.

Although one example does not prove a general point, this painting was one of the best known in the United States, and the bequest received much publicity. The commentary in the press was complimentary, indicating that the stress on the public's access to important works of art, as opposed to private ownership, was in vogue as it had not been earlier. This shift of outlook was affected, in part, by the growing importance of the Metropolitan Museum and also by the growth of museums in other major cities. Even Meissonier was pleased. He wrote to Hilton, who shared the contents of his letter with the *New York Times* (July 13, 1887): "It is a royal gift and your city should be proud of claiming you as one of its citizens." Hilton may have been more imitative than generous. At the same auction, Cornelius Vanderbilt, through his agent Samuel P. Avery, purchased *The Horse Fair* for $53,000, and then donated it to the Metropolitan. In his letter of donation Vanderbilt stressed the importance of enabling the public to see fine works of art. The painting, he wrote, "should be in a position where it can be permanently accessible to the public." In the acceptance letter from the museum's secretary, Di Cesnola, Vanderbilt was praised for contributing "to the instruction and enjoyment of the multitudes . . . ."

The respective acts of the first and second presidents of the Metropolitan Museum, John Taylor Johnston and Henry G. Marquand, whose homes were included in *Artistic Houses*, may also reflect the growing strength and significance of the city museum in the 1880s. Johnston gave generously to support the early purchases of European collections, but he also continued to develop his own collection, and in 1876 offered for sale 200 oils and 125 watercolors in one of the largest art auctions of the decade. The *Times* did not rebuke him for ignoring the new Metropolitan Museum, but noted wistfully that it was a shame such a fine group of paintings could not become a public possession. Turner's *Slave Ship*, which Johnston had loaned for the first exhibition of the museum in February 1872, was sold for $10,000.

A month before Henry G. Marquand assumed office in 1889 he gave the museum 33 paintings, among them works by van Eyck, Hals, Lucas van Leyden, Vermeer, Van Dyck, Velázquez. This bequest was the finest series of old masters the museum had ever received. According to the *Times* (January 17, 1889), "the donor had noticed with pleasure the public interest manifested in the pictures, and, being convinced that the collection would be of greater service in a public gallery than in any private one, he had determined to offer the pictures unconditionally to the Trustees of the Museum." No doubt there were particular reasons why Marquand shared his collection and Johnston did not, but their respective decisions were symbolic and reflected their times. Sheldon's photographic record of interiors was published at the height of the popularity of the private, residential art gallery and shortly before the public museum replaced it as the focal point of a city's artistic activity.

Regardless of the size of the painting collection, and whether it was displayed in a special gallery or was to be found in Boston, New York, Philadelphia or Chicago, these works were painted by the same artists. How surprising that such affluent Americans, whose fortunes had been made by authoritative decisions and the courage to take the risks of a gambler, were so attentive to those who determined which artists were in and which were out. Art critics of the early 1880s, including Sheldon, knew what names constituted a fine collection and then looked for the obligatory Bouguereau, Detaille, Fortuny or Schreyer. If the roster was incomplete, a collector would often hunt for an example by the missing artist. According to the gossip of the day, William H. Vanderbilt was told so many times that his collection was not balanced without a Corot that he eventually bought two of them.

By examining Sheldon's text and photographs and by checking the inventories of collections in *The Art Treasures of America: Being the Choicest Works of Art in the Public and Private Collections of North America,* a three-volume work compiled by Earl Shinn between 1879 and 1882, we get a rough listing of the most popular painters of these years. Sheldon named approximately 220 different artists, a total that may appear to contradict the assertion that there was a defined stable of fashionable painters, and referred to more than 430 different paintings. Shinn's anthology included nine of the collectors Sheldon visited: Cornelia M. Stewart, Henry C. Gibson, Charles S. Smith, Henry Hilton, Mary Stuart, William H. Vanderbilt, John T. Martin, J. Pierpont Morgan and John Wolfe. If we add the references to an artist named in *Artistic Houses* to those in Shinn's catalogues of these nine collections, we are able to estimate the relative popularity of desired painters. Accordingly, they were Diaz, Bouguereau, Detaille, Corot, Meissonier, Schreyer, Merle, Vibert, Fortuny, Madrazo and Meyer von Bremen.

Narcisse Virgile Diaz de la Peña (1808–1876), born of Spanish parents, lived in France. A painter of nymphs and gypsies or allegorical figures in woodland settings, he was also respected for his Barbizon landscapes in which vivacious colors illuminated skies, trees and glens. Influenced strongly by his years in Italy, Adolphe-William Bouguereau (1825–1905) painted in a skillfully smooth (though anachronistic) manner portraits, mythological and anecdotal themes and sentimental genre pieces. After joining the army during the Franco-Prussian War, Jean-Baptiste-Édouard Detaille (1848–1912) concentrated on military history and moments from the daily life of soldiers, subjects that he executed easily in a realistic manner. Of the painters sought after in the early 1880s, Jean-Baptiste-Camille Corot (1796–1875) has received the most favorable treatment from twentieth-century historians and critics. His popularity in the United States rose after his death. American collectors liked his quiet landscapes more than his portrayals of meditative women, but both were considered poetic antidotes to literal, didactic painting.

Jean-Louis-Ernest Meissonier (1815–1891) was the teacher of Detaille. Buyers in the United States preferred his military paintings, though several collections contained his portraits and historical genre scenes which he based on exhaustive research. Adolf Schreyer (1828–1899) was born in Frankfurt am Main, Germany. "A master of emotional, as well as he is of prismatic, effects," according to a St. Louis critic, he succeeded with scenes of mounted Arab horsemen or wolves attacking winter coaches in the forests of Russia. Hugues Merle (1823–1881) painted genre works with titles like *The Secret* or literary-historical descriptions of moments, such as *Get Thee to a Nunnery*. His sweet academic style was influenced by fellow French painter Pierre-Paul Prud'hon.

The artist who dominated the ecclesiastical genre market was Jean-Georges Vibert (1840–1902). Painting in exquisite detail, he caught Catholic clergy, particularly cardinals, in literal vignettes that gently mocked their pride, gluttony and foolishness. Mariano Fortuny y Carbo (1838–1874) was born in Spain but also studied in Rome. Impressed by the colors and light of North Africa in 1860, he subsequently produced Moorish and Spanish genre scenes marked by brilliant hues. Though technically facile, he was not a deep thinker. Don Federigo de Madrazo y Kuntz (1815–1894), having studied in Paris with Winterhalter, became the painter to the Spanish court. He was noted for his portraits. Paintings by Johann Georg Meyer, better known as Meyer von Bremen (1813–1886), were included in seven of the nine *Artistic Houses* collections catalogued by Shinn. He depicted children in morally edifying but cloying moments and gave them titles such as *The Little Rogue, The Little Knitter, The Little Pleader. First Sorrow*, in the Stewart collection, depicts a heartbroken child and a dead canary.

Only slightly less popular among American millionaires of the day were paintings by Zamacois, Ziem, Troyon, Millet, Van Marcke, De Neuville, the American Eastman Johnson and the British-American painter George Henry Boughton. But the point has been made that in the years just prior to 1883 wealthy art patrons on the East Coast and in Chicago and St. Louis were not buying old masters, French romantics, English landscape painters, mid-century realists, and certainly not Degas, Manet or the Impressionists, who first exhibited as a group in Paris in 1874. There were exceptions. A. T. Stewart owned a Titian *Madonna and Child* and a Hobbema *Moonlight Landscape*, but at the sale where *Friedland, 1807* and *The Horse Fair* stirred such blockbuster bids, the Titian went for $800 and the Hobbema for $350. In Boston, Mrs. D. N. Spooner had found a *Holy Family* by a pupil of Rubens, a sunset landscape by Claude and an original attributed to Domenichino. Samuel Colman, himself an artist, had Delacroix's second version of *Dante and Virgil Crossing the Styx* and a portrait head supposedly by Rembrandt.

Fig. 16. Samuel Colman house, Newport, Rhode Island.

Several collectors who later developed magnificent holdings of medieval, Renaissance and Baroque art were relatively uninformed art patrons in the early 1880s. Isabella Stewart Gardner, of the Gardner Museum in the Fenway, Boston, had purchased a copy of a Boucher painting but did not acquire her first major old master until Bernard Berenson led her to Botticelli's *Death of Lucretia* in 1894. Aside from a few poetic French and American landscapes, J. Pierpont Morgan in these years was buying the same kinds of explanatory paintings as William H. Vanderbilt and Marshall Field. In summary, the 60 percent of the families included in this study which purchased contemporary paintings tended to buy canvases of relatively conservative French artists of the last half of the nineteenth century or to buy paintings by Spanish, German and sometimes Hungarian and Italian artists whose styles and themes reflected those of the French.

Many of these families represented new wealth created by the astounding economic development of the United States in the nineteenth century. Some had made fortunes which dwarfed generational fortunes in Britain or France, some could command resources that would have upstaged the princely families of fifteenth-century Italy. Yet this American aristocracy of wealth did not support Yankee painters who were using their creative talents to explain the beauty, breadth and unlimited potential of the United States. The *New York Times* lamented this in an editorial on December 2, 1876:

Nevertheless, our picture-buying public is largely commercial. It demands "potboilers." It is hardly necessary to add that it gets them. Is it any wonder, then, that the progress of art among us is slow? Of course, we make no account of the prevalent complaints of those struggling geniuses who are "unappreciated," and who, like other equally worthy men in other professions, have mistaken their calling. It is true that hundreds of deserving artists are restrained from doing violence to the noblest ideas of art because they cherish a spark of devotion to their ideal, and not because an enlightened public taste has withheld them. A rich picture-buyer hangs a canvas on his wall and glows with honest pride as he points to the signature of its European painter.

American painters were plentiful, talented or gradually improving, concerned with many of the themes purchasable in Paris, and certainly needed a generous national patronage, but most of the families included in *Artistic Houses* treated them as second-class artists. "Fine art" meant art produced across the Atlantic.

American painters were not ignored, but they represented a fraction of the total holdings in these houses, approximately 20 percent. The preference for foreign artists was also measurable in the prices paid at auctions between 1876 and 1883. At the John Taylor Johnston sale in December 1876, the highest price, surprisingly, was paid for an American work—$12,500 for *Niagara Falls* by Frederick Church—but the next highest bids were for foreign paintings: $9700 for Troyon's *Autumn Morning, Landscape and Cattle;* $8600 for Meissonier's *Marshal Saxe and Staff;* $8350 for the *Turkish Patrol, Smyrna,* by Decamps; and $8000 for Gérome's *Death of Caesar.* At the Claghorn auction the following year, the highest figures were $4100 for *In the Fields,* by Ludwig Knaus, $4000 for *The Disputed Point,* by Zamacois, and $3225 for *Arabs in Ambush* by Adolf Schreyer. The top price for an American-born artist was $700 for Church's painting of a landscape in Connecticut. No American works were auctioned at the sale of the John Wolfe collection in 1882.

Fig. 17. Frederick F. Thompson house, New York, New York.

Among the collectors who patronized American painters were Dr. Henry C. Haven, who bought works by Elihu Vedder; Joseph H. White, who owned works by George Fuller and George Inness; and Robert Stuart, who had landscapes by Church, Cole, Cropsey, Doughty, S. R. Gifford, William Hart, Huntington, Inness, Kensett, McEntee and J. F. Weir. Prior to his auction, Johnston owned not only *Niagara Falls* but also Homer's *Prisoners from the Front,* which brought $1860, and all four of Cole's *Voyage of Life* series, which realized a total of $3100. The remaining collectors in this anthology who supported American artists were Frederick F. Thompson, William G. Dominick, Clara Jessup Moore, Clarence H. Clark, Samuel M. Nickerson, J. Pierpont Morgan and William F. Havemeyer.

The most distinctive fine-arts collection included in *Artistic Houses* was that of James L. Claghorn, who probably knew more about his thousands of prints than others did about their scores of oils. In April of 1877 Claghorn sold his numerous predictable paintings for $76,635 in order to concentrate on prints, which at his death in 1884 numbered between 30,000 and 40,000, representing the efforts of more than 1500 printmakers who lived between the fifteenth and the nineteenth centuries. He

owned at least 185 Rembrandts, including states of *The Three Crosses* and *Ecce Homo,* and 85 impressions by Albrecht Dürer. This collection was exceptional nationally, not just among those singled out by Sheldon. Philadelphians were unhappy when all of these prints were purchased by Robert Garrett of Baltimore for $150,000 in 1885.

So similar in subject matter were these collections that it is possible to identify categories and to suggest their relative popularity. Obviously, there were variations—Robert Stuart bought a much larger percentage of landscapes than did Judge Henry Hilton, who liked military paintings and scenes from North Africa and the Middle East—but even these personal preferences do not invalidate the generalization.

Approximately 50 to 60 percent of the average collection consisted of genre themes. These could be divided into descriptive genre, moralistic genre and sentimental genre. Descriptive paintings were given titles like *The Lost Night Key, The Poor Student,* or *The New Shoes*—titles that provided a general introduction to a specific moment in the life of the individual or individuals depicted. These paintings were essentially frozen narratives. The obligation of the painter was to link the title to the painted scene by supplying enough visual clues for the viewer to reconstruct the narrative correctly. Because the correct reconstruction was crucial, the clues were usually numerous, didactic and difficult to ignore. In such paintings the artist had to be a master coordinator, insuring that the roles of all persons in the scene were understandable and, at the same time, subordinating their actions to the primary issue illuminated by the title. These paintings, usually overclarified, seldom risked subtleties that might be misconstrued. Didactic texts, like the following commentary on *The Effects of a False Note* of 1875 of Antonio Casanova, which appeared in the sale catalogue of the John T. Martin collection in 1909, left little room for imagination:

> The young marquis has a birthday! and so the floor of his spacious salon is littered with presents—toy soldiers, a model kitchen, and what not. A number of notables have called to pay their respects in the stately style and gorgeous costumes of the middle eighteenth century. And of course there is a band, a hautboy and a cello, a violin and a trombone. And the trombonist, in the kindness of his foolish old heart, had decorated the bell of his instrument with a fearsome dragon's head, and proceeds to wind him a most raucous note, full of bellowings and the shrieks of a monster. A second shriek answers him, and the poor little marquis, toys flung aside and terror in his noble heart, flies to his mother for rescue, while the horrified ladies tug at the poor trombonist's coat-tails.

A subcategory of descriptive genre dealt with the life of the Catholic clergy—the first sermon of a nervous priest or a monk dancing with a colorfully attired Spanish woman. Moralistic or edifying works employed titles such as *Worldly Thoughts, Take Care* or *A Difficult Choice.* These were visual sermons about pride or avarice, or they recreated moments common to human experience from which lessons could be taken. Sentimental paintings exploited babies and ingenuous children, as well as kittens, lambs and other newborn, nonviolent animals to posit an innocent paradise on earth.

The second most common subject in these paintings was landscape, a theme that appeared about one-third as frequently as genre scenes. In 1883 American patrons were purchasing more paintings of attractive country scenes, particularly by Barbizon and Hudson River artists, than they had ten years earlier. Although American patrons seemed more willing than previously to take nature as it existed, appreciating the beauty of the ordinary, they were still impressed by landscapes made more beguiling by the light of early morning or twilight. And they certainly remained enthusiastic about paintings of exotic locations and dramatic scenery. Landscape is a difficult category to define neatly because painters also used it as a backdrop for pictures with titles like *End of the Day,* in which returning cattle became a human metaphor, or as the setting in which simple but admirable peasants rested from their work.

Depictions of life in the Middle East and North Africa followed genre and landscape in popularity. Because the "Eastern" painting included views of Venice, Constantinople or Cairo, these could also be classified as landscapes. However, this kind of subject was usually geographically vague—*Moorish Girl Dancing* or *Arabs at a Ford*—but romanticized life in distant regions. Next came military paintings, a field dominated by the French, who concentrated on the battlefield glories of Napoleon or skirmishes from the recent Franco-Prussian War. American collectors also bought encampment descriptions of roll calls and soldiers playing cards.

The remaining categories appeared much less frequently. Occasionally, these collections contained paintings based on historical events or scenes from literature. Likewise, myths, allegories and religious subjects were rare and still-life arrangements even rarer. Portraits tended to be of current family members or of ancestors.

What did these American collectors want in painting? Their choices suggest that they accepted the primacy of subject matter, that they enjoyed paintings that could be translated easily into words in order to minimize the ambiguity of the scene and, finally, that they were happier with themes evoking a European past than with those documenting an American present.

They respected the ability of a painter to command artistic means, lively colors or strong brush strokes, for example, but they regarded these means as subordinate to theme. Their definition of a good painting probably would have excluded the spatial experiments, questions of perception or the reality of flux that increasingly intrigued innovative French artists of the 1860s and 1870s. They expected artists to account for a reassuring or a romantic world, not to inquire about the independent possibilities of formal elements, and they assumed brushwork would be thematically descriptive rather than an expressive indicator of a period's pulse.

Secondly, the paintings they bought were "verbal" paintings, works of art that described places, told stories, explained situations, accounted for events. These canvases narrated, discovered or contrived moments cleansed of ambiguity and confusion. Unlike the ineffable Rembrandt portrait that demands imagination and risk and may change in content from day to day as variables in the interactive process change, these paintings offered little room for interpretation. Their statements, reflecting a world viewed in terms of categories rather than possibilities, were easily read and easily discussed. They encouraged talk—talk that would confirm the evidence the artist had cleverly worked into the explanatory scheme.

Finally, the subject matter these collectors enjoyed had relatively little to do with the dynamic forces that had transformed the United States and had made them financially secure. We do not find paintings of rolling mills, railroad yards or grain elevators. This could be explained by arguing that painters on both sides of the Atlantic ignored such subjects. Yet these patrons regularly commissioned artists in Paris and in New York and could have requested works that showed the vitality and achievements of the country's industrial and commercial transformation. They were also surprisingly modest about their own activities. Where are the paintings depicting J. Pierpont Morgan at the office or A. T. Stewart in his department store? Instead, owners preferred scenes of a rural, preindustrial world, pictures set in the small towns of France or Germany, in European fields plowed for centuries or in the tranquil valleys of Connecticut or the mountains of the Catskills.

The people in these rural places recall for us the good old days. Their actions, expressing the positive and negative of their humanness and their persistent failure to remember the lessons of the past, were socially instructive but politically innocuous.

Not all subjects were comforting. Arabs on horseback, sheiks entering harems or generals quizzing recently captured prisoners provided excitement and variation, but such exotic events in distant places were taken by American as enchanting fairy tales, not disturbing realities. Curiously, the pragmatic businessman, who was seldom quiet about the virtues of American life and enterprise, wanted his art to romanticize a European past.

WHAT THE PHOTOGRAPHS REVEAL

Sheldon and D. Appleton and Company, the publishers, selected 203 photographs for *Artistic Houses* to illustrate their contention that "The domestic architecture of no nation in the world can show trophies more original, affluent, or admirable." Of the 97 buildings photographed, four (nos. 17, 174, 199, 203) were not private residences. The rooms featured in the 93 private houses and apartments were the spaces in which the whole family met or entertained the public. Sheldon selected 53 plates of halls, entrées and stairways, 47 of dining rooms, 36 of drawing rooms, parlors, salons and sitting rooms, 30 of libraries, 11 of picture galleries and five of reception rooms. There were also two photographs of music rooms, two plates of Japanese rooms and one each of a smoking room, conservatory, ballroom, pavilion and tapestry room. Thus, 96 percent of the interiors in these houses were public rather than private spaces, rooms in which the family would normally entertain friends and guests.

Only eight of the photographs described rooms (five bedrooms and three boudoirs) that probably were used only by the members of the household. Sheldon chose interiors to photograph which, though usable informally by the residents, were central to formal occasions. He ignored basements, attics, kitchens and servants' quarters, support areas for the functioning of the household without which the "effortless" entertaining that occurred in the dining room and living room would have been impossible. He also avoided areas in which family and guests might let their hair down or perform private functions, such as the billiard room and bathroom. The interiors he featured were, undoubtedly, the ones of which a family was most proud and also the ones a curious public would have wanted to see. They were also the best to prove his contention that American domestic architecture was unrivaled for trophies "original, affluent, or admirable."

The photographs of these formal spaces published in 1883 and 1884 reveal a surprising similarity in appearance despite obvious exceptions. The exceptions that stand out are those usually explainable by the kind of house, its function, location or age. Many of the New York houses were restricted to 25′ or 50′ widths, such as the homes of George F. Baker and William H. De Forest, while those of William I. Russell (no. 74) and O. D. Munn (no. 130) were freestanding structures located in the bucolic settings of planned communities. A few of the houses included were summer or weekend houses, not the primary residences of their owners. The halls of the Newcomb house at Elberon, New Jersey (nos. 84 & 85) and the Goelet house at Newport, Rhode Island (nos. 27 & 28) are spacious, informally furnished and located at the centers of radiating plans. Their shape, size, purpose and character differ markedly from those of their owners' town houses in New York City. The Moorish pavilion (no. 72) near the Ottendorfers' house overlooking the Hudson River is singular in this series. Geographical differences are also noticeable. The interiors of several houses in Boston—for example, those of Walter Hunnewell (nos. 147 & 148), John Charles Phillips (nos. 163–165) and Charles A. Whittier (nos. 169–172) appear to be less crowded, roomier and more comfortable than the houses erected in New York at the end of the 1870s and the first years of the 1880s. The collection also includes houses built decades earlier but later remodeled to keep up with decorative trends. Though fashionable for the 1880s, the dining room of Samuel J. Tilden on Gramercy Park South (no. 111) does not look like dining rooms of new houses erected uptown in these years.

Fig. 18. Robert Goelet house, Newport, Rhode Island.

Another exception to the general appearance of these interiors is attributable to the work of L. C. Tiffany & Associated Artists. Tiffany and his colleagues were responsible for the interior decoration of several of these houses; the best examples of their touch are seen in the photographs of the dining room and library of Tiffany's own apartment (nos. 15 & 16) and in the George Kemp salon (no. 140). In these rooms the decorative energy comes from the square and rectangular panels of varied materials that make up the wall surface rather than from the arrangement of discrete objects. The result is a mosaic of shapes held together tenuously in a plane, conveying an implication of flux not found in the majority of these rooms.

Despite these exceptions, these interiors share a marked family resemblance as if they were created at the same moment, according to agreed-upon decorative criteria, by designers who had taught one another. We find the same materials and preferences over and over: partially covered parquetry floors; three-part walls consisting of a strong dark wainscoting, a middle neutral ground of paper, brocade or leather, and a decorated frieze at the top; ceilings usually paneled in dark wood but sometimes finished in painted plaster; brass sconces and chandeliers; centered, shelf-supporting overmantels with tiles below; fine woods and superior wood carving; exquisite hangings of plush and velvet; heavy embroidered portieres; firm but appealing colors—crimson, dead gold, bronze; stamped leather chairs in the dining room; Oriental and Moorish accents; bric-a-brac from the world over—"Egyptian waterbottles, Japanese cups, Thuringian porcelain, crackleware, cloisonné, Spanish faience"—and on the walls original oil paintings by familiar names of the modern French, German, Spanish and Italian schools.

These homogeneous interiors tend to be dark because of the dominant mahogany, walnut or stained-oak paneling and because the windows are not adequate to overcome their prevailing seriousness. Perhaps the photography unduly affects this conclusion. The light that does enter does not lift these interiors but bounces from the exquisitely finished surfaces of the wood and from the scores of well-crafted objects within the rooms. The reflected lights from these objects compete with one another and with the glistening surfaces of the panels. Despite attempts to draw attention to focal points such as fireplaces, sideboards or paintings, these rooms lack areas to contemplate. There are not enough voids or neutral zones to permit visual rest, and the competition between objects, major and minor, prevents us from appreciating any one. Space is displaced by fastidious arrangements of unlimited, disparate possessions. Quantity triumphs over character and presentation over discovery.

The inclination of the wealthy elite in the United States in the early 1880s to define, clarify and order Society extended also to Society's art, particularly art within the home. Just as there were authorities in the field of manners, there were authorities in the field of art and decoration to protect couples, some with little artistic training or sensitivity, from embarrassment and to reassure them that their domestic environment would properly reflect their position in society. With a few exceptions the homes Sheldon visited had not been decorated by their owners.

Mrs. Burton Harrison observed in *Harper's Monthly* (August 1884): "In plain words, the decorative 'craze' has had its day. Amateurs no longer creep in where artists dare not tread. The legitimate adorners of our homes breathe a long sigh of relief." Amateurs were out; the experts had entered the interiors Sheldon photographed. How much control the decorator exerted varied, but in many of these houses, as a member of the New York firm of Pottier and Stymus explained in 1882, the work could be extensive. "We generally get a house from the mason, that is, when the mason work has been finished, and have charge of the entire woodwork decoration. . . . Sometimes we get *carte blanche* for everything—style, design, quality, and price."

Home owners, particularly the women, were encouraged by those who wrote columns on interior decoration to indulge their caprices, but those included in *Artistic Houses* tended to do so within the artistic framework determined by a decorator. Sheldon praised Mrs. John A. Zerega for her pencil drawing which John La Farge transferred into the portiere at the end of her drawing room (no. 25) and Mrs. F. W. Hurtt for the furniture she had selected in Morocco for their Moorish library-parlor (nos. 95 & 96).

The surprising similarity of these interiors, referred to earlier, was caused by several factors. Most of them were created, reconstructed or refurnished in the major cities of the Eastern seaboard—Boston, New York and Philadelphia—within a few years of each other in the late 1870s and the early 1880s. They were designed and furnished by decorating experts who guaranteed homeowners fashionable, contemporary rooms reflecting their wealth and social status. Despite variations among decorating firms and acts of self-expression on the part of the owners, the need and reassurance of proper behavior, extended to the design of the home, transcended them.

In addition to the similar appearance of the large majority of these rooms, they are also similar in that they contain no people—for that matter they contain few signs that human beings have used them recently. The photographs show no proud wife and husband sitting in their newly decorated drawing room. Many of these couples had at least four children—the Cheneys had 11—but there is no child posing in these photographs or even surreptitiously watching the photographer at work from behind a grandfather clock. The photographs are strangely devoid of indications of informal family life responsible for those untidy piles of items which, at the end of day or before the guests arrive, are picked up and returned to their proper locations. Such evidence of messy human use is hard to find. In fact, any evidence of human use is rare. The slip of paper that Maria Vanderbilt left in her book to mark the place where she stopped reading (no. 124) is one of the few reassurances that the owners read the books that are seen in these photographs.

We cannot find children's toys or games, even playthings neatly put away. Sometimes we can see a newspaper or a magazine on a lower shelf, but not where it will be clearly documented in the photograph. Sometimes we find a letter opener, but rarely the opened letter. Ashtrays are cleaned and pipes removed, pencils picked up, sewing put in the basket. Occasionally, we notice imperfections that take on positive qualities in the face of such fastidious housekeeping. Someone has neglected to set both candles perpendicularly in the Joys' library (no. 30) or to straighten the books in the Willings' unique hall in Chicago (no. 153). In short, these photographs do not document the casual or accidental reminders that human beings lived at these addresses.

On the other hand, there is evidence to suggest that the families and servants worked hard to get the house ready for the arrival of Sheldon and his photographer. They have cleaned the fireplaces and polished the metal plates at the rear of the fire opening or they have lit a fire (nos. 165–167)—another sign of life. They have arranged scarfs carefully to accent railings (no. 88) or pinned back a portiere to reveal the entrance to another room (no. 23). In many rooms they have aligned objects on tables as if working from a graph-paper pattern or they have stacked books to obtain arty asymmetrical balance (no. 203). Likewise, chairs have been placed in drawing rooms in locations that would have frustrated conversation but won awards for artistic distribution (nos. 100, 116, 129). In shooting numerous dining rooms, the photographer has suggested that the two closest to the camera be pulled out from the table to funnel the response of the viewer.

As they prepared for the photographer, the owners and servants tried to give their interiors a spit-and-polish look before they became permanently frozen on the pages of *Artistic Houses*. This is not surprising. However, the intensity with which they wanted to leave the impression of domestic perfection is surprising. They purged the accidental and the casual in their quest for the appearance of impersonal and impeccable order. They wanted to be recognized by the contemporary public and by history for their flawless arrangements rather than their personal imprints. In addition to getting ready for dress inspection, many actually staged the scene that was to be photographically preserved by rearranging rooms to strengthen the intended impression. This can be observed by examining rooms photographed from two different positions, good examples of which are the John T. Martin picture gallery (nos. 149 & 150) and the Hurtt library-parlor (nos. 95 & 96). Martin's prize painting was a Millet study of a male and female peasant walking to work. In number 149 it appears behind the divided sofa at the near left; in number 150, the same room photographed from the opposite end, the Millet reappears on the easel at the distant right. Similarly, the objects on the central table have been changed and shifted to suit each perspective. In the Hurtt interiors, the statue of a strumming musician was moved to appear each time in the foreground room, the round table has been substituted for the three-legged table and the objects on the latter have been changed.

These are small reminders that photography is not necessarily neutral. Some of these house owners were willing to manipulate their domestic settings in exchange for the impact they thought the photographs would have on the public. *Artistic Houses* is a valuable record of interior decoration and the life-style of the wealthy in the early 1880s. It was also an active agent that discouraged revelations of family idiosyncrasies and normal patterns and encouraged steps that left the impression of elegant and ordered homes.

The photographs in *Artistic Houses* document interiors that do not look like the interiors of houses built earlier in the nineteenth century. This is to be expected because changes in fashions meant different materials for hangings, different woods and styles of furniture, or the increasing popularity of Oriental rugs and stained-glass windows. However, the difference between many of these interiors and those of the decades preceding the 1880s was not, primarily, caused by changes in furnishings but by a new function of the wealthy American town house, particularly the town house in New York City. A large number of residences celebrated in *Artistic Houses* have been transformed from traditional domestic environments stressing elegance, comfort and convenience into domestic museums. The *American Architect and Building News* recognized this new phenomenon (August 9, 1884): "But a man's house, which used to be his castle, is now his museum, and the purist understands that things are to be considered as unticketed specimens, the tokens of the collector's prowess or the souvenirs of his travels." Clarence Cook noticed the tendency to fill houses with objects as early as 1876 in his series on the house written for *Scribner's Monthly* (February 1876):

A New York parlor of the kind called "stylish," where no merely useful thing is permitted, and where nothing can be used with comfort, is always overcrowded; things are bought from pure whim, or because the buyer doesn't know what to do with her money; and as the parlor is only used on what are called state occasions, what would be the good of having easy-going, comfortable things in it. So everything bought for show goes there; and as the temptation to New York rich people is to be all the time buying things for show, the inevitable result is, that in time the intruding camel crowds out the occupant of the tent.

This description certainly does not apply to all of the metropolitan interiors published in *Artistic Houses*. It is not true of the drawing room of Walter and June Hunnewell (no. 148), or the dining rooms of Dr. Haven (no. 80) and Jane and John Charles Phillips (no. 165). But these were interiors in Boston, not New York, where Society's definition of what an important house should look like was discussed and heeded more frequently than in Boston or Philadelphia.

Americans for generations had displayed prized possessions within their homes. The difference between the traditional approach and the new one evident in so many New York interiors is that, as Cook predicted, the objects were crowding out the family. So jammed with stuff are some of these spaces that we may wonder if the owners asked the photographer for a few minutes' delay in order to bring in special objects from surrounding rooms. In the drawing room of Judge Hilton (no. 78) so many chairs, stands, tables and easels block the way that they must have affected the traffic patterns of the house. Egerton Winthrop's reception room (no. 54) looks like a warehouse of exotic but not very functional furniture. Even the established families of old New York were smitten by bric-a-brac mania, as the drawing room of Hamilton Fish (no. 52) demonstrates.

In such houses the museum mentality seems to have replaced the idea of the home as a protective environment serving the physical, social, spiritual and cultural requirements of the family. As the importance of domestic exhibition space increased, comfort, convenience, movement, intimacy and repose decreased. When the William H. Vanderbilt mansion was first opened to 2000 friends of the family on March 7, 1882, the reporter for the *Times* searched for signs of domesticity amid the glitter:

There is nothing exactly loud, or anything which "swears." Still, the effect is crushing. Eyes distended to their utmost are palled, as the gustatory sense is sometimes cloyed by overtasting. One longs to find out if there is not one simple room where there might be found some repose.

This writer may have been reacting particularly to the Japanese room (no. 118).

An ironic consequence of the museum mentality was the failure of many of these interiors to express the distinctiveness their families assumed they were expressing. Believing that a house should reflect who the family was and what the family did, owners displayed proudly Japanese screens, Bristol faience, modern Louis XVI furniture from Paris, fragments of Venetian tapestries—artwork they had labored to find or traveled abroad to purchase. And they commissioned Tiffany windows and worked to add a Diaz painting to their collections.

Unfortunately, there were other families trying to find distinctiveness through the same objects. One display of bric-a-brac looked like another display of bric-a-brac, one family's series of modern conservative masters matched that of another family. Reassured of being correct, they were not reassured of being distinctive in their choices. Furthermore, works of art in many well-appointed houses looked like works of art in a museum, an assemblage of disparate objects. Collected for ulterior reasons, the displays in the new domestic museum often were not held together by a personal point of view. These assemblages of prized possessions, intended to reveal the family, frequently revealed the characterlessness of the formulation of the collection.

Sheldon's informative but critically timid commentaries do not alert us to trouble spots which then or later might dim the brilliant new day of American domestic art. He would have seconded M. E. W. Sherwood's conclusion about the country's participation "in the full floodtide of modern art improvement and beauty." He did not refer to the possibility that these interiors may have resembled one another even though he praised owners for including certain names within their painting collection and implied the sophistication of collectors who display the particular bric-a-brac that was fashionable in 1883–84. The decision to eliminate people from the photographs and to focus on the objects and settings was undoubtedly his idea. These scenes of impersonal perfection delighted him. His enthusiasm for what he saw was unchecked, as is evident in his repeated phrases lauding owners and decorators for their ability to produce results without flaws. His text is filled with compliments like "perfect harmony runs through the walls," "furnished throughout with rare good taste," "surroundings in perfect accord with the desires of a cultivated taste." Nor is Sheldon aware of the vulnerability of these interiors to charges of ostentatious display. To the contrary, he repeatedly reassures his readers that the opposite is true. Of the Childs' drawing room (no. 202) he wrote, "Not the slightest attempt at show appears in this room, or, indeed, anywhere throughout the house." "Nothing has been done for ostentation" in the Anderson parlor, the decoration of the Goddard library (no. 161) "shows no haste to be something for its own sake," and even in the palatial Villard houses "no attempt at ostentation appears in any part of the architectural outline or the decorative scheme." Sheldon tried to convince readers that all of these interiors had been discreetly integrated to obtain the ideal balance, "to secure style without pretension, luxury without danger to homely, domestic effect, simplicity without monotony, and dignity without severity," as he characterized the William Clark house.

Perhaps we could attribute Sheldon's relentlessly positive conclusions to the circumstances of the publication. He had asked important and wealthy citizens to permit him to describe and photograph their houses. Once they consented, he was not in a good position to tell them how to arrange them better. The entire text contains no negative criticism, not even a highly qualified reservation. Even when he seems to be heading toward an inevitable rebuke, Sheldon will either find a positive implication or will leave the impression that there is nothing wrong. An example of the latter is his response to the drawing room of the Vanderbilts (no. 116). "The effect is gorgeous in the extreme: everything sparkles and flashes with gold and color—with mother-of-pearl, with marbles, with jewel-effects in glass—and almost every surface is covered, one might say weighted, with ornament . . . ."

Sheldon was positive because he could not risk offending subscribers, because he believed the contemporary interiors of no nation could match those of the United States and because the text and photographs in *Artistic Houses* were the "worthiest extant representative" of this superiority. He had reasons to be confident. Never before in America had the most influential and

wealthiest citizens of the largest cities been so involved in art. They wanted beautiful homes. They hired noted architects to build them and noted decorators to furnish them. They collected works of art to display in their houses, sometimes traveling abroad to find appropriate items. They read about the increasing quality of American architecture and decoration in newly-formed art journals and in the increasing number of articles that appeared in such popular monthlies as *Lippincott's* and *Harper's*. They were proud of the high quality of craftsmanship in their houses and enjoyed the intricate and extensive evidence of that skill in the houses of their friends. They knew that the finest of American homes were now testimonials to the country's rising cultural and artistic taste. *Artistic Houses* confirmed the reality of this "exceedingly fresh and brilliant morning."

Fig. 19. Hollis Hunnewell house, Boston, Massachusetts.

Yet this artistic dawn was not entirely American. "A journey through France might not produce an impression half so Gallic as an entrance into Mr. Hunnewell's ballroom," Sheldon had written. On the other hand, if affluent Americans were buying the old treasures of Europe, Europeans, restless under the long shadow of the Renaissance, were beginning to discover refreshing characteristics in American domestic architecture. This began in the years the volumes of *Artistic Houses* were published. By 1887 architectural journals in Germany, France and Britain had called attention to American houses because they were so "curiously instructive." These characteristics were not those discussed by Sheldon or stressed in his photographs; in fact, they were not the same houses he had selected.

Europeans overlooked the town houses and concentrated on the freestanding houses, usually of wood, that had been built for the middle and upper-middle classes in the suburbs and the countryside. What they admired were features which the photographs in *Artistic Houses* tended to obscure or to demote. They liked the unpretentious informality which indicated the family was "at home," the simplicity and absence of show, the spatial openness made possible by central heating, the internal flexibility that enabled owners to link or isolate rooms, the importance of comfort, the laborsaving mechanical innovations and shortcuts that increased domestic convenience, and the architects' extended authority (built-ins, closets, chimney seats) over the appearance and the function of the interior.

Ironically, European architects and critics turned their backs on the new urban architecture that had inspired *Artistic Houses* and Sheldon's pronouncements of national achievement, but found an "exceedingly fresh and brilliant morning" in the suburban houses based on a longer and broader American tradition.

ILLUSTRATIONS
AND
CAPTIONS

CORNELIA M. STEWART HOUSE

Cornelia M. Clinch (October 20, 1803–October 25, 1886), the daughter of an established ship chandler in New York, married Alexander Turney Stewart (October 12, 1803–April 10, 1876) in 1825. Their three children all predeceased their father. Born in Ireland, Stewart had emigrated to the United States when he was 16. In his early twenties, Stewart inherited about $5000, purchased Irish laces, and sold them at a small shop in New York City. In 1846 he moved into a new five-story dry-goods store at the corner of Chambers Street and Broadway. Because business prospered, in 1862 he commissioned a second store, which became known as the Uptown Store. Designed by John Kellum (1807–1871), it contained eight floors and was a wonderfully equipped, popular and extremely profitable operation on Broadway between East 9th and 10th Streets. Stewart's success may have marked the apogee of the influence of the merchant class in the United States before it was superseded by industrialists and bankers.

In the late 1850s the Stewarts purchased, for $225,000, the splendid town house of Dr. Samuel P. Townsend, the largest brownstone in the city, which had been built recently on the northwest corner of Fifth Avenue and West 34th Street. Initially, Stewart intended to strip the interior to the floor joists but reconsidered and ordered all vestiges of the original mansion, even the foundation stones, removed. However, his vaunted business efficiency was not evident in the building process. The project, also designed by Kellum, required 500 workers, who labored in fits and starts over a five-year period, and ultimately cost more than $1.5 million. Completed in 1869, the mansion commanded the attention and encouraged the wagging tongues of New Yorkers. Its dimensions, 120′ along 34th Street and 72½′ along Fifth Avenue, were huge for a city house of its day. Despite its mixture of Greek, Renaissance and modern French elements, the Stewarts' "Marble Palace" was an orderly composition. Compared to its discreet but costly dignity, the William B. Astor II brownstone, directly across 34th Street, now looked decidedly second-class.

Inside, the brick walls of many of the Stewart house's 55 rooms were finished in Carrara marble or painted panels. The floors of major rooms were covered with either marble or tile resting on brick-arch construction spanning iron girders. The main floor, entered from the wide steps on West 34th Street, led to the principal social rooms: hall, reception, dining, music, drawing and picture gallery. The floor above was also divided into eight rooms with 18′9″ ceilings; the plans of these two floors varied little because of the weight of the brick-and-iron construction.

Beside the Stewart house, the finest brownstones of the city would have looked drab and unrefined on their exteriors, and though they might have been comfortable and even elegant within, they were neither as opulent nor as commanding. The drawing room in particular (no. 3), expressed the grandeur, scale, artistic fashion and cultural sophistication that distinguished this house from its New York contemporaries. Yet some observers argued that the house did not look like a home. According to *Harper's Weekly* (August 14, 1869):

> The building, with scarcely an alteration in the arrangement of its rooms, could be transformed into a magnificent art-gallery. It almost astonishes us to hear the architect speak of this as a reception room, of that as a breakfast room, and of another as the parlor. The beautiful wardrobe and bath rooms are the only portions of the house which distinctively suggest the idea of a private residence.

After Mrs. Stewart's death in 1886, the *Times* asserted that there was no question but that the mansion's grand staircase, spacious halls and picture gallery suited it ideally for club use. In 1891 it was leased to the

Manhattan Club, which occupied the structure until 1899, when the club was unable to meet its costs. The house was demolished early in the first decade of the twentieth century.

The Stewarts and their architect had conceived a unique residence and executed the idea, apparently with little self-doubt. The "Marble Palace" was immediately noticed but not immediately loved. Before it was finished *Appleton's Illustrated Guide* claimed, "of all the famous buildings on Fifth Avenue, none will ever be so famous. . . . Words are absolutely inadequate to describe its beauty and unique grandeur." The *New York Sun* praised Stewart for a private act with handsome public results. But architect P. B. Wight, acknowledging the cost, wondered how "any one surrounded by works of art, as was Mr. Stewart, could have had so little understanding of what constituted a work of architecture" (*American Architect and Building News*, May 6, 1876). Despite such reservations, Jay Cantor, in his thorough account of the Stewart house (*Winterthur Portfolio*, vol. 10), contended that subsequent New York mansion builders were profoundly affected by its challenge.

New Yorkers were intrigued by the anomaly of two relatively plain people living in this conspicuous, palatial house. A contemporary biographer noted Stewart's abstemious personal habits and his unwillingness to wear diamond pins, watch chains or glittering rings. Obituaries praised his "thrift" and "plain dealing." Living in a house ideal for social events, he and his wife shunned society. In his last years only close friends and selected art authorities were invited inside.

When Cornelia M. Stewart died in 1886, the *New York Times* gave her death front-page coverage, but not because she had been a social, political or intellectual force in the life of the city. She had few friends and spent summers quietly in Saratoga and winters in the "Marble Palace." The coverage reflected local curiosity about the size of the Stewart fortune, estimated in 1876 to be at least $35 million, and her will. She left $15 million less than she had inherited, the difference being attributed to her gifts to charities and relatives and the transfer of property to Judge Henry Hilton (nos. 78 & 79), her financial adviser and confidant of her husband for 30 years. Of the remaining fortune, approximately half went to Hilton in trust and half to the members of her family.

3

1. Hall, Cornelia M. Stewart house, 1 West 34th Street, New York, New York; John Kellum, architect, 1864–69; demolished ca. 1901. The main hall ran north–south through the middle of the main part of the house. Visitors were dwarfed by the lofty ceiling, silenced by the ghostly statues and paced by the obtrusive but dry Corinthian columns. Although the sculptures chosen by Stewart were in vogue when the house was completed, most would have been considered old-fashioned by the New York art establishment when *Artistic Houses* was published. The first pair in this photograph was created by Italian sculptors. On the left was the *Water Nymph*, by Antonio Tantardini (1829–1879), and on the right was the *Fisher Girl* by Scipione Tadolini (1822–1892). Behind these, respectively, were *Demosthenes* by Thomas Crawford (1813?–1857) and *Zenobia* by Harriet Hosmer (1830–1908), both Americans. Behind *Zenobia*, was a clock, 14′ high, from the Eugène Cornu factory of Paris. At the end of the hall on the right was one of the scores of copies of *Nydia*, by Randolph Rogers (1825–1892).

The hall also served as an introduction to the picture gallery beyond. We can see the canvas of *Beatrice and Benedict* by French artist Hugues Merle (1823–1881).

2. Reception room, Cornelia M. Stewart house. This room linked the hall with the drawing room, which can be seen through the doorway. Sheldon noted the costliness of objects and surfaces not only here but throughout the house: "Money flowed abundantly during the seven [five] years when this white marble palace was building for a merchant prince. . . ."

The rosewood table in the center was covered with a slab of Mexican onyx. The bronze and gilt panels of the rosewood cabinets in the corners were decorated with figures in relief. Complementing the design of the ceiling was a commissioned Aubusson carpet. Stewart paid an Italian painter more than $15,000 to beautify the walls and ceilings. Here the decorative panels compete with the paintings. On the left of the doorway was a portrait of a lady by G. J. Jacquet (1846–1909); on the right *Marguerite*, by G. J. Ferrier (1847–1914). Carved casings of Carrara marble framed the doors and windows. Blue silk covered the chairs and sofas and was also used for the hangings.

3. Drawing room, Cornelia M. Stewart house. The left wall contained three enormous windows that faced Fifth Avenue. Between them were two equally impressive mirrors. This sequence of A-B-A-B-A was repeated on the opposite side of the room, where three entrances—from the music room, side hall and reception room—were separated by two cabinets, each 9′ long and 4′ high. The pattern of the carpet was also divided into three bays and reflected the ceiling's design, painted in encaustic. Reinforcing the axis were gasoliers and tables below. The drawing room was also divided into three parts vertically: the first contained the gilded whitewood furniture covered with pale yellow satin, the second the mirrors, windows, doorways and gold-toned wall panels and the third the cornice and ceiling decoration.

There were no paintings in this room, but sculptures were carefully placed to maintain the insistent balance: *First Love*, by American-born R. H. Park (1832–after 1890), stood before the central window and was flanked by two $10,000 Sèvres vases. In front of the 34th Street window was *Maternal Love* by Salvatore Albano (1841–1893).

4

4. Music room, Cornelia M. Stewart house. Rooms designed solely for music were not common in American domestic architecture in these years, but were included in some of the larger and more pretentious houses. The ideal music room was expected to have a high and coved ceiling, a minimum of draperies to insure satisfactory sound, and a varied decor that was neither too heavy nor too fanciful.

The major pieces of furniture in this room were of rosewood. The table in the center was highlighted at regular intervals on its skirt by bronze reliefs symbolizing the seasons. This room also contained three cabinets, the panels of which were decorated in silver and bronze high reliefs. The frames of the doorways and windows, as well as the mantel (not visible here), were finished in white marble. In general, the color scheme was quiet but not somber. The cream of the Aubusson carpet, the white marble and the light green that covered the darker portions of the walls and ceiling provided an effective background for the heavier colors of the paintings. However, the Stewart house was so extensively decorated that pictures could not be hung well. Furthermore, the metallic rod-and-chain system of support did not blend easily with the marble and *faux-marbre* walls. The most satisfactory solution to this problem, rarely employed in other interiors of this series, was the curtained niche at the left, a formal and imposing means of displaying a work of art.

Through the doorway can be seen the end of the main hall and the newel post and first steps of the curving marble staircase, called by an anonymous observer the "most beautiful specimen of architecture of that kind" in the United States.

5. Library, Cornelia M. Stewart house. We know surprisingly little about Stewart's personal life. He apparently enjoyed books and admitted to friends that he read selections from the *Aeneid* in Latin before work each morning. His collection of books, however, was less impressive and celebrated than his collection of paintings. The highest

prices paid for titles at the sale of his library in March 1887 were $1350 for an original edition of Audubon's *Birds of America*, issued in four volumes 1827–38, and $252 for a first edition of the *Viviparous Quadrupeds of North America* by Audubon and Backman. The books were kept in eight black-walnut cases placed around the room, while the larger portfolios were stored in the drawers of the two 10′ tables.

Although her husband had died approximately seven years before this photograph was taken, Mrs. Stewart had probably made few changes in this room. She commissioned the posthumous portrait of Stewart by Thomas Le Clear (1818–1882), on the easel to the right, and placed her own portrait, by Jeannette Loop (1840–1909), opposite it. Above each, like patron saints from a royal past, were portraits of Elizabeth I of England and Alexander II of Russia. Compared to other libraries in this series, the Stewart's was larger, less intimate and more formal.

6. Mrs. Stewart's bedroom, Cornelia M. Stewart house. The main bedrooms were on the second floor in addition to the sitting and billiard rooms and the library. Above the library was the principal guest room, known as the "General Grant Room." Because the floor dimensions and ceiling height of the family rooms on the second floor were identical to those of the social or public rooms below, and because the decorative character of these rooms was coordinated, form certainly did not follow function in the Stewart palace. Specific activities were claimed from generalized spaces largely through the impact of the furniture, which, in this room, does not blend well with the exuberant curves of the gasolier or with the repeated catenaries of the draperies. Without closets, the bedroom was essentially a marble-and-plaster box, a very expensively finished box. After the plaster was laid on the iron furring, four layers of underground paint were applied before the application of the final design.

5

6

7

8

7. Picture gallery, Cornelia M. Stewart house. At the end of the main hall was the entrance to the picture gallery, a windowless space approximately 75′ long, 30′ wide and 50′ high. Built as a block on the north side of the house, it was illuminated during the day by natural light that came through the skylight of glass and iron. Evening viewing was made possible by three gasoliers that hung from the skylight. The gallery's wall was obscured by the tightly fitted frames, a system that enabled the Stewarts to display about 150 works in this space. When Earl Shinn itemized and discussed the Stewart collection in *The Art Treasures of America* (ca. 1879–82), he listed 179 paintings and 19 pieces of sculpture.

Because these works of art were collected between 1846 and 1875, they constituted a collection older than most featured in *Artistic Houses* and did not reflect post-Centennial New York art trends. Nevertheless, it contained paintings by several French artists who were still popular in the United States in the early 1880s: three by Jean-Léon Gérome (1824–1904), three by A. D. Bouguereau, and four by Jean-Louis Meissonier. But the didactic and chromatically conservative character of the Stewart paintings appealed less to later critics. *The Art Amateur* of November 1879 declared that it was "not exactly the shrine of a poet-painter. You do not go thither to see examples of Delacroix, Descamps, Millet, Corot, Rousseau. . . ."

The sculpture in the immediate foreground is *Proserpine* by Marshall Wood (d. 1882) and behind it to the left is a seated *Flora* by Chauncey B. Ives (1810–1894). To the right of *Flora* were two works by Hiram Powers (1805–1873): *Eve Tempted*, with apple in hand, and one of the six copies of his *Greek Slave* of 1843. "Ghosts of connoisseurs of 40 years ago," was the verdict by a critic of the early 1880s of Stewart's sculpture collection.

8. Picture gallery, Cornelia M. Stewart house. The Stewarts' best-known paintings were *The Horse Fair* (1853) by Rosa Bonheur (1822–1899) and *Friedland, 1807,* (completed in 1875) by Meissonier. Seventeen feet long, *The Horse Fair* dominated the west wall of the gallery. The painting's size, strength and susceptibility to anecdotal embellishments made it one of the most popular works of the period. Meissonier's interpretation of Napoleon the soldier is in the center of the north wall near the *Greek Slave* and underneath *Niagara from the American Side*, an 8′ × 5′ canvas by Frederick Church (1826–1900).

Stewart probably paid between $4 and $5 million for the 1011 objects offered for sale in New York in 1887. $513,750 were bid on the paintings. *Friedland, 1807*, sold to Henry Hilton for $66,000, brought the highest price. Cornelius Vanderbilt purchased *The Horse Fair* for $53,000 (the second highest price) and immediately donated it to the Metropolitan Museum of Art. That these two paintings, generally considered two of the most important horse paintings of the nineteenth century, were in the United States was cited often by Americans as evidence of the rising sophistication of Yankee buyers.

9. Print gallery, James L. Claghorn house, 222 North 19th Street, Philadelphia, Pennsylvania; architect unknown, late 1850s; demolished 1917. Claghorn (July 5, 1817–August 25, 1884) was one of the more informed collectors in the country from the 1860s until his death. A banker, Claghorn served for 12 years as president of the Pennsylvania Academy of the Fine Arts. After buying more than 300 American paintings and then turning to works by contemporary Europeans, he sold his oils to concentrate on prints, of which he eventually owned between 30,000 and 40,000.

Prints hung on the side wall were exposed to light continuously, but those at the end were hung on sliding panels that would have provided some protection. Rather than offering study space, flat surfaces, such as the Renaissance Revival parlor table at the right, held ceramics from around the world—in this case, a Wedgwood urn and a Satsuma vase.

10

10. Drawing room, E. Rollins Morse house, 167 Commonwealth Avenue, Boston, Massachusetts; Sturgis and Brigham, architects, 1880–81; standing. Morse (October 21, 1845–September 10, 1931) was a banker and investment broker who, in partnership with his brother Charles J., operated a firm at 28 State Street in Boston. He married Marion R. Steedman on May 29, 1873; she died on May 1, 1920. With considerable assets, social standing and social mobility—the couple also lived in New York and Washington—Mrs. Morse became a hostess of renown, one of the great hostesses of Newport, according to Mariana Van Rensselaer. This building still stands as an attached masonry house on Commonwealth Avenue but has been converted to apartments. Stylistically, the exterior is a combination of delicate Federal motifs and heavy pseudo-Romanesque forms. The main entrance is set within a segmental archway and is adjacent to a broad curving bay window that extends through the three main floors of this four-story building. The ground floor is faced with brownstone, the upper floors with red brick and stone trim.

This room was on the second floor, frequently treated as the main level in Back Bay houses. Because of the relatively quiet walls of stamped leather in old gold and the painted panels of the rather high ceiling, divided diagonally by strips of darkened oak, the center of gravity of this room was unusually low. Furthermore, with its spacious dimensions, modest and comfortable furniture and limited bric-a-brac, the room contrasts markedly with a contemporary type of New York interior (nos. 24, 52, 100, 131) in which the living space doubles as an exhibition area. Works of art were exhibited in the Morse drawing room, but they remained subordinate to the character of the space. The painting of the seated woman in evening dress is by B. C. Porter (1845–1908) and a Venetian scene, on the left side of the fireplace, by Félix Ziem (1821–1911). At far left is a frond of the palm tree that stood in the center of the bay window overlooking Commonwealth Avenue.

---

11. Drawing room, Hollis Hunnewell house, 315 Dartmouth Street, Boston, Massachusetts; Sturgis and Brigham, architects, 1868–70; standing but altered. Hollis Hunnewell (November 16,

1836–June 11, 1884) was the son of dynamic Horatio Hollis Hunnewell (1810–1902) and the father of Hollis Horatio Hunnewell, who was born in 1868. As a child he lived in Boston and in Paris, where his father was involved with the banking house of Welles and Company. Hollis graduated from Harvard in 1858, worked in Paris with his father, and in April 1867 married Louisa Bronson (April 4, 1843–November 10, 1890) of New York City. By December of 1883 he was ill with an unspecified sickness and he died the following summer.

Designed in the late 1860s, the original house was three bays wide, of brick and brownstone and capped by a mansard roof four stories high on one side and three stories high on the other. On December 18, 1876, a fire severely damaged the structure, which was rebuilt in the early 1880s. The family moved into the house during May 1884.

The Hunnewells had collected, during their residence in Paris, European paintings, the largest of which in this room is the *Madonna and Child* after Giovanni Bellini (ca. 1430–1516), furniture and heraldic plaques, combined them with fine Chinese porcelains and then pushed all of these items in their drawing room to the edges to clear the central space for traffic. The result is a large cocoon of impressive objects from varied times and cultures.

12. Tapestry room, Hollis Hunnewell house. This room is appropriately named for the tapestry that encircles it and determines its character. Remarkably, the scenes depicted on the wall continue around the room, even across the draperies, without interruption. The conspicuous border of the tapestries is continued to the center of each window, where the top and bottom borders are joined by side borders to complete each scene. Because of the exact conformity of the scenes in the tapestry to the height and width of each wall and because of their use in the window drapery, these textiles must have been commissioned expressly for this space. In order to show off these richly decorated surfaces, the number and obtrusiveness of pieces of furniture and other objects have been controlled. The furniture is low and delicate, the carpet fine but relatively subdued, the ceiling painted a solid color and the cornice restrained.

11

12

13

14

13. Hall, Louis C. Tiffany apartment, 48 East 26th Street, New York, New York; architect unknown, date unknown; demolished. Louis C. Tiffany (February 18, 1848–January 17, 1933) inherited over $13 million in 1902 on the death of his father, Charles L. Tiffany, founder of the well-known jewelry firm, now Tiffany & Co. Instead of joining his father in business, Louis studied painting in the United States and in Europe. In 1879 he and three friends—Samuel Colman (1832–1920), Lockwood De Forest (1850–1932) and Candace Wheeler (1828–1923)—formed Louis C. Tiffany and Company, Associated Artists, a firm dedicated to the revitalization and modernization of interior design. Although this partnership ended four years later, its influence on interiors in the Eastern United States was cited often in art publications of the 1880s. Sheldon included several interiors by Associated Artists in *Artistic Houses*, among them numbers 17, 18, 52, 67, 68, 108, 139–142 and 198.

Tiffany and his family—his wife, Mary Woodbridge Goddard, whom he married on May 15, 1872, and their three children—moved in 1878 into the top story of the Bella Apartments on East 26th Street. Two years later *The Art Journal* (vol. 6) featured his redesigned quarters in an article on New York studios. The author, John Moran, warned his readers that "some might think that Mr. Tiffany pushes his decorative ideas to an extreme . . . ." He had combined disparate elements, his "finds," in tenuous but refreshing relationships, produced an impression of spontaneity without disregarding artistic balance, and articulated wall surfaces in flat patterns freed from Renaissance weight and independent of Renaissance illusionistic space. After the death of Mary in 1884, Tiffany moved to a multifamily, 50-room house at the corner of East 72nd Street and Madison Avenue.

The hall contains numerous unexpected, seemingly incompatible, objects. Visitors, entering from the elevator through the door at the near left, were confronted by a stack of weapons and equipment that partially obstructed the passageway to the right. More weapons, hanging ungracefully at the intersection of the two corridors, directed attention to the crude, heavily gouged pine rafters. This gabled section

was painted brown, and the walls, parts of them covered by bronze and bronze studs, a warm India red. In *The Art Work of Louis C. Tiffany* (1914) by Charles De Kay, there is a reference to a window in the gable area raised by a large wooden wheel and chain. In the 1880s it was not common to incorporate functional equipment, in the manner of the contemporary British architect James Sterling, in the public spaces of a city residence. At the right is another example, a blunt gas jet attached to the wall by its hose. This jet was placed there to cast a flickering light on the stained-glass window behind it. According to Moran, the abstract design of the window was inspired by one created by daubing the residue of Tiffany's palette knife. This early window is similar to one he installed in the dining room of the George Kemp house (no. 141).

14. Drawing room, Louis C. Tiffany apartment. According to Sheldon, when Tiffany decorated a room in a former style, as he did his "Moorish" drawing room, he did not follow that style closely. "By Moorish decoration the reader is to understand, not a copy of anything that ever has existed or still exists, but only a general feeling for a particular type." Sheldon also explained: "In this drawing-room, for instance, the Moorish feeling has received a dash of East Indian, and the wall-papers and ceiling-papers are Japanese, but there is a unity that binds everything into an *ensemble*, and the spirit of that unity is delicacy." In other words, the original was a catalyst for Tiffany's imagination.

The buff Japanese ceiling paper contained glittering pieces of mica. The high screen supported by Moorish columns on the east side of the room separated this space from the hall. Its portieres, reflected in the mirror of the divider, were made from Japanese materials. On the other side of the divider the wallpaper was pink. To the left of the fireplace was Tiffany's 1879 watercolor of his family, *In the Fields at Irvington*. To attract attention to the relatively small fireplace, he exaggerated the width of the tiled panels to either side, lifted the mantel and filled the opening below with a translucent screen of mica in a spiderweb pattern, and completed the overmantel with three mirrors and shelves.

15

16

17

15. Dining room, Louis C. Tiffany apartment. In this room Tiffany placed circular forms against rectangular sections. The forms are present at all levels, from the tray on the bottom shelf to the fan carving of the eighteenth-century mantel front, the Oriental porcelain charger in the middle of the mantel and the plates to either side, the rounded turkey and pumpkin of the overmantel painting (probably by Tiffany) and, finally, the repeated blue disks of the ceiling. The rectangle of the extremely simple oak table was repeated in the rectangular sections of the walls. The dining room should look more cluttered than it does, considering the number of objects it contains, but because Tiffany concentrates on two geometric shapes, the potential of each to distract is lessened. Furthermore, these forms and surfaces are essentially flat. Even the Japanese wallpaper, with its embroidered borders, and the ceiling paper are space-denying patterns. Tiffany liked wall sections that contrasted in color, design, texture and materials. For example, the fire opening was faced with tile; above it was the carved-oak mantel, the band of dark paper and finally the painting with its strong colors of yellow, red and blue. In stacking these contrasting sections, Tiffany was ignoring the sculptural handling of the fireplace area commonly used by his contemporaries.

16. Library, Louis C. Tiffany apartment. In contrast to most of the dining rooms in this series, which were treated as isolated rooms, Tiffany's could also be used as an extension of the sitting room or library. The doorway between the two rooms was wide, there were no portieres to obstruct vision or movement (though there probably were sliding doors), and from either space one could see through the leaves of the transom. Yet these two rooms were not similar in character. If the dining room looked nervous and thinly paneled, the library appeared to be busy and stuffed with substantial pieces. The padded wicker chairs were common in such settings, as was the table with multiple shelves for folio volumes. The fireplace was the dominant three-dimensional element. Three decades later, Tiffany was still pleased with the "novel manner" in which he had handled the book shelving around the fireplace. By "novel" he also meant the "irregular balance" he had substituted for the predictable symmetry of fireplace decoration. The wall panels, some left bare but most hand-painted, were also placed without concern for symmetry. These walls seem haphazard and probably too taxing for the tired eye. We should remember that this apartment was remodeled rather than reconstructed. Without denying

the planarity of the walls he inherited, Tiffany infused them with an unconventional energy.

---

17. East Room, The White House, 1600 Pennsylvania Avenue, Washington, D.C.; James Hoban and others, architects, 1792, 1815–17; standing. Because of structural deterioration, new beams, supported by columns at either end, were added to the East Room in 1873. At the same time huge crystal chandeliers were ordered from Germany for this room and for other principal rooms in the house. In 1882 President Chester A. Arthur, having failed to persuade Congress to erect a larger and more elaborate mansion, hired Louis C. Tiffany and Company, Associated Artists, to redecorate the room in keeping with the design standards of the era.

The work was relatively modest, costing a total of $30,000 and requiring only seven weeks to complete; however, Tiffany was able to introduce an aura of splendor and refined taste ideally suited to the temperament of the resident of the White House, for Arthur was a man deeply concerned with appearances and social graces, one who preferred elegance to showy gestures.

In the East Room Tiffany was constrained by the major design features and structural elements already present. The entranceway was the work of Benjamin Latrobe (1764–1820); the frieze, with its Grecian motif, designed by Thomas U. Walter (1804–1887) and the chandeliers, beams, supporting columns, fireplace mantels and overmantel mirrors dated from the 1873 remodeling. Tiffany left these features intact as well as the dominant color scheme of white and gilt. In this 80' × 40' space he laid a new Axminster carpet of a sienna color to harmonize with the existing decoration. He applied mosaic pattern to the ceiling in silver leaf, creating shiny surfaces that reflected the carpet below.

Tiffany's work extended to other public spaces in the White House, notably the Blue Room, Red Room and dining room. He considered his chief contribution a curtain of opalescent glass that separated the downstairs living space from the corridor. In 1902 President Theodore Roosevelt commissioned the firm of McKim, Mead and White to renovate and redecorate the White House completely. When this half-million-dollar project was finished, the work by Tiffany had been erased.

18. Dining room, William T. Lusk house, 47 East 34th Street, New York, New York; architect unknown, 1867–68; demolished. Lusk (May 23, 1838–June 12, 1897) was the author of *The Science and Art of Midwifery* (1881), which was a standard text for the next two decades. He was also one of the few gynecologists to perform caesarean operations successfully. Ironically, his first wife, Mary Hartwell Chittenden (August 18, 1840–September 13, 1871), whom he married in 1864, died with her child during her fifth delivery. He married Mrs. Matilda Myer Thorn in 1876. Lusk had opened his practice in New York in 1865 and in 1871 joined the faculty of Bellevue Hospital Medical College. In 1894 he became president of the American Gynecological Society.

Lusk was the physician to the Tiffany family during these years, and Tiffany's daughter married Lusk's son. The dining room and the parlor of this 34th Street house were decorated by L. C. Tiffany & Associated Artists. The room is a fine example of the firm's rejection of dark, sculptural effects in favor of planar, reflective surfaces. The woodwork was stained pine, a material most of the owners of these interiors would have considered too cheap and too common. The first register of the room was lined with disciplined right-angled parts—the cupboard, tiled fire front and wood box on the left and the buffet and diminutive doorway to the pantry on the right. Between the woodwork and the bronze frieze, the wall was covered with quiet Japanese paper. On the distant wall this register was dominated by two transoms composed of square panes of diffused amber glass. These transoms distract one from the stubby windows of transparent glass below. Tightly organized and visually charged, this interior was an American counterpart to the energy and impermanence found in the contemporary paintings of Degas and Cézanne in France.

---

19. Library, Clarence H. Clark house, 4200 Locust Street, Philadelphia, Pennsylvania; architect unknown, late 1850s; demolished 1916. Probably erected in the 1850s and later enlarged, this house was one of the grand mansions of West Philadelphia. The formidable structure was eventually composed of a three-story ashlar block in the center with two-story wings at either side, and a one-and-a-half-story projection from each wing. Horses and carriages swung in from Locust Street along a wide, curving driveway to deposit women and gentlemen before a large and highly ornamented portico. Behind the house was an extensive park open to the public. The site is now occupied by the University City New School.

The library was contained in one of the projections and terminated a vista of more than 125′ across the rooms of the main floor. Spatially distinctive, this room expanded into deep alcoves, one of which is visible at the left, and was covered by the octagonal ceiling approximately 20′ above the floor. This ceiling was divided by oak beams into geometric sections filled with embossed leather. Below the beams was a window frieze of stained glass that included at intervals the words of a Goethe sentiment: "Like a star that maketh not haste, that taketh not rest; be each one fulfilling his God-given hest." One of Clark's "God-given" hests was to cover his walls with embossed leather. The art and bric-a-brac in this room were combined without much concern for stylistic or cultural unity. Between a reproduction of the Ghent Altarpiece of 1432 on the left and a miniature copy of the statue of Augustus of Primaporta of 20 B.C. on the right were exquisite ceramics from the Orient and nineteenth-century American and European paintings. The two portraits on the left wall were probably painted by George Munzig (1859–1908) of Boston. The tall volumes on the lower shelf, rarely seen in the libraries included in *Artistic Houses,* were probably well-bound runs of art or architectural journals to which Clark subscribed.

20. Dining room, Clarence H. Clark house. The son of banker Enoch W. Clark and the father of banker Clarence H., Jr., Clark (April 19, 1833–March 13, 1906) possessed one of Philadelphia's major fortunes. He was regarded as a leading art collector of Philadelphia and served on the Board of Directors of the Pennsylvania Academy of the Fine Arts from 1871 until 1905, from 1892 as vice president. He preferred anecdotal, didactic paintings. Although the Oriental scene on the left, by E. L. Weeks (1849–1903), an American follower of J.-L. Gérome, was a prized picture, it was not well displayed. It was hung too high; overlapping the woodwork was not common. Furthermore, the woodwork and the Victorian mahogany table and chairs were too strong and too shiny for the good of the painting. Even the fireplace and overmantel, with the delicate Chippendale brass andirons, look somewhat frivolous in this ponderous, dark setting.

18

19

20

21

22

23

21. Flemish ballroom, Frederic W. Stevens house, 2 West 57th Street, New York, New York; George Harney, architect, 1875–76; demolished. Few rooms in New York in the early 1880s were as formal and historically correct as this one. Stevens and his first wife, Adele Livingston Sampson, whom he married on October 8, 1862, had the room shipped over from Ghent, Belgium, where it had been used for more than a century. Conscientious about authenticity, they claimed to have recreated the original, with its Gobelin tapestries, carved marble mantel, the wood carvings of the doors, corners and walls, the floor of oak parquetry and the furniture covered with Beauvais tapestries. Though the act was questionable, the result was socially incontestable. By treating the evolution of interior decoration as conservatively as possible, they had at least protected themselves from the risks of short-lived vogues or unrealized blunders.

Stevens (September 19, 1839–January 20, 1928) was one of the blessed people of the nineteenth century, the son of a wealthy New York merchant and the grandson of Albert Gallatin, Secretary of the Treasury under Jefferson and Madison. His education—Yale—was proper, his church affiliation—Episcopal—was proper, he summered at Newport in a house designed by McKim, Mead and White and actively supported the New York Public Library and the Metropolitan Museum of Art. Trained as a lawyer, he became a New York banker. Society-conscious, he maneuvered two of his daughters into marriages with European nobility. One of the few flaws in Stevens' public image was his divorce from his wife in 1886. He married Alice Seely in December 1904.

22. Drawing room, Frederic W. Stevens house. The character of the ballroom was expressed through its obvious balance and careful coordination, its impression of a delicate space bounded by relatively flat, thin planes and by the discreet placement of finely finished objects and functional parts. By contrast, the drawing room, more representative of expensive New York interior decoration of about 1880, was not ruled by such stringent symmetry. One of the fireplaces was centered against its wall, the other was not. Although the furniture was appropriate for this setting, its colors and shapes and its effect on

surrounding space were rather dramatic and varied. The darker walls and ceiling were divided into sections by gilt strips and shallow beams, making these surfaces appear more vigorous and plastic and less precious. Finally, the room presented a moderately helter-skelter appearance. This can be seen in the right foreground where the casual but calculated placement of disparate objects is visible. From her father's house Mrs. Stevens brought old velour hangings and furniture, covered in deep garnet velvet on a gray satin ground. The shelves of books in a drawing room were unusual for a house that possessed a separate library.

23. Hall, Frederic W. Stevens house. Montgomery Schuyler (*Harper's New Monthly Magazine*, September 1883) and Mariana Van Rensselaer (*Century Magazine*, February 1886) praised the exterior of the Stevens house. It was a freestanding structure on the southwest corner of Fifth Avenue and West 57th Street, an area in which prominent New Yorkers were building in the early 1880s.

Even in this period of rich interiors, this hall, entered from West 57th Street, was profusely decorated. Stevens claimed that the tapestries in this space, describing the story of Psyche, had been manufactured in Brussels in the late sixteenth century. Additional tapestries were used as portieres or were draped over railings of the floors above. Few surfaces remained quiet; the carved table, metal clock, English mosaic floor, twisted colonnettes, individually designed balusters, stuffed peacock, fluted supports (matching those in the tapestries), the massive urn in the center and double-clustered brass chandelier designed by Cottier & Co. of New York all demanded attention and examination. The profusion of objects and competing surfaces obscured the quality of the oak paneling.

Nevertheless, contemporaries gave the hall high marks. According to Mrs. M. E. W. Sherwood in *Harper's New Monthly Magazine*, October 1882: "The grand hall . . . is a picture in itself. This house is thoroughly artistic and in the modern style. . . . It shows that all the study and talk about high art is not nonsense, but that it means harmony and perfection."

24. Drawing room, John A. Zerega house, 38 West 48th Street, New York, New York; architect unknown, 1882–83; demolished. Although the Zerega residence was situated near some of the legendary Fifth Avenue mansions of the late nineteenth century, and was by no means a cheap building, it probably would have been placed in the second tier of mansions: buildings that were smaller and had fewer ceremonial rooms, and were often erected on restricted lots that allowed little external expression of luxury and wealth. Mr. Zerega, born about 1826, was a stockbroker who was known at the Exchange as "the Pirate," possibly because he had been a clipper-ship operator in his father's shipping business as a youth or because, according to the *Times*, "he had tender scruples against selling out a customer when his margin became exhausted." Information about Mrs. Zerega is scant. Both were listed in the *Social Register* of 1910.

Noteworthy in this drawing room is the clear reliance on furnishings rather than architectural finish to carry its decorative statement. Competing surfaces—the carpet, sofa covering, mantel cloth, blue-and-gold floral paper—animate this space to the point of diminishing returns. Not until the eye reaches the plain frieze of raised gold does the visual cacophony stop. Likewise, the ceiling, articulated with geometrically laid ribbing against a plain background, is treated as a relatively neutral surface. But below, the primary objective was to compose a "pretty" symphony of floral patterns and colors, an objective difficult for us today to understand. The central-heating system in this house enabled the family to open one room to another, as is evident in this photograph. However, the Zeregas, like the majority of owners in this series, treated the rooms of their open plan as separate exhibit spaces rather than emphasizing freedom of movement or spatial linkage.

25. Drawing room, John A. Zerega house. This view of the drawing room proves the popularity of embroidery in city quarters in the early 1880s. At the immediate right, three panels of the piano were covered with embroidered and painted kid. In the right corner of the room was an embroidered screen depicting a woodland nymph, based on a painting by John La Farge (1835–1910). The work that thrilled Sheldon, however, was the artistic hanging of the archway. "This splendid portiere, easily the principal feature of the apartment, was designed by Mr. La Farge, after a pencil-drawing by Mrs. Zerega, and executed by the ladies in Miss Tillinghast's studio. It is a sunset landscape . . . casting its flush of evening splendor in silver gleams of sunset on a high ground covered with peonies, in the midst of an environment of exquisite rich browns, olives, and golds, a great feeling of atmosphere, a solid study of varied hues and contrasted textures, a broad and harmonious wealth of *chiaro-oscuro*, a wise balancing of tones, a finely-harmonized scheme of coloring, and a rare capacity on the part of the artists to see their subject as a whole, so that we may speak of this portiere as an epoch-making work of picturesque embroidery. . . ."

26. Dining room, John A. Zerega house. This room was a one-story extension at the rear of the main portion of the house. Its location meant that it would be near to the kitchen and the servants' area and could be constructed at a cost lower than that of rooms within the confines of a multistory building. In order to accommodate the long extension tables needed for entertaining, dining rooms in late nineteenth-century residences were often the largest single space in the house, and the solution of a one-story block was an economic way to obtain the necessary dimensions. A projecting block also permitted more light. Here windows were placed in the four short sides of the octagonal plan, producing enough light to require curtains to regulate it. For the clerestory windows above these curtained windows, the Zeregas chose Latin words felicitously suited to dining in the 1880s: *Hospitalitas, Amicitia, Familia,* and *Prosperitas* (hospitality, friendship, family and prosperity). The muted glow from these stained-glass panels was especially noticeable at sunset.

The fireplace mantel of mahogany extended almost to the mahogany frieze at the top of the wall. Mahogany was used throughout the room, in the sideboard (not visible) and in the furniture upholstered in stamped leather colored to match the woodwork. The stamped wallpaper was gold, the rug on the floor based on Smyrna patterns.

Mrs. Zerega painted the three canvas panels of the screen in the center of this photograph, proof of the interest of cultured women of this era in the arts.

27

28

29

27. Hall, Robert Goelet house, corner Narragansett and Ochre Point Avenues, Newport, Rhode Island; McKim, Mead and White, architects, 1881–83; standing. Although Goelet (September 29, 1841–April 27, 1889) listed himself as a lawyer, his principal occupation was managing his numerous real-estate holdings. Like many of the New Yorkers included in Sheldon's anthology, the Goelets—he married Henriette Louise Warren in 1879—lived in grand style with a town house on Fifth Avenue, a fall and winter retreat at Tuxedo Park, New York, this summer house at Newport, a 306'-long steam yacht, the *Nahma,* and memberships in more than 20 social and civic organizations.

In October 1881 Goelet purchased this prized 7½-acre site on the Newport Cliff Walk for $100,000. By December of that year McKim, Mead and White had finished the plans for one of their finest summer "cottages," regarded today by historians as a monument of the shingle style. "Southside" was large (150' × 50'), brick on the ground story and shingled above, and asymmetrically picturesque.

This hall, much less playful than the exterior, especially the ocean facade, is one of the memorable interiors of American resort architecture of the early 1880s. It is exceptionally large (44' × 30' and 24' high), centrally located in the plan and, spatially, the primary link in the traffic movements of the first floor and between the first and second floors. The opening to the left leads to the drawing room, that to the right to the sitting room. Because of its central function in family life, its scale, oak paneling, tapestries that recall hanging banners and the large, simple and strong fire opening, the room is reminiscent of the manor halls of late medieval England. The bamboo lounge and rocker, however, remind us that this is an American summer haven.

28. Hall, Robert Goelet house. This photograph was taken from the entrance to the drawing room visible in number 27. The bracket of the fireplace is at the far left. From this position the space looks more like a living hall. The owners have confidently but nonchalantly thrown together such disparate pieces as the tiger skin on the floor and the Jacobean open armchair against the paneling. Most of the pieces of furniture were easily movable, suggesting that the social occasion

rather than the formality of the hall determined where one sat. The main feature of the room from this perspective was the hand-carved canopied bed, which had been transformed into an upholstered retreat. The ferns on the top of the bed and the casually draped cloths on the balustrade humanize a space large enough to be intimidating.

Stanford White's upper gallery was a brilliant complement to a hall that at ground level was so strong and elegant. Though not incompatible, its tone was different—quicker, lighter, spatially more intriguing.

29. Library, Samuel Colman house, 7 Red Cross Avenue, Newport, Rhode Island; McKim, Mead and White, architects, 1882–83; standing. "Dignified yet rural," was Mariana Van Rensselaer's verdict on this relatively modest Newport cottage designed for Samuel Colman (March 4, 1832–March 27, 1920) and his first wife, Anne Dunham. Colman was a popular landscape painter and a founder and first president of the American Society of Painters in Water Colors. He also developed one of the earliest and finest American collections of Oriental prints and pottery. Colman joined Louis C. Tiffany, Candace Wheeler and Lockwood De Forest in 1879 to create Louis C. Tiffany and Company, Associated Artists.

His primary responsibility with Associated Artists was designing fabrics and wall and ceiling papers. The fabric over the mantel reflected his style: a plant or organic motif conventionalized and repeated in an allover, vacuum-abhorring pattern. This field of stylized energy was surrounded by a neutral border, a scheme similar to that of the ceiling, where the framing of the border was inspired by Japanese architecture and the field within—a network of ebony over Japanese silks—was inspired by his visit to Morocco. He also combined Moorish and Oriental references in the fireplace. One reason this interior seems so busy is Colman's reluctance to permit the surfaces of his walls to be quiet. It is also cluttered by furniture and books that have not been neatly arranged. We see this room not "on display" but as it probably looked during a normal day.

30

30. Library, Charles H. Joy house, 86 Marlborough Street, Boston, Massachusetts; Sturgis and Brigham, architects, 1873; standing. Numbers 86 and 82 Marlborough Street are paired Ruskinian row houses, three stories high with octagonal bays and mansard roofs. An illustration of this library appeared in an early issue of the *American Architect and Building News* (January 15, 1876). The room measured approximately 17′ by 19′ and was 11′ high. Black walnut was used for the low built-in bookcases, for the panels that reached to narrowly set beams and for the ceiling. In the frieze panels were scenes created by J. Moyr Smith, a British architect Sturgis may have met in London. To relieve the serious, almost heavy-handed treatment of the paneled walls and ceiling, the Joys covered the floor with colorful rugs in lively patterns and the architects finished the fire opening with decorative tiles taken from a convent in Spain.

The statuettes on the mantel were paired figures of Henry IV of France and his wife, Marie de Médicis, owned until a few years earlier by "a noble French family." Opposite the carved French chest in the middle of the far wall and not visible in this photograph was a rectangular bay illuminated by ten stained-glass windows. The room also contained a portrait of a Joy ancestor, supposedly by John Singleton Copley (1738–1815), and a portrait of Joy's great-grandfather, possibly in the overmantel, attributed to Thomas Gainsborough (1727–1788).

Little is known of Joy (1844–1892). An obituary notice in the *Boston Evening Transcript* called him the "last of an old and wealthy Boston family," despite his five children, three boys and two girls, who came from his marriage in 1865 to Marie Luise Mudge. He held memberships in the Somerset Club and the Eastern Yacht Club, and had a summer home in Groton, Massachusetts.

---

31. Parlor, Ulysses S. Grant house, 3 East 66th Street, New York, New York; architect unknown, date unknown; demolished 1933. After serving two terms as President of the United States (1869–1877), Grant (April 27, 1822–July 23, 1885) toured the world with his wife, the former Julia Dent (January 26, 1826–December 14, 1902). He returned in triumph, but nearly penniless. With an income of approximately $6000 a year, they settled first in Galena, Illinois, and then moved to the Fifth Avenue Hotel in New York, where they received special rates. Aware of their limited resources, 20 friends, among them George W. Childs, Hamilton Fish and J. Pierpont Morgan, collected money to enable the couple to purchase a brick home in the city. Mrs. Grant was ecstatic:

> It was a much larger and a more expensive house than we had intended (or had the means) to buy, but it was so new and sweet and large that this quite outweighed our more prudential scruples. . . . And how happy I was all that autumn in ordering the making of my handsome hangings, the opening of my boxes, and the placing of all the souvenirs collected during our long and eventful journey around the world.

The walls and ceiling of the parlor, a room exceptionally simple for a former President, were painted in an unvaried light hue. Likewise, the woodwork of the doorways, mantel and ceiling was restrained. Against these neutral surfaces, the Grants arranged many of the objects they had received on their trip, among them the two teakwood cabinets in the corners, the porcelains near the fireplace and the embroidered screen depicting a cock and a hen that rests against the wall below a version of *Sheridan Twenty Miles Away* by T. Buchanan Read (1822–1872). In addition to these gifts from Japan, the Mikado personally gave them the pair of large silver vases on the mantel. Mrs. Grant purchased the rug in India.

32. Library, Ulysses S. Grant house. In 1884, a private banking firm in which Grant had invested failed, leaving him with immediate debts. To meet these, he began writing his memoirs in this second-story library. He completed them four days before he died of throat cancer in an Adirondack cottage.

The bulk of his book collection was given to him by the citizens of Boston. This room also contained gifts—canes, swords, medals, decorative boxes—from European cities. The plain walls and simply decorated ceilings, plus the absence of wainscoting in the rooms of the Grant house, contribute to settings that were restrained for a posh New York town house of the day. Mrs. Grant sold the house for $130,000 in 1894. The house had been used as a four-story tenement before it was razed in September 1933.

32

OLIVER AMES HOUSE

Oliver Ames was near the height of his political and business career when he erected one of the finest mansions in Boston. Built in 1882, the Ames residence occupies one of the city's most prominent corners, Commonwealth and Massachusetts Avenues. Ames was born on February 4, 1831 in North Easton, Massachusetts, and died on October 22, 1895. His father, Oakes Ames, was a successful businessman who operated a shovel factory. Oliver combined educational activities at various academies and at Brown University with working in his father's factory, where his physical labors included work at the shovel forges. In 1860 he married Anna Coffin Ray (1840–March 11, 1917) of Nantucket and fathered two sons and four daughters.

The pivotal event in Ames's career came in 1873, when his father became implicated in the Crédit Mobilier scandal involving the unscrupulous sale of federal lands to Western railroads owned in part by him. The elder Ames, at the time a member of Congress, was censured by his associates for his role in the affair. Upon the death of Oakes Ames in 1873, Oliver inherited the responsibility of managing a vast railroad and industrial empire that was on the verge of financial collapse in the wake of the scandal. Pledging his own fortune, Oliver finally succeeded in liquidating his father's debts and honoring all obligations. He once remarked, "If I could efface the record of that [Congressional] vote of censure, I would willingly bring my political life to a close." This desire to redeem his father's name morally and financially led him into politics. Though he was never elected to Congress, he was elected Lieutenant Governor of Massachusetts in 1882 and served for four years before his election as Governor in 1886. Neither a distinguished public speaker nor a creative politician, Ames was a moderate who gained the respect of the electorate and the Bostonian business community. Clinging to his principles of free trade, he retired from politics a few years after his third term as governor. As a vocal opponent of the high tariffs that were supported by his own party, Ames was denied a seat at the 1892 Republican Convention.

The interest of Oliver Ames in regaining the respect of the public in the wake of his father's censure extended not only to the fields of politics and business, but also to architecture. In conjunction with his brother, Oakes A. Ames, he erected the Ames Memorial Town Hall (North Easton, Massachusetts; H. H. Richardson, architect; 1879–81) in memory of his father. His fine mansion on Commonwealth Avenue in Boston may also have been inspired by the same sentiment. Sheldon described it as "one of the largest and costliest of the many fine residences which line both sides of Commonwealth Avenue."

Ames and his brother employed Henry H. Richardson (1838–1886) to design a number of buildings on their behalf, such as the Ames Building (1882–83) in Boston, the Ames Memorial Library (1877–79) in North Easton and the Ames Monument (1879) in Wyoming. These buildings for the Ames family were typically Richardsonian—rock-

faced exteriors with simplified Romanesque styling. Richardson was initially employed by Ames to prepare the design for his Boston mansion. As part of the design, Richardson proposed a drawing room in "pearly white" and gold, with ultramarine walls. This decorating scheme was retained in the drawing room of the final version even though Richardson was replaced by the lesser-known Boston architect Carl Fehmer.

Resolute below, the finished house expressed materially a confidence that was apparent in the struggle of Ames to clear his family name. However, the weight and serious mien of the lower floors were relieved by the picturesque roof level, where overscaled dormers and prominent chimneys made a lighter public statement. Fehmer utilized a brownstone surface composed of smooth-cut rectangular blocks accented by classical ornamentation concentrated around the window and door openings and on a broad horizontal band between the first and second floors. It is unknown why Ames replaced Richardson with Fehmer, although it is possible that the widely traveled and well-educated Ames desired greater archaeological accuracy and a higher degree of ornamentation than was present in the plans by Richardson. This trend toward greater reliance on stricter interpretation of European precedent in architecture and decorative arts was to become more prevalent later in the decade.

---

33. Hall, Oliver Ames house, 355 Commonwealth Avenue, Boston, Massachusetts; Carl Fehmer, architect, 1882; standing. The house is entered through a vestibule which, in the 1880s, was lined with statuary and richly colored marble. These figures were grouped beneath a vaulted stained-glass ceiling of softly tinted colors. The hall in this period was finished with cherry woodwork and colored in soft gray-blue. A large, ornately carved wood screen, which appears in the left foreground, partially divides this enormous hall, somewhat lessening the dramatic scale of the room. The center of the attention in this view is the large fireplace placed between two windows. Above the fire opening was a carved arch containing relief figures and at the sides peculiar columns, classical below with unclassical caryatids above,

supporting the high mantel. While the basic character of this space is Renaissance-inspired, the vigorous ornamentation, with its human, animal and composite figures, lends a medieval flavor.

34. Hall, Oliver Ames house. This view shows the large stairway that winds to the second floor beneath an enormous stained-glass dome in strong colors. On the first landing is a painting by Jean-Gustave Jacquet, *The First at the Summit.* At an auction of the Ames estate held at the American Art Galleries in 1919, this painting was sold for $425. The major spaces on the first floor open onto this great oak hall—the library, music room, reception room and dining room. The drawing room was not pictured in this publication, though a period photograph appears in *The Tasteful Interlude* (1981) by William Seale.

33

35

35. Library, Oliver Ames house. This room has a more refined elegance than the animated decorations of the hall. It was decorated by C. H. George of New York with a dominant color scheme in a soft greenish hue with contrasting deep red mahogany woodwork. The walls are covered with a copy of old Venetian silk in tones of green and brown. This green was also used for the hangings and to upholster the furniture. Like other parts of this room, the finely painted embossed ceiling, arranged in octagonal sections, was created to be impressive to the eye without being distracting. Judging from the shelves and available work area, the books in this library were used as much for decorative value as for their intellectual stimulation. Although the windows of this space provided good interior light, the light could be reduced by drawing the hangings. Stained glass fills the clerestory panels.

Examples of the valuable collection of paintings and art objects that Ames collected are visible in this room. The collection was liquidated in 1919 for a total value of almost $60,000. Although he hung in his library paintings by popular European artists, among them Mihaly Munkacsy (1844–1900), J. J. Lefebvre (1836–1911), Charles Landelle (1812–1908) and C. E. Delort (1841–1895), the canvases that brought the highest bids were two by the American landscape painter George Inness (1825–1894). Opening directly from the library, but not visible in this photograph, is the music room, decorated in golden plush drapery and gilded woodwork.

36, 37. Dining room, Oliver Ames house. This large room spans the entire breadth of the house at its rear, separating the formal rooms of the front section from the extensive rear servants' wing. The room is finished throughout with oak woodwork. The paneled wood ceiling is supported at its edges by large caryatids depicting characters from mythology. Looking toward the west, we see five of the seven windows in this spacious room and matching niches containing identical vases, while toward the east we see an enormous sideboard of oak flanked by similar niches. To complement the oak color, the wall of silk tapestry was dull blue and the hangings a warm madder red. Polished brass fittings sparkled in the fireplace. Also of oak, the tables and chairs were created in an early German Reniassance style.

The bedrooms, located on the upper floor, were ornamented in a variety of colors. In its dazzling decor and opulence, this house is symbolic of the wealth and prestige attained by Oliver Ames and of his triumph over his family disgrace. The decoration of these interiors also displays quite dramatically some important concepts in late nineteenth-century American interiors: the implication of age, created by darkened wood and ornamental motifs inspired by medieval and early Renaissance styles; the ever-present clutter of small decorative items that leaves few voids; and the mixture of styles from room to room and even within each room. Because the owner evidently took such a direct role in the shaping of this residence, as indicated in the selection of the architect and involvement with various decorating firms, the house was an informative document of Bostonian wealth and social-political power in the early 1880s.

The Oliver Ames house was converted into luxury office space in the course of a 1981 renovation, resulting in the restoration of the major rooms of the first floor and the creation of additional office space in the basement and attic—a total of six floors of offices. Using federal income-tax incentives for historic preservation, restorers have reclaimed the stained-glass windows, gilded ceilings, wood paneling and grand stairway. The Ames house is among the minority of houses in this book that survives in a respectable state of preservation.

38

39

38. Library, Rudolph Ellis house, 2113 Spruce Street, Philadelphia, Pennsylvania; Furness and Hewitt, architects, ca., 1874; standing. The house of Rudolph Ellis (November 20, 1837–September 22, 1915) and his wife, Philadelphia native Helen Struthers (whom he married April 26, 1866) was either built or remodeled by Furness and Hewitt about 1874. In 1889 the house was remodeled again for R. Winder Johnson by Furness, Evans and Co. Ellis returned to Philadelphia after service as a captain in the Civil War. He formed R. Ellis and Co., a brokerage firm. In time he held several directorships, including one on the board of the Pennsylvania Railroad, and in 1901 became president of the Fidelity Trust Co. of Philadelphia. In his last years he moved to suburban Philadelphia, serving as a trustee of Radnor Township and president of the Radnor Hunt Club.

Judging from the pieces on the shelves around the mantel, the Ellis bric-a-brac was fashionable but not exceptional, consisting of Japanese ceramics, bronze statues, a metal clock, a brass container. However, the ceiling of the library was unique. Apparently, it was arranged in squares outlined in oak blocks. The field of each square was highlighted in crimson, the same color used for the portieres and the window draperies. Ceilings of such height and decorative complexity were not common in domestic libraries because these rooms usually were designed to appear intimate and peaceful. In the ideal library the books were expected to be the focus of the decorative scheme; here they were not. On the other hand, we could conclude from the manner in which they have been stacked on the shelves that these owners used them more frequently than most whose libraries appeared in *Artistic Houses.*

The woodwork around the mantel, like that of the ceiling, was eye-catching and complicated. Lathe-turned, inlaid supports, resting on plinths, not only stabilize the mantel but also pass through it to support a higher shelf at each side of the mirror. Were these supposed to be the stalagmites complementing the stalactites in a ball-and-rod motif that hung from the blocks of the ceiling and secured the overmantel shelf? In the middle of this intricate support system was a dark oasis, a plate-glass mirror backed by velvet rather than the usual quicksilver. This room probably was much lighter than it appears in this picture because the drapes have been drawn to aid photography.

39. Hall, Henry M. Flagler house, Edgewater Point, Mamaro-

neck, New York; architect unknown, date unknown; destroyed by fire 1924. In its obituary notice, the *New York Times* referred to Flagler (January 2, 1830–May 20, 1913) as "one of the world's richest men." His oil-refinery partnership with the Rockefeller brothers in Cleveland was reorganized as the Standard Oil Company in 1870. Although Flagler remained an officer of Standard Oil until 1908, he concentrated his energies after the mid-1880s on the development of Florida, building the hotels and railroads that helped to transform the state into a winter resort.

He rented this house at Mamaroneck in the summer of 1881 and purchased it the following year for $125,000. He may have rented the house as a means of keeping his family together after Mary, his wife of 28 years, died in May of 1881. Two years later he married Ida Shourds, but their relationship deteriorated and in 1897 she was committed to a mental sanatorium. A week after he obtained a divorce on grounds of insanity in August 1901, he married 34-year-old Lilly Kenan.

According to biographer S. Walter Martin, "By January 2, 1885, Flagler had spent $330,992.51 on the Mamaroneck property. The house was completely renovated inside and out. New fixtures were installed throughout the dwelling and attractive furniture was bought. Even the chandeliers were according to Flagler's own ideas." The appearance of the inlaid wood floor suggests that this part of the house had been renovated when this photograph was taken.

The hall of this 40-room summer retreat was probably large with a high ceiling and ample natural lighting. It is a good example of American open planning of the early 1880s, which often resulted in vistas passing through linked rooms of the main floor and even vertical perspectives between levels. The carved newel posts, supports and cornice were designed in a simplified Renaissance style. Less conservative was the balustrade of the stairs with its carved panels and truncated, lathe-turned elements. The landing of this staircase was unusual. A large mirror, reflecting the space in front of it, contributed to the spatial complexity of the hall. The area of the landing was large enough to provide room for a rocking chair. The outside face of this peculiar alcove contained a complicated carving of two griffins facing a central urn. From a hook or nail above, someone has hung a carved elephant tusk that cradles a dried starfish. Another odd feature is the block of wood, attached to the railing by a common rope, that balances the stuffed peacock.

40

40. Dining room, Julia T. Harper house, 4 Gramercy Park West, New York, New York; architect unknown, 1847; standing. Julia Thorne (1821–1902) married James Harper (April 13, 1795–March 27, 1869) in 1848, a year after his first wife of 24 years, Maria Arcularius, died. Their residence overlooked Gramercy Park, one of two fenced parks in New York City to which only the owners of surrounding houses had keys. In front of the Harper house were two wrought-iron lampposts, mayor's lamps—symbols reminding pedestrians that he had held the highest office in the city (1844–45). The lamps, as well as the iron portico of the porch, still stand in front of the relatively unchanged four-story exterior.

After an apprenticeship to a printer, James, with a younger brother, formed the printing firm of J. & J. Harper in 1817. In 1833 it became Harper & Brothers, one of the most successful publishing houses in the United States in the nineteenth century. Historians credit James for conceiving of *Harper's New Monthly Magazine,* which appeared in 1850. Mrs. Harper was not philanthropically active after his death, in part because she was an invalid for most of her life.

In 1879 her son, James Thorne Harper, and his wife commissioned Stanford White to create this dining room at the rear of the house. Solid and unpretentious despite an abundance of whatnots, it attracted Sheldon by its moderation and cohesiveness. "A fine sense of repose belongs to surroundings in perfect accord with the desires of a cultivated taste, and full of evidences of a sensitive observation at the disposal of a trained and knowing hand." The principal woods— mahogany for the wainscoting and oak for the paneled ceiling—were choices often seen in elegant dining rooms of the period. The embossed leather, covering the wall between the wainscoting and ceiling, was another material considered quite proper though also quite expensive. This leather was a discreet blue-green, highlighted with touches of bronze paint. Like the walls, the chairs were mahogany padded with embossed leather. Sheldon appreciated such a carefully coordinated unit: "Nothing glares; nothing stares." The dark propriety of this dining room was distinctly unlike the rooms of the Tiffany (nos. 13–16) and Colman (no. 29) houses, in which the decorative means were varied and competitive and their impact less subdued and stable.

On the other hand, the Harper dining room was not featureless. Above the table the splendid chandelier of cut glass that concealed the gas jets was set in a coved octagonal recess. At the side wall were windows of intricately leaded glass, partially veiled by the thin curtains. Warm, serious and protective, this dining room was a formal expression of the sentiment cut in the marble over the fire opening, "Tis Home Where The Hearth Is."

41. Library, Clara Jessup Moore house, 510 South Broad Street, Philadelphia, Pennsylvania; Charles M. Burns, architect, 1875; demolished 1958. Despite Clara Jessup Moore's (February 16, 1824–January 5, 1899) reputation as a writer, the *Philadelphia Directory* of 1883, reflecting the period's reluctance to credit women as professionals, identified her as a "widow" living at 510 South Broad Street. Granted, this information was true. Her husband, Bloomfield Haines Moore, the owner of Jessup & Moore, a paper-manufacturing firm, had died on July 5, 1878, leaving her this house in a French château style that *King's Views of Philadelphia,* as late as 1902, described as "unquestionably the handsomest residence on South Broad Street and one of the finest in the city."

The couple were married on October 27, 1842. They raised three children, one of whom, Ella, became the Countess von Rosen, wife of the chamberlain of the King of Sweden. Clara Jessup Moore wrote on social etiquette—*The Young Lady's Friend* (1873), *Sensible Etiquette of the Best Society, Customs, Manners, Morals and Home Culture* (1878), *Social Ethics and Society Duties* (1892)—several novels, (including *On Dangerous Ground* of 1876, which enjoyed many editions and was translated into French and Swedish), books for children (among them *Master Jacky's Holidays,* which went through more than 20 editions), poems and even *The Role of Doctor and Nurse in Caring for Insanity* (1881). She wrote under the pseudonyms Bloomfield-Moore, Clara Moreton and Mrs. N. O. Ward.

Number 510 South Broad Street was an address closely associated with art collecting in Philadelphia. In 1882 Clara Jessup Moore gave many pieces of furniture, pottery, textiles and other types of decorative art to the Pennsylvania Museum, later the Philadelphia Museum. In 1883 she donated 100 paintings from her collection and in 1899 gave 20 more. Two other collectors, Francis Thomas Sully Darley and John G. Johnson, subsequently lived in the house.

Where Clara Jessup Moore wrote is not known; here the library does not appear to contain any writing equipment. The room certainly was a distinctive space, one independent of contemporary views of how to furnish interiors correctly. The high ceiling confirms the approximate date of the house, 1870–75. The mantelpiece was gigantic, imaginatively designed and plastically aggressive—somewhat similar to a few exteriors in Philadelphia designed by Frank Furness. A veritable medieval bestiary haunted the gable of the overmantel, while below Burns transformed familiar elements of old architecture into peculiarly modern shapes. So strong was the wooden frame of the fireplace that it overwhelmed the decorative contributions of shelf objects and figured andirons. Through the window at the right, unusually broad for an interior window in these houses, we can see the drapery, chandelier and exterior window of the adjacent drawing room. The marble statue of Cupid, seen from the rear, was in the drawing room; in front of the glass were two bronze figures representing *Science Guiding Industry.* Despite these architectural peculiarities, the room looked more comfortable than staged. There were Chinese porcelain fishbowls serving as planters on either side of the window, a Chinese-silk fire screen, ancestral pictures on the walls, black-walnut bookcases and modest furniture.

42. Dining room, Clara Jessup Moore house. The Moores had collected much of their furniture during trips to Europe. Some of their finest pieces were displayed in the dining room—the sideboard carved in high relief in the left corner and an oak cabinet, also carved, opposite it. This cabinet was filled with choice pieces of Capodimonte, porcelains initially manufactured in the royal palace of Capodimonte under the patronage of Charles III of Naples in the mid-eighteenth-century. At the immediate right was a mantel with an oval mirror, the frame also in high relief. Through the doorway at the rear can be seen the picture gallery, which may have been an addition to the original house.

43. Hall, Clara Jessup Moore house. To the left of the hall were the library and the drawing room, directly ahead the dining room and picture gallery, and to the right the stairway and a front reception room. The hall was an exhibition area, a preliminary space that announced the finer attractions beyond. The exhibition consisted of an assortment of chairs on which people seldom sat, examples of the owners' porcelains and inlaid tables, a collection of Moorish arms over the arch—proof that the Moores had traveled in exotic lands—and copies of the *Venus de Milo, Augustus of Primaporta,* and *Nydia* by Randolph Rogers (also seen in the Stewart home, no. 1). The most unexpected elements of this stylistically eclectic setting were the pre–Art Nouveau flowers of the stairwall.

41

42

43

G. B. BOWLER HOUSE

The owner of this house was Mrs. G. B. Bowler, about whom information is scarce. A contemporary source referred to those who lived here as "the ladies who make this house their home." "Chatwold," as it was called, was designed by the Boston firm of Arthur Rotch and George Thomas Tilden in a spirited though awkward combination of half-timber work, stone and shingles. For its time and, particularly, for its location, the house was expensive and self-consciously historical. Sheldon tried to explain this when he discussed "Chatwold" in *Artistic Country-Seats* of 1886–87: "The effort has been to combine the solid attractions of a city home with the less solid attractions of a typical home by the seaside, although, as at Newport, the tendency toward long sojourns grows, and with it the disposition to make the seaside abode as comfortable as urban tastes demand."

Illustrations of the Bowler house were published in the United States and in Europe during the 1880s. The leading American architectural journal, *American Architect and Building News*, featured it on March 3, 1883, and two excellent photographs of its exterior appeared in *L'Architecture Américaine,* published in Paris in 1886 (reprinted by Dover Publications as *American Victorian Architecture*, 23177-1). On September 10, 1887, the *Deutsche Bauzeitung* included a sketch of it to point out that the house was dependent on English prototypes and not really representative of the simplicity and verve of recent American domestic design that had attracted the attention of its editors. Writing in *The Century* in July 1886, American critic Mariana Van Rensselaer praised its combination of exterior colors—the gray stones of the tower, gray granite walls with red granite trim, the dark red framing between panels of light plaster dashed with red pebbles and the dark stained shingles of the roof.

44. Hall, G. B. Bowler house, Scooner Head Road, Bar Harbor, Maine; Rotch and Tilden, architects, 1882–83; demolished 1945. Despite its debts to English architecture, the exterior of "Chatwold" was unmistakably an American house of the early 1880s. The plan was, furthermore, a fine example of the "internal vista" made possible by central heating. Four rooms, a hall (34′ × 24′) with a dining room on the right and drawing room and library on the left, could be opened to each other to form a spatial corridor 80′ long. This major axis intersected a shorter one—shown in this photograph—that connected the main entrance with the rear terrace. From the terrace the view across the tree-lined lawn to the ocean below was spectacular.

Rotch and Tilden created an exceptionally large landing, the near side defined by a barrier of stained ash and the far by windows offering an excellent view of the ocean. The landing and the hall below borrowed heavily from the theater; there were curtains, an abundance of entrances and exits and a balcony impatient for a soliloquy. Underneath the landing was a cozy sitting room, approximately 24′ × 11′, with a deep fireplace on the right. This was the pivotal space of the house, the center of both horizontal and vertical movement. However, the ornate mahogany chairs and the oak table were not compatible with the setting. This furniture is too large for the space and does not complement well the clean lines of the rafters and windows or the light that flooded this hall. Above, the paper, imitating alternating stone courses of medieval structures, and the somber tapestries seem out of keeping with the casually strewn drapery on the railing and the ungainly drawn portieres of the main level. The furniture appears to block access to the terrace doors. On the cabinet at the right is a large polychromatic rooster, inspired by Italian majolica.

44

45

45. Japanese library, Edward H. Williams house, 101 North 33rd Street, Philadelphia, Pennsylvania; architect unknown, 1872–73; demolished 1912. Like many of the visitors to the Philadelphia Exposition in 1876, the authors of *The Illustrated History of the Centennial Exhibition* were impressed by the work of the Japanese. "We have been accustomed to regard that country as uncivilized, or half-civilized at the best, but we found here abundant evidences that it outshines the most cultivated nations of Europe in arts which are their pride and glory, and which are regarded as among the proudest tokens of their high civilization." Similarly intrigued by this work, Dr. Edward H. Williams (June 1, 1824–December 21, 1899) began collecting Japanese bronzes, porcelains, lacquered ware, inlaid boxes, cabinetry, screens and wall pictures and displayed them in his home.

Graduating in 1846 from the Vermont Medical College, Williams served as an intern in New York City and as a doctor in Proctorsville, Vermont. But a few years later he returned to his originally intended career—railroad engineering. After working for numerous lines in Canada and the Midwest, he became the general superintendent of the Pennsylvania Railroad in 1865. He became a partner in the Baldwin Locomotive Works of Philadelphia five years later, a position requiring trips to Europe, South America, Egypt, Australia, India and Japan. Williams endowed buildings at Carleton College and the University of Vermont. On June 15, 1848 he married Cornelia Bailey (d. July 16, 1889) of Woodstock, Vermont; they had three children.

This Japanese library or sitting room, executed between 1880 and 1882, was considered by contemporaries to be one of the most conscientious efforts to create a Japanese environment in an American home. Beguiled by the result, Sheldon claimed extravagantly that "the pervading impression of this beautiful room seems as native to Japanese soil as the venerable and venerated Fusiyama [Fujiyama]

itself." It is surprising that such an ambitious act of cultural plagiarism occurred in Philadelphia for, despite the local impact of the Centennial, the enthusiasm for Japanese objects and decor was stronger in New York.

Between the top of the frieze and the central rectangular window of stained glass was a blue coved ceiling depicting storks and picturesque trees. The frieze was highlighted by a series of frames containing bronze dragon reliefs. Above the mantel at this level was a miniature temple roof. The wall panels of Japanese flowers against an Indian-red ground were painted by George Herzog (1851–?), an accomplished Munich-trained designer. Written in characters on each of these panels was a verse of a poem about winter and homesickness. The glass bookcases and the flanking cabinets, shaped like small towers and capped with pagodalike roofs, were made of ebony and ebonized cherry. Above the fire opening, Yokohama tiles depicted a procession of grasshoppers, attended by harmless wasps, carrying banners and persimmons. The four hanging lanterns, two of which are visible, were made by Schneider, Campbell and Co. of New York. The rug on the floor was Chinese. When this room was illustrated in *The Decorator and Furnisher* (December 1884), more pieces of Western furniture had been added to this room than appeared in this earlier photograph.

Sheldon was wrong; this room, filled with Japanese objects and art, was still radically different from those "native to Japanese soil." In Japanese houses interior decoration was essentially an act of reduction; in the United States in 1882 it was an act of accumulation. The Japanese library of Dr. Williams was too heavy, overloaded, dark, unplanar and even stylistically mixed to be mistaken for a Japanese equivalent. Williams may have acquired Japanese objects, but not an appreciation for their environmental simplicity.

46. Reception room, Henry C. Gibson house, 1612 Walnut Street, Philadelphia, Pennsylvania; architect unknown, ca. 1870; demolished 1928. Henry C. Gibson (1830–1891) was a millionaire active in the art market of the period who has been neglected by twentieth-century art historians. Sheldon claimed his collection was regarded as one of "the largest and most valuable" in the country. His estate, valued at $7 million in 1891, marked him as one of the wealthier men of Philadelphia, yet published sources then and now tell us little about him or his family. The son of a distiller and importer of wines, he joined his father's firm in 1853, two years after he began studying viticulture and the distilling process in Europe. In 1865 he took over John Gibson's Son and Co. There were at least two children, a son and a daughter, from his marriage to Mary Klett.

Gibson supported many of Philadelphia's cultural and scientific organizations dedicated to public enlightenment, but probably devoted most of his energy to the Pennsylvania Academy of the Fine Arts. He served on its board from 1870 until his death and as its vice president in 1890. Despite the Academy's decision to emphasize American work, it accepted his 1892 bequest of 102 works—the majority by Barbizon and French academic painters.

Although this house was probably built in the late 1860s or the early 1870s, it may have been remodeled in about 1880 to display the Gibson collection more effectively. In 1879–80, Gibson and his children had gone to Europe on an art-purchasing trip. The perfect fit between the objects displayed under the triple arch—two Japanese porcelain vases and a group depicting Hector taking leave of Andromache and Astyanax—and the pedestals on which they rest suggests that this art may have conditioned the setting. Gibson and his architect appear to have been less concerned with the coherence and functional quality of the interior rooms than they were with the display of individual pieces, which, as was also true of the library, were jammed together regardless of their diverse origins and styles. Despite the simplicity of its walls, the systematic organization of the wooden screen and the neatness of the glass chandelier, the reception room looked overstocked—the Italian marble-mosaic table competes with the figure group of Mercury and a maiden on top—cramped and didactic. It was a room easier to contemplate than to enter.

47. Library, Henry C. Gibson house. Sheldon realized this house had been arranged to show off Gibson's art collection. "Instead of building for them [the paintings] a distinct and lofty gallery, the owner has constructed a series of apartments called cabinets, that not only open into each other, but are integral parts of the house itself." These "cabinets" are visible in this photograph of the library.

The two compartments in this photograph look less like a library than a gift shop. There was a print of Raphael's *La Belle Jardinière* and next to it an unidentified portrait. Egyptian heads ornamented the gasolier and two large Oriental incense burners were placed under the pointed horseshoe arches characteristic of Saracenic architecture of Spain and North Africa. In the center of the second compartment, crammed with vases, plates, pictures and busts, was a stuffed owl. On the distant wall hung a Roman mosaic of a bacchante recently unearthed in the excavation of the Via Praenestina. Beneath this mosaic was an elephant tusk. This frenzied exhibition of materials and objects from around the world raises questions about the extent to which Gibson and his wife were aesthetically sensitized by the art they had collected.

48. Dining room, Henry C. Gibson house. *The Herd,* signed and dated 1869 by Émile van Marcke (1827–1890), dominated the rear wall of the dining room and was reflected in the great mirror opposite it, thus reminding diners at either end of the table of the original state of their sirloins. To its right was another animal painting—goats and sheep—flanked by two large marble groups, probably mid-nineteenth-century American, and below in the center a diminutive bronze version of the *Dying Gaul* or *Dying Trumpeter* of the third century B.C. Under the archway was a tall candelabrum, one of a pair that reportedly was owned by Napoleon. The furnishings and art of the dining room were not well integrated. The clock of the mantel would be incompatible with most settings.

46

49

49. Picture gallery, Henry C. Gibson house. American collectors often commissioned paintings by their favorite French artists, but Gibson apparently preferred to buy his on the market, usually through Goupil and Co. of Paris. He liked mood landscapes by Barbizon painters or touching descriptions of cattle or sheep with such titles as *Seeking Shelter.* He was also fascinated by exotic locales, collecting topographical and genre paintings of Venice and Constantinople. Among his many possessions that taught lessons were the three largest in this photograph of the gallery. On the far wall was *Charge of the Ninth Regiment of Cuirassiers, Village of Morsbronn, Day of the Battle of Reichshoffen, August 6, 1870,* painted by Detaille in 1874 to show the bravery of the French troops. Above it was a vignette of human fortitude tested by the rigors of nature, *Traveling in the Ukraine* (6′ × 3½′), painted in 1877 by the Polish artist Josef Chelmonski (1850–1914). On the right wall was *The Potato Harvest* by Jules Breton (1827–1906). Below it was *The Wrestlers* by Munkacsy.

Two of the best-known paintings in the photograph, *Landscape* by Corot, to the right of the capital of the column, and *The Return of the Flock* by Millet (1814–1875), hidden by the incense burner at the front of the table, have been sold by the American-oriented Academy.

50. Library, Charles S. Smith house, 25 West 47th Street, New York, New York; architect unknown, 1875–76; demolished 1938. "Charles Stewart Smith [March 2, 1832–November 30, 1909], noted in the commercial, financial, political, artistic, and social affairs of this city for years," was the way the *New York Times* began his obituary. He had long been a dry-goods commission merchant, retiring in 1887 from Smith, Hogg and Co., was the director of numerous banks of the city, a trustee of the Metropolitan Museum and the Presbyterian Hospital and, from 1883 until 1890, president of the Chamber of Commerce. In 1894

he headed the celebrated Committee of Seventy that temporarily replaced Tammany Hall with the reform administration of Mayor William L. Strong.

Relatively free of furniture and lined with paintings as well as bookcases, the library was treated as a continuation of the picture gallery visible in the distance at the right. The open Moorish archway and the high, round-arched doorways between rooms suggested that Smith wanted the principal spaces of his house joined more fluidly than was typical of a New York city residence. Mrs. Smith (Henrietta Caswell, who married Charles in 1869, six years after the death of his first wife, Eliza Bradish) painted the copy of Millet's *The Angelus* on the gold satin portiere stretched across the center opening—a rare example in this series of an owner's contribution to the decoration of a house.

At the right is an Italian reproduction of *Cupid and Psyche,* by Antonio Canova (1757–1822), and over the mantel was *The Golden Horn: Pilgrims Starting for Mecca* by Ziem. The mantel contains two of the 450 pieces of Japanese porcelain and faience the family collected.

51. Picture gallery, Charles S. Smith house. The Smiths' painting collection was modest in size (less than 100) and contained works by many of the fashionable European artists of the period: Meissonier, Diaz, Dupré, Daubigny, Detaille, Troyon, Gérome, Gleyre, Knaus, J. Breton, Boldini, Zamacois, Millet, Fortuny, Corot, E. Frère, Ziem, De Neuville, Schreyer, van Marcke, Munkacsy, Villegas, Vibert, von Bremen. With its small dimensions, fireplace, and simple furniture, this gallery was more intimate and informal than most of the galleries illustrated in *Artistic Houses.* Above the mantel were *Watching the Flock* by Edmond Tschaggeny (1818–1873) and *Abelard Lecturing* by A. C. E. Steinheil (1850–1908). To the right of the mantel shelf was Detaille's *Calling the Roll,* depicting a sergeant checking off the names of Prussian prisoners.

50

51

52

52. Drawing room, Hamilton Fish house, 251 East 17th Street, New York, New York; architect unknown, 1867–68; demolished. Born in New York City on August 3, 1808, near the site of this residence, Hamilton Fish married Julia Kean (December 19, 1816–June 30, 1887) in December 1836 and died six years after her on September 7, 1893. He was one of America's leading elder statesmen at the time his house on Stuyvesant Square was remodeled by L. C. Tiffany & Associated Artists. His long and distinguished political career had been crowned by his eight-year tenure as Secretary of State under President Grant. Although Fish had been retired from active politics for several years when this photograph was taken, his New York City residence was still the scene of many newsworthy political and social gatherings.

Although the Fishes were old-school social leaders, they could not have hosted many guests in their drawing room, crowded as it was. In fact, this space seems more like a disheveled library than a newly renovated drawing room. Certainly, L. C. Tiffany & Associated Artists would not want to take credit for this varied inventory of competing objects. If the company had recently reconstituted this space, where is the evidence of their special touch? Not in the carved marble fireplace, the anchor of the room, which had been there previously. We have to look past the profusion of objects to the wall surfaces to see the new work, specifically the checkerboard wainscoting to the right and left of the fire opening, the frame of the central mirror, the sections of beveled glass that border the central pane and the square panels of teakwood from Southeast Asia that border the sections of beveled glass. We should also include the repeated low reliefs in bronze and related colors that form the broad frieze, the tilelike pattern of the ceiling and, possibly, the four Venetian chandeliers. The two pieces of sculpture, a portrait bust by Hiram Powers near the fireplace and *Indian Girl* by E. D. Palmer (1817–1904) between the rooms, were falling from favor with critics in 1883–84.

53. Drawing room, Egerton Winthrop house, 23 East 33rd Street, New York, New York; Richard Morris Hunt, architect, 1878–79; demolished. Although born and raised in America, Winthrop (October 7, 1839–April 6, 1916) spent many years in Paris, where he acquired a deep interest in French art and culture. According to Sheldon, "Few apartments in this city have been treated with such persistent determination to reproduce in all respects the forms, color and feeling of a particular era [Louis XVI]."

Born to a family that traced its roots back to John Winthrop, who settled in America in 1630, Egerton was raised in an environment of culture and wealth. He married Charlotte Troup Bronson. At the outbreak of the Civil War, they sailed to Paris, where the family lived until 1870. Winthrop then returned to New York and his legal career, but after the death of his wife in 1872, he returned to Paris and resided in New York only occasionally until 1886.

Not surprisingly, Winthrop chose Hunt (1827–1895), trained at the École des Beaux-Arts, to design the exterior of the house in a Second Empire style. Much of the ornamentation, including the papier-mâché decoration of this Louis XVI room, was imported from France. Also imported was the furniture, reproduced from period models and heavily gilded. In this room were displayed some of the family's choicest tapestries, a few after paintings by Charles Le Brun (1619–1690), and examples of its Sèvres and Chelsea porcelains.

54. Reception room, Egerton Winthrop house. The importance many owners attached to the history of their objects and furnishings was revealed effectively in Sheldon's comment on this reception room, a comment that implies his endorsement of Winthrop's reverence for age and provenance:

> The mantel is a copy of one in the Louvre, of Henry the Second's time, said to be the work of Goujon, who executed for that monarch the celebrated recumbent statue of Diane de Poitiers . . . . An old Portuguese cabinet, with intricate brass ornamentation, stands near an old French cabinet, probably a reproduction of a Ducerceau. All the stuffs—French and Italian brocades, principally—are old . . . . A Stuyvesant clock, on one of the cabinets, is chiefly remarkable for having been in the Stuyvesant family one hundred and seventy-five years.

Edith Wharton, identifying Winthrop as her first real friend and intellectual companion, called this house the first in New York City in which "an educated taste had replaced . . . rubbish 'ornaments' with objects of real beauty in a simply designed setting."

53

54

Marshall Field House

Field (August 18, 1835–January 16, 1906) hired the rising Richard Morris Hunt of New York to design this house in 1871, just before the outbreak of the Great Chicago Fire. Untouched by the conflagration, construction continued until the structure was completed in 1873, at a cost of approximately $250,000. At that time Field and Levi S. Leiter were partners in Field, Leiter and Company, Chicago's most successful dry-goods firm. In 1881, when the annual volume had reached $25 million, Field encouraged Leiter to retire and renamed the business Marshall Field & Co.

He had been married to Nannie Douglas Scott for ten years when they moved into their new house on Prairie Avenue. This residential street near the Loop—Field walked to work—attracted millionaires. Until the 1890s, when they began to move to more fashionable locations, the residents were known as the "Prairie Avenue Set." The Fields had two children, in whose honor they invited 500 guests to their famed Mikado Ball in January 1886, and were active socially, although their marriage was not the kind that poets write about. She died in 1896, and he remarried a widowed friend, Mrs. Delia Spencer Caton, in 1905, shortly before he died of pneumonia. The house was bequeathed to the Association of Arts and Industries in 1937 to be used as a school of industrial arts. After the building was remodeled, the school opened under the name of the New Bauhaus, directed by László Moholy-Nagy, who had worked with Walter Gropius at the original Bauhaus in Germany. This venture failed financially, and the school was closed.

Compared to the house erected in New York City by his dry-goods counterpart Alexander T. Stewart (nos. 1–8), Field's town house was modest. It was certainly much less expensive, smaller, was finished in brick and sandstone rather than marble, and though designed in the popular Second Empire Style, it did not challenge the art world as Stewart's palace had. The principal west facade comprised a high basement, two conservatively ornamented floors and a tall but uninteresting mansard attic. The house was neither gracefully designed nor expressive of a clear artistic idea. Visually more attractive was the asymmetrical south facade, containing the glassed conservatory.

55. Library, Marshall Field house, 1905 Prairie Avenue, Chicago, Illinois; Richard Morris Hunt, architect, 1871–73; demolished 1955. Though this criticism may be unfair because there is no clear evidence to support it, this library seems to be composed of compatible objects that have been chosen and collected without a workable definition of a library to guide these choices. In other words, the inventory is there, but the parts do not mesh easily into a unit that reflects definable personal ideas and a specific functional goal. Perhaps a safer way to state this is to argue that Hunt designed a room with character that the Fields confused.

There is considerable power and fine craftsmanship in the double doors to the hall, in the cornice, ceiling and built-in bookcases that serve also as the wainscoting of the room. There are also focal points in the room—the bay window opposite the double doors to the hall and the elaborate fireplace opposite the doors to the drawing room. But the furniture has been placed without concern for the intentions of the designer. Ineffective for conversation, the chairs at the right also suggest that the glass doors of the bookcases were seldom opened. The closeness of the table to the fireplace may mean that logs were seldom burned. This table and its lamp obscure the beautiful tiles around the fire opening, while the containers and candelabra on the mantel shelf obstruct our view of the delicate stained-glass window behind. This apparent stress on the inclusion of items without much concern for their functional and artistic integration raises the possibility that this room was used primarily for display.

The Fields owned paintings by Millet, Schreyer and Meissonier, among others, but none of the paintings in the library can be identified with certainty.

55

56

57

56. Hall, Marshall Field house. From Prairie Avenue granite steps led to the main door, which opened into the vestibule, with its marble floor and mahogany woodwork, and then into this peculiar hall, cut through the center of the house. On the left of the hall were the drawing room, decorated as a French salon of the seventeenth century, and behind it the library. On the right side was the reception room and behind it a short passageway that led from the bulge in the center of the hall to the conservatory on the south side.

In an obvious attempt to counteract the length and emptiness of this hall and also to deemphasize its traffic function, the center of this space was widened. Domestic touches—the hearth, rug and chairs—were added, but the result looked contrived and not very inviting. Furthermore, the graceful stairway at the end of the hall, bathed by light from stained-glass windows above and faced below by imaginatively designed woodwork, a stairway that deserved an uninterrupted view, was diminished by the chandelier and the projecting furniture and heavily articulated entranceway. There is so much friction between this wide space in the hall and its objects that we may wonder if the photographer did not take the picture after the furniture companies had disgorged their wares and before these pieces had been carried to their intended rooms.

---

57. Hall, Asa P. Potter house, Nantasket Beach, Massachusetts; architect unknown, date unknown; demolished. What a contrast

between this hall and the hall of the Field mansion! In the latter the potentially intriguing space was given character through very respectable pieces and by fine details such as those on the embossed walls or on the frescoed frieze and ceiling. Because these specific objects invited individual attention, it was impossible to move from the vestibule to the stairs without engaging in a series of acknowledgments. At the Potter house, overlooking the Atlantic Ocean, the great space of the hall was more impressive than anything in it. The planners and owners did not clutter it with furniture and kept its structural details to a minimum. In the hall of the Field house visitors understood that, interrupted as it was, they had to pass through it to participate in family life. In the Potter hall visitors were more likely to stand still, watching for signs of family activity on three levels. These differences were encouraged undoubtedly by the differences in purpose and location of the two houses. One was a solidly built city residence in Chicago's most prestigious neighborhood, the other a summer house of wood overlooking the shore.

The Potters lived at 244 Commonwealth Avenue in Boston and relaxed in this house at Nantasket Beach. Asa P. Potter was born in 1838 and died on June 17, 1929; Mrs. Potter died on February 14, 1916. They had two daughters and four sons. Beginning in the paper business, he shifted to banking and became president of the Maverick National Bank of Boston.

58

58. Hall and stairway, Frederick F. Thompson house, 283 Madison Avenue, New York, New York; McKim, Mead and Bigelow, architects; 1879–81, demolished. A founder and long-time director of the 1st National Bank of New York City, Frederick Ferris Thompson (June 2, 1836–April 10, 1899) was a banker throughout most of his adult life. In 1857 he married Mary Clark (December 27, 1835–July 28, 1923), the daughter of the governor of New York. Thompson was a gregarious and intellectually lively individual who gave generously to educational institutions (Williams College, Vassar College, Columbia Teachers College) and to organizations encouraging the arts and the study of folklore, geography, archaeology and photography. He operated his own printing press, publishing a small paper dedicated to the advancement of photography. After his death, Mrs. Thompson gave money to Williams for a chapel and to Vassar for a library.

The house cost approximately $66,000. Ten steps from the sidewalk led to a high first floor, permitting a well-lighted basement that contained a billiard room and a rare bowling alley erected over brick-arch construction to limit noise.

There were many conveniences and safeguards built into the house at the request of the Thompsons. In one of the two vestibules was an exposed steam coil to warm the cold feet of waiting telegraph boys. The inner vestibule had a concealed door that admitted those familiar with the house to use the toilet facilities on the second floor before making their formal entrance down the main stairway of the hall. There was also a hydraulic elevator with several safeguards.

Though Montgomery Schuyler (*Harper's New Monthly Magazine,* September 1883) did not think the exterior noticeable, the main hall was unquestionably distinctive. Completed by Stanford White after

Madison Avenue entrance (right).

he replaced Bigelow as third partner of the firm in September 1879, it was large (38′ × 18′) for a New York town house and, in character, reminiscent of halls this firm designed for country houses in the early 1880s. Used as a connecting link, it was sparsely furnished. European visitors were often surprised by such internal openness as the inviting entrance to the library at the left, accustomed as they were to compartmentalized entering halls that protected the privacy of the family. In the same spirit, the route to the upper floors was open and clearly marked; in fact, the visitor was challenged to climb to the summit by the stained-glass windows illustrating *Pilgrim's Progress.*

59. Hall, Frederick F. Thompson house. The recessed fireplace under the elliptical arch on dwarfed columns was on the north side of this hall, which paralleled Madison Avenue. The scene carved on the Caen stone mantel frieze depicts calla lilies and ferns; the panels above have signs of the Zodiac: Pisces, Aries and Scorpio. The right angles of these mantel panels were repeated in the small square oak panels of the walls and the ceiling of the same wood. Two brass ewers were the only objects on the short mantel shelf. In this warm but well-disciplined setting, the glass globes of the wall sconces look exceptionally delicate. At the foot of the stairs was an unexpected piece of contrasting decoration, a carved plant that wrapped around the column with the freedom of a fully developed Art Nouveau motif.

60. Library, Frederick F. Thompson house. Among the libraries illustrated in these photographs, this was one of the largest and, judging from the setting, one of the most functional and frequently used. The room, 30′ square, held approximately 3000 volumes stacked on maple shelves, some equipped with slides to support the book being consulted. There were enough tables and flat surfaces for work. The unmatched furniture—the slat-back Windsor armchair, bentwood chairs with cane backing and well-used stuffed armchairs—was not selected primarily for display. Similarly, the bric-a-brac was mixed and not obtrusive. Above the shelves, 7½′ high, the wall space was painted a neutral color and hung with portraits. The Moorish flavor of the room came mainly from the arabesques of stucco in some of the ceiling panels and the tile designs painted on the underside of the wooden divider. As in every major room of the house, there was a ventilator in the center of the ceiling to circulate the air and to remove cigar smoke and gas leaking from the chandeliers.

59

60

61

62

63

61. Dining room, Frederick F. Thompson house. The principal rooms of these houses of the early 1880s were often designed and furnished to look distinctly different from each other. In the Thompson house, dissimilarities were particularly striking, as if each space had been designed by a different hand. Since the architects were paid approximately $6500 for interior furnishings, they may have been responsible for finishing these rooms.

The dining room was not timidly designed; it contained features that could have affected the whole negatively if they had not been skillfully controlled. The space could have been overwhelmed by the woodwork that rose to the cornice above the sideboard and almost to the height of the doors in other sections. To avoid this, the lively stained-glass windows, depicting birds, trees and flowers, counteracted the prominent sideboard below. At the sides of these windows were thin, curving shelves that also counteracted the weight of the sideboard.

To create plate shelves above the panels and above the lintels of the doors, the designers projected the frieze instead of allowing it to remain flat, adding to the possibility that the woodwork was too high and too heavy for the room. On the other hand, the floral pattern of this projecting frieze may have added more energy than weight to these sections. The same rippling effect is apparent on some registers of the terra-cotta overmantel. This floral pattern connected the woodwork and the terra-cotta to the plant life of the stained-glass window and also to the textured paper below the cornice. Furthermore, the profile of the supporting plate and pot shelves announced the coved ceiling, where the architects knew better than to include the heavy timbers of ancient banqueting halls. Instead, the ceiling was divided by relatively light strips of mahogany. The higher ceiling permitted higher wall decoration. Above the table was a square stained-glass skylight.

62. Dining room and conservatory, Frederick F. Thompson house. The woodwork of the dining room would have been more oppressive without the grand conservatory bay. Conservatories were commonly attached to dining rooms because plants gave off a pleasant fragrance that could also combat odors from the kitchens nearby. (Some architectural writers and arbiters of etiquette warned that prolonged exposure to the smells generated by plants could adversely affect guests. Consequently, the opening between dining room and conservatory was usually much smaller than it was here, or could be closed off.) From the evidence of this photograph, the dining room could not be sealed off from the conservatory. The main feature of this large conservatory, framed in brass, was its centrally located fountain.

63. Drawing room, Frederick F. Thompson house. Unlike most of the drawing rooms in this series, the walls and ceiling of the one in the Thompson house were treated as flat, neutral areas that set off the heavy coved cornice above and the paneled dado below. Except for the border lines and geometric designs in the corners, the buff ceiling was plain. The walls, painted a dull Indian red to complement the red cherrywood of the mantel, furniture and window trim, provided a suitable background for the paintings and Chinese embroidery that hung from the picture rail. Among the few wealthy New Yorkers who did not concentrate on French academic painting, the Thompsons had a small but respectable collection of works by Americans (Alexander Wyant, William Hart, John Kensett, Emanuel Leutze). Over the mantel is *Venice*, by Sanford R. Gifford (1823–1880).

The unifying cornice was composed of bronze panels depicting sunflowers and tiger lilies in relief. Strips of bamboo marked the panels of the dado, and bamboo was also used in the decoration of the mantel. Related stickwork appeared in the Japanese Revival sidechairs and in the cabinet in the right corner. This open and movable cabinet held prized small pieces which in most of the living rooms of *Artistic Houses* would have been displayed on fixed shelves attached to the fireplace. At the far left is another arrangement not seen often in these photographs, the bay filled with planters and the rod-and-curtain system that could separate this section from the main part of the room.

THE OPULENT INTERIORS OF THE GILDED AGE　77

64. Library, Mariana Arnot Ogden house, Fordham Heights, New York, New York; Calvert Vaux, architect, ca. 1855; demolished. Following her husband's death in 1877, after only two years of marriage, Mrs. Ogden managed "Boscobel" (beautiful wood) and its exquisite grounds until the relentless expansion of New York City transformed this area. Once a paradise of unusual trees—linden, weeping ash, purple beech, catalpa, cypress and Austrian, Weymouth and Cembra pines—this estate became an untenable oasis after the nearby Washington Bridge over the Harlem River opened in March 1889. The house, constructed of stone quarried on the site, was built for another family. William Ogden (June 15, 1805–August 3, 1877) purchased the property in the spring of 1866 but did not spend much time there until his marriage on February 9, 1875, four years after he moved to New York following the Great Chicago Fire. As the first mayor of Chicago, he was more closely tied to the first four decades of that city than any other single person.

Evidence suggests that this room was planned as the drawing room and the drawing room as the library. If true, this would explain its appearance, atypical of separate domestic libraries in the early 1880s, which would have been smaller, more intimate in character and less formal in decoration. The ceiling was tightly frescoed in a geometric pattern, the ebony jambs and lintels of the openings were unusually triumphal and the hangings and wallpaper smacked of "good taste." On the other hand, the furniture, light and movable, made the room appear less formidable than its walls and ceiling implied it should be. The room was probably more important as a spatial extension of the drawing room than as a functioning library.

65. Drawing room, William F. Havemeyer house, 86 Harrison Street, East Orange, New Jersey; architect unknown, ca. 1871–78; demolished 1960s. William F. Havemeyer, Jr., (March 31, 1850–September 7, 1913) was born in New York, married Josephine L. Harmon in 1876 and began his career with the Havemeyer Sugar Refining Co. He retired from the sugar business in 1889 but continued to be active in banking. As a collector, Havemeyer concentrated on second-level American painters. He later concentrated on another hobby, collecting George Washington memorabilia.

The Havemeyer drawing room was not a memorable interior, despite its recent decoration by Roux and Co. of New York. Although it was finished in chestnut and mahogany with fretwork panels on the ceiling and Japanese paper of armor designs on red for the walls, and although much effort had been spent on the fireplace and overmantel—the peculiar coal scuttle on the left, the Victorian fan screen that echoed the rising-sun motif at the top, and the numerous display shelves in the middle—the room lacked distinctiveness and focus.

66. Drawing room, Knight D. Cheney house, 50 Forest Street, South Manchester, Connecticut; architect unknown, ca. 1860; standing but altered. This drawing room was one of the largest and most expensive included by Sheldon. It consumed space as if it were unlimited and cheap, in the manner of the great living halls that such architects as McKim, Mead and White created at the center of their resort houses of these years. Like those halls, this encouraged varied functions without appearing to be subdivided into obvious sections. Its appearance of unity was achieved by the fixed height of the wainscoting, the mantel shelf and bookshelves, and by the continuous wall covering of leather and the coved frieze above. Its appearance of breadth was due, in part, to the mirror of the mantelpiece, the vast carpet and the beams of the hand-painted ceiling that led the eye to the edges. Its appearance of comfort owed much to the softness of the upholstery, such as the Turkish frame armchair and ottoman at the left, the generous table coverings and the carpet.

The beautiful fabrics and coverings of this room were probably influenced by the owners' business activities. Knight D. Cheney (October 9, 1837–August 13, 1907) became in 1876 a director of Cheney Brothers of Hartford and South Manchester, Connecticut, pacesetters of the American silk industry. In 1894 he became the firm's president. On June 4, 1862, he married Ednah Dow Smith of Peterborough, New Hampshire. With 11 children, the Cheneys probably needed this family space.

The house was built as a three-story clapboard structure; the renovation of 1878–80 is attributed locally to Henry Hobson Richardson.

64

65

66

WILLIAM S. KIMBALL HOUSE

The large and expensive house built for William S. Kimball (March 30, 1837–March 26, 1895) and his second wife, Laura Page Mitchell, was considered too pretentious and extravagant even for Rochester's third ward, at that time the "ruffled shirt" district of the city. A fine example of the oversized and overdesigned mansions of the early 1880s, it was three-and-a-half stories high, contained 30 rooms and cost $500,000 to build and furnish. Composed asymmetrically of a variety of materials, horizontally laid stone below and vertically oriented half-timber work above, and enlivened on its sides by numerous voids and projections and on top by prominent chimneys and gables, "Kimball's Castle" expressed well the exuberance and confidence of the period as well as its spatial and material excesses. The house was used for only 41 years, one more instance of a later generation's inability to support a personal monument it had inherited. Uninhabited after the death of the second Mrs. Kimball in 1922, the deteriorating structure was taken over by the city in 1938 and sold ten years later for $1000 to the Rochester Institute of Technology, which razed it.

If the cubic footage of houses were proportional to the municipal importance of their owners, the dimensions of this one made sense. Kimball's obituaries agreed with nineteenth-century histories of Rochester that he had been more closely identified with the growth of his city than any of his contemporaries. In 1863 Kimball left the Union navy for Rochester, where he established W. S. Kimball and Co., later known internationally as the manufacturers of Peerless and Vanity Fair tobaccos. The company employed 800—the largest work force in Rochester—and was respected for its efficient organization and relatively humane treatment of its workers. It was the first major company of the city to require only a half day of work on Saturdays. Kimball was also president of the Union Bank, the City Hospital and the State Industrial School, and served as director of numerous financial and railroad enterprises. He married his first wife, Marion Elizabeth Keeler (1836–1879), on October 7, 1858 and, a year after her death, his second. There were two children from each marriage.

Kimball was capable of bold but quirky decisions. In the early 1880s he commissioned his brother-in-law, sculptor Guernsey Mitchell (1854–1921), to create a mammoth statue of Mercury that was placed on top of the tobacco factory, where it remained as a symbol of Rochester until its removal in 1951. The exterior of Kimball's house did not reveal his independent streak, but other aspects did. His greenhouses protected what may have been the finest collection of orchids in the country. His deep wine cellar was air-cooled. His carriages were lifted by elevator in the two-story brick stables. A diversified collector, he had acquired 1200 pepper boxes from around the world. One of the bedrooms, lined with bamboo, was finished in a pseudo-Japanese style, a step that would have been considered unusual even in the major cities of the Eastern seaboard. On the third floor were the quarters for 20 Japanese servants.

The interior was the startling feature of this house, primarily because Kimball, for unknown reasons, selected L. C. Tiffany & Associated Artists to furnish it. If the exterior made its point through plagiarized, bulky divisions, the interior, at least the hall and the library, seemed to shimmer. Tiffany's intricate combinations of materials and patterns suggested impermanence and lightness, qualities frequently expressed by the artists of the twentieth century.

67. Hall, William S. Kimball house, 145 Troup Street, Rochester, New York; architect unknown, 1881–82; demolished ca. 1948. Here the decorators from New York took risks and transformed the hall into space attractive primarily because of its surfaces. The main feature was the wooden screen on the right, composed of panels of East India teak. Because it reached almost to the 13'-high ceiling, this screen separated the hall from the stairway beyond it, yet it was so open that the hall and the stairwell could be read as a single space. Paradoxically, this was an inviting barrier. Note the variations of patterns in these panels. The disciplined energy of this elegant divider was also expressed in the carpet and in the papers of the walls and ceiling.

In contrast to these small-scaled designs, the fireplace of Siena marble and oak seemed strong and calm. This strength was also evident in the oak beams of the ceiling. The stairway behind the screen led to a musicians' gallery that overlooked the room in which Kimball hung his collection of nineteenth-century French, German, British and American paintings. The gallery also contained a large organ whose pipes could be seen through the screen from the hall below.

68. Library, William S. Kimball house. In several respects the library was typical of its day and class. It was well illuminated by natural light by day and by the gas chandelier and the kerosene table lamp at night. Warm wooden beams added both strength and intimacy, and the top of the bookcases served as a shelf for a variety of expected items: a stuffed owl, globe, vases, bowls and a relief sculpture. The relief is a Nubian head in which the features of a beautiful white woman are painted a dark red-brown on a molded plaster cast. A relief showing her male counterpart is on the table opposite. The well-padded, comfortable furniture, encouraging a slower and less formal pace, was also popular. The central table was large enough for folio volumes and also contained storage drawers. The fireplace, often an ornament in the drawing room or dining room, was actually used in this and most libraries.

Less typical, however, was the visual impact of the fireplace designed by Associated Artists, probably in 1881. Usually the mantel area was the anchor around which the remainder of the room was arranged. Here the fireplace looks like a late addition, as if it were a glittering box shoved into a quiet niche once terminated by a wall of glass. Though small in size, this box was visually prominent. Tiffany played surface against surface, the stained glass of the windows against the glass tiles and the glass tiles against the polished squares of mahogany in the overmantel.

67

68

69

Bradley Martin House

A lawyer from Albany, New York, Bradley Martin (December 18, 1841–February 5, 1913) married Cornelia Sherman (d. October 24, 1920), whose father left her an inheritance of almost $6 million in 1881. Financially secure, they studied the social mountain to determine the best method of climbing, reaching the summit with their famous, though controversial, ball of February 10, 1897.

In the 1880s they established addresses on both sides of the Atlantic. Between 1881 and 1883 they remodeled and transformed the adjacent houses of 20 and 22 West 20th Street into a single residence 52′ wide. In 1882 the Martins bought a house in London and two years later became country gentry by leasing a fine hunting preserve in Scotland called "Bal Macaan."

The climbing strategy of the Martins was a simple one—stage a major event periodically and invite large numbers of very important people. On January 26, 1885 they invited 400 guests to a dinner dance. To accommodate the crowd, they commissioned a temporary banquet hall (68′ × 25′) for the rear of their house. It was a unique occasion, described by the *Times* reporter as "the most superb dance that has ever been given in New York or in America."

The Martins gained additional social points on February 8, 1890, when they entertained 300 guests at a cotillion dinner at Delmonico's. Again, the *Times* was ecstatic: "the most magnificent dinner probably ever given in New York." Their standing was further improved when their 16-year-old daughter Cornelia married the impoverished Earl of Craven in 1893.

Mrs. Martin's long-promised attempt to surpass in splendor the celebrated Vanderbilt ball of 1883 was held at the Waldorf Hotel on the night of February 10–11, 1897. For weeks New York's milliners, dressmakers and wig makers had been besieged with requests for authentic costumes of personalities from German, French and British

history. From 11:00 P.M. until 6:30 A.M., 600 guests danced and feasted, consuming 61 cases of champagne and $369,000 of the Martins' fortune. Though a dazzling spectacle that became a landmark in the social history of New York, it was also tainted. Led by Dr. Rev. William Rainsford of St. George Episcopal Church, critics condemned the irresponsibility and insensitivity of wealth. Mrs. Martin fired back that during an economic recession it had been "an impetus to trade." A year later the Martins settled permanently in Great Britain.

69. Drawing room, Bradley Martin house, 22 West 20th Street, New York, New York; architect unknown, date unknown; demolished. This salon, like the Martins' public posture, was costly, pretentious, contrived and dependent on association. The "unity" of this setting was neither the result of functional considerations nor the quest for stylistic integrity despite the reminders of the period of Louis XIII. This room was held together by the pedigree or source of its objects. Since guests might not know the European background of each item, the Martins had to talk in order to bring this "unity" to life. Even if each item was genuine, the easy familiarity with history that the Martins conveyed was not. In exploiting the past to enhance their image, they created a skillful display of expensive kitsch.

70, 71. Dining room, Bradley Martin house. Judging from this room, the Martins' ambition to acquire and exhibit was ultimately frustrated by the limits of their space. They also appear to have abhorred a vacuum. The wainscot and ceiling were paneled and carved in English bog oak. Beauvais tapestries covered the walls and were used for the window hangings. The impressive portieres that separated the dining room and the music room were made out of Mexican saddle cloths and Spanish altar cloths, their silver and gold threads set off against a ground of garnet plush. In the ornate niche above the fireplace was a portrait of one of their two daughters, probably Cornelia, by the French painter Carolus-Duran (1837–1917). On the chair backs the family coat-of-arms was embroidered in silver and gold. Fragments of tapestries edged the tablecloth.

72

**72. Main room, Oswald Ottendorfer pavilion, between West
135th and 136th Streets on Riverside Drive, New York, New
York; William Schickel, architect, 1879; demolished.** The 1880
edition of the guidebook *Hudson River by Daylight* referred to a
recently erected pavilion that had become one of the landmarks for
riverboat passengers. Oswald Ottendorfer (February 26, 1826–December 15, 1900) and his wife, Anna Behr Uhl Ottendorfer (February 13,
1815–April 1, 1884), had built the unusual $30,000 structure on the high
bluffs overlooking the Hudson on the property where they had a
weekend and summer house. Designed in the then-popular Moorish
style, the one-story pavilion was approximately 36' × 42' on its exterior
and on the west had an open piazza that provided panoramic views of
the river.

This photograph shows the central space of the building, measuring
25' × 34' with a ceiling 32' high. It was defined as Moorish because of
the geometric character of its surface decoration applied in an allover
manner, the horseshoe arches resting on dosseret blocks supported by
slender columns, the *mihrab* or prayer niche in the corner of the room,
and the incipient stalactite vaulting of the upper section of the walls.
However, this was an age in which consistency was not necessarily a
requirement in restating a style. Definitely un-Moorish were the shield
of stars and stripes above the horseshoe arch of the doorway, the
flocked paper of the walls and a lengthy passage in German on the
ceiling.

The Ottendorfers were the premier citizens of New York's immigrant
German community at this time. She was a much-beloved philanthropist and former manager of the leading German newspaper of the
country, the *Staats-Zeitung*, and he the editor of that newspaper since
1858, a year before their marriage. He was also a political reformer of
unblemished reputation.

**73. Dining room, Robert Treat Paine, Jr., house, 6 Joy Street,
Boston, Massachusetts; Alexander Parris, architect, 1824;
standing.** Lydia Lyman Paine (April 29, 1837–March 9, 1897) grew up
in this house, built by her father in the 1820s. She had been married to
Robert Treat Paine, Jr. (October 28, 1835–August 11, 1910) for almost
20 years when she returned here with her husband and children after
her father's death in 1881. To meet the needs of their family and their
social obligations, they added this dining room, 35' × 30', to the original

structure. Oak was used generously in the resolute mantelpiece and
also in the high-relief ceiling. The author of *Artistic Houses* reached the
conclusion: "The intention of the architect seems to have been to
combine utmost quietude and reserve of effect with a lavish expenditure of material and decoration . . . ."

The rug was Indian and the wall covered with paper that looked like
stamped leather. The wide mantel was the focal point. Below the shelf
the woodwork continued the pattern of the wainscoting of the walls;
above the shelf on each side was a shallow niche, ensconcing an
Apollo Belvedere on the left and an Amazon on the right. At the
rounded corners of the overmantel were open shelves framed by small
panes of glass. In front of the mirror of beveled glass was a statue of
Aristides. Below it was a lion's head carved on the cornice of the
mantel shelf and at the rear of the fire opening a cast-iron head
designed by Elihu Vedder (1836–1923). Paine had retired from his law
practice at the age of 35 to devote his energies and time to social and
international problems.

**74. Hall, William I. Russell house, corner Knollwood Road and
Wells Lane, Short Hills, New Jersey; Lamb and Rich, architects,
1881–82; destroyed by fire 1934.** Russell (ca. 1850–March 5, 1925)
described his personal peaks and valleys in a frank, nostalgic
autobiography entitled *The Romance and Tragedy of a Widely Known
Business Man of New York* (1922). One of the leading metal dealers of
New York until 1894, he suffered financial problems and tried to
commit suicide in January 1903.

An early resident of Short Hills, a planned community adjacent to
Millburn, New Jersey, Russell recounted his family's happy life at their
first home in Short Hills, "Sunnyside," and their enthusiasm for this
their second and larger home, "Redstone":

> ["Redstone"] was a delight to the eye. . . . Through a massive doorway one
> enters a hall of baronial character . . . finished in oak, with open-beam
> ceiling, and above the high wainscot a rough wall in Pompeian red.
>
> Two features of the hall are the great stone fireplace with its old-fashioned
> crane and huge wrought iron andirons and the stained-glass window on the
> staircase, a life-sized figure of a "Knight of Old."

This imaginative, asymmetrical space easily accepted stuffed animals,
a bust, medieval weapons, Oriental ceramics, a colonial settee and a
recent painting of Arab horsemen.

73

74

75. Drawing room, Edward N. Dickerson house, 64 East 34th Street, New York, New York; McKim, Mead and Bigelow, architects, 1877–79; standing. The Dickerson house was the earliest urban house of McKim, Mead and Bigelow. A century ago, however, critics discussed it primarily for its mechanical innovations, many of them conceived by the owner, and for its interior decoration. Dickerson's ideas improved the economy and efficiency of operation. He devised a way to flush water so forcefully through the toilet bowl that candles held near the toilet fluttered in the instant breeze. He claimed to have taken steps to reduce the number of tons of coal required in a year to heat this house. He had also patented safety devices that prevented the elevator of the house from moving with the doors open or opening except at specific floors.

In her article praising recent New York interiors (*Harper's New Monthly Magazine*, October 1882), Mrs. M. E. W. Sherwood included the Dickerson house. A new artistic age had begun: "We can not look through the tasteful and artistic interiors of New York without a pleasurable sense of having lived through a very dark night, to be rewarded with an exceedingly fresh and brilliant morning." She thought the stained-glass windows and subtle color scheme of this drawing room were proof of this dawn. (Sheldon was also impressed with its quiet tonal harmonies—the woodwork and furniture of satinwood, the light blue satin damask wall panels and the ceiling's gold pattern on a pale gray ground.)

This room illustrated a number of Mrs. Sherwood's arguments. She encouraged "caprices," meaning the willingness to experiment. The Dickersons had mixed their collection of Japanese pottery with a painting of an Eastern European peasant girl and a Louis XV mantel centerpiece of silverwork on blue porcelain. She also would have approved of their accents and highlights. There were no heavy scrolls or weighty furniture here; the scene was bright, lively, eccentric. She liked rooms "festooned with pink and blue silk . . . all roses and blue ribbons" combined with a few straight-backed chairs, long mirrors and portieres suggesting days of old.

76. Library, Edward N. Dickerson house. Dickerson (February 11, 1824–December 12, 1889) graduated from Princeton with honors at 18 and was admitted to the bar when he was 21. He married Caroline Nystrom on October 11, 1848; they had three children—two daughters and one son. He was a busy patent lawyer, a Sunday scientist and an authority on the efficiency of steam engines. In 1864 he argued before the Supreme Court against a decision of the Secretary of the Navy in planning a new steam navy. His laboratory for optical and electrical experiments was directly above this library. On the roof was his observatory.

Visual evidence suggests that Dickerson used this library constantly. There were sufficient shelves for his large collection, special drawers for folio volumes, a central table with adequate space for taking notes and comfortable chairs to read in. The character of the room was carried mainly by the dark surfaces, the black walnut and French walnut paneling, the embossed-leather ceiling and the carefully crafted woodwork of the fireplace. This was a study in which bric-a-brac gave way to books.

77. Dining room, Edward N. Dickerson house. Mrs. Sherwood also admired the dining room of the Dickerson house, especially the stamped-leather walls, the carved buffet that contained a blue Bohemian glass punch bowl (reportedly purchased by Thomas Jefferson in Paris) and the sixteenth-century brass sconces. Her endorsement of eclecticism was based on the assumption that, if they were well made, pieces of varied cultures and periods could be combined.

The most publicized feature of this room was a carved Oriental screen (not visible in this photograph) that had been exhibited at the Philadelphia Centennial. Ventilators, hidden below and in the decorated panels of the ceiling, could remove after-dinner cigar smoke.

This four-story house (25' × 100') was projected to cost about $30,000. Montgomery Schuyler (*American Architect and Building News*, April 23, 1881) called it "the first of the distinctively Queen Anne houses."

78

79

80

HENRY HILTON HOUSE

By New York standards Henry Hilton (October 1824–August 24, 1899) was a successful man. He lived in a splendidly decorated brownstone, owned a recognized collection of paintings, and left an estate valued at $6 million. But many contemporaries disliked and mistrusted him. The *Times* called him a vandal and an ignoramus during his tenure as a commissioner of the Department of Public Parks of New York City. Henry Ward Beecher and William Cullen Bryant, among others, reacted publicly to his refusal in 1877 to accept Jews at his Grand Union Hotel in Saratoga Springs. Even in death he seemed petty; he left no bequest to any charity.

Journalists and social critics questioned millionaires who sidled up to somebody else's hard work, and they could be sharp with those who failed to develop fortunes entrusted to them. Hilton did both. An undistinguished lawyer, he was elected judge of the Court of Common Pleas in New York but retired to concentrate on his role as adviser to the dry-goods merchant A. T. Stewart. Hilton's wife, Ellen Banker (March 20, 1828–February 20, 1885), was a cousin of Mrs. Stewart. His influence increased steadily; the public gossiped about the judge's manipulative powers. When Stewart died in 1876, his estate, estimated to be between $35 and $60 million, was placed under Hilton's control. Twenty years later only a fraction of the great fortune remained.

78. Drawing room, Henry Hilton house, 7 West 34th Street, New York, New York; architect unknown, date unknown; demolished. The Hiltons moved into this house in 1878, after hiring the same decorator who had worked on Stewart's Marble Palace to do the plaster relief and design of this ceiling and its neutral encaustic walls. The doorways were redone in silverwood. Matching mantels, east and west, were constructed of silverwood and ebony highlighted with ormolu and gilt. Hand-stamped blue-garnet plush was used for the tufted chairs in the foreground. Despite these features, the room was a distant echo of A. T. Stewart's drawing room (no. 3).

The Hiltons were forced to crowd their drawing room with prized urns, statues and paintings because the house lacked a proper picture gallery. The art obscured or competed with the expensive furnishings and decoration. Many of these pieces were sold at auction in February 1900, but the sale was discouraging. Considered old-fashioned, the collection of 132 paintings was sold for $118,715. It included C. E. Delort's *Arrival of the Cardinal* (beside the mantel) and *Young Woman Reading* (beside it on an easel) by the German artist J. E. Anders (1845–?). The bronze busts on either side of the mirror between the doorways, *Woman of Smyrna* and *Zeibecke*, were both by E. C. H. Guillemin (1841–1907).

79. Dining room, Henry Hilton house. In the dining room the Italian decorator was responsible for the flat wall panels painted with garlands, urns and busts and edged with a Greek key pattern, the heavier plaster brackets supporting the plaster entablature, and the composition of the ceiling. The principal wood of the room was ebony inlaid with a lighter wood. It was used for the sideboard, wainscoting, mantel, casing of the doors and the chairs and table. Even the chandelier, its design attributed to the judge, was partly of ebony. This room also contained impressive examples of sewing and weaving. The chairs were covered with flowered silk tapestries on a ground of light blue. The inlaid screen, hiding the butler's entrance, was composed of three panels on which appliqué work and embroidery on silk depicted late-medieval figures. On the mantel was a clock topped by a sleeping Ariadne by Ferdinand Barbedienne (1810–1892).

80. Dining room, Henry C. Haven house, 195 Commonwealth Avenue, Boston, Massachusetts; J. Pickering Putnam, architect, 1881–82; standing. Haven (September 13, 1852–February 19, 1915) was a bachelor physician when he commissioned this $40,000 house. A graduate of Amherst College in 1873 and of the Harvard Medical School in 1879, he specialized in the diseases of infants. His reception room and examining office were located in the front of the house, separated from the dining, drawing and music rooms.

The differences between this dining room and the Hiltons' are marked. The latter was "decorated," resulting in a display of intricately crafted and highly detailed objects that did not share a common origin or conform to restricted visual criteria, and were often included for nonfunctional reasons. By comparison, the Haven dining room was spare, serious, dark and heavy, reflecting Bostonian tastes and preferences of the period just as Hilton's reflected those of the New York fashionable set. The character of the room was determined by the architect, not the decorator. Cherry was used for the paneling and sideboard and dark oak for the chairs and table.

81. Drawing room, H. Victor Newcomb house, 683 Fifth Avenue, New York, New York; McKim, Mead and White, architects, 1881–82; demolished. In the design for the drawing room of H. Victor Newcomb's city residence, the architects and decorator were influenced strongly by European precedents. Although the room was lavishly furnished and intricately detailed, its elements were combined effectively to create an environment more unified than the majority of the drawing rooms in this series. Absent is the easy mixture of medieval and Renaissance elements characteristic of so many residential interiors of the affluent. The unity of the room is even strong enough to absorb the exotic accent of the tiger-skin rug. The style of the room is Louis XIII, reflecting the influence of the early Italian Renaissance on French design, in which the ceiling and cornice ornamentation was of papier-mâché painted and highlighted with gold. The basic colors of the room were pink, salmon and light blue. The fireplace mantel on the left was carved from bluish-green marble, the drapery was pink plush and pale blue plush, and the carpet, woven in England, was salmon.

In the drawing room hung works by De Neuville, Vibert, E. Frère and Loutaunau. On the easel in the right corner is the *Watercarrier* by Millet. Above the mantel is a large octagonal mirror in a gilded frame and opposite it, over the entrance, is an allegorical canvas by Pierre-Victor Galland (1822–1892). Another Galland painting, reflected in the mirror, is located above the entrance to the library.

Son of the president of the Louisville and Nashville Railroad, Horatio Victor Newcomb (July 26, 1844–November 2, 1911) began life comfortably. He married Florence Ward Danforth in December 1866. Succeeding his father as head of the railroad, he moved from Louisville to New York in about 1881 and became president of the United States National Bank. However, mental illness, which had also afflicted his mother, incapacitated Newcomb in 1891. Court cases to determine whether or not he was sane, and thus responsible for his fortune, continued into the twentieth century.

82. Library, H. Victor Newcomb house. The library was quite different from the drawing room, the principal room of the house. Its dark natural woodwork, robustly carved, and the deeply tinted wall fabrics with vigorous patterns give this room a quality associated with the earlier Italianate and Second Empire styles. The primary decorative features, located above eye level, include the floral panels that are either of wood or painted dark to match the tone of the surrounding woodwork, the substantial wooden cornice supported by large consoles spaced at regular intervals and the wide papered frieze. Paintings were hung against the neutral middle section of the wall; the only identifiable one is the scene of mounted riders by Jean-Richard Goubie (1842–1899), above the mantel.

83. Conservatory, H. Victor Newcomb house. The room was fully glazed on one side and was covered by a coved ceiling of glass supported by wrought iron. Though not obligatory in the large city residence, the nineteenth-century conservatory was popular as a place to display exotic tropical plants. The plants could be moved to other rooms for special occasions or could be placed outdoors during warm weather to highlight an entrance, terrace or small city plot. The conservatory also added diversity to interior decoration. With its extreme lightness, openness and greenery, the conservatory could be a marked contrast to the other major rooms of a residence. In a New York City house, such as this one with its restricted lot size, the conservatory was even more essential—a rural oasis in urban density. Furthermore, the profusion of plants complemented the heavy inventory of items.

Like most conservatories in the city, this one was adjacent to the dining room and kitchen at the rear of the house; the dining room, in an adapted Henry II style, is visible in the distance. It was paneled to a height of six feet in mahogany, the same material used for the ceiling, creating a stately though somber setting for dining.

81

H. Victor Newcomb House, Elberon

This house attracted much attention in the 1880s and has continued to appeal to later generations of architectural critics. Bruce Price, an architect and contemporary of McKim, Mead and White, described the first time he saw the Newcomb house (*Scribner's Magazine*, July 1890): "I was driving from Sea Girt to Long Branch at the time, and, unaware of its existence, came suddenly upon it. The whole scheme, form, and treatment of the house were new to me, and I looked upon it with mingled feelings of surprise and pleasure." Price emphasized new treatment and his emotional response. He was referring to the shingles that covered the asymmetrical exterior and bound the centrifugally oriented volumes within. It was, he thought, "the forerunner" of the shingle houses that gave both character and coherence to American domestic work of the early 1880s.

But Price was also probably delighted by the broad, sloping foreground of grass, the blue-gray background of sky and sea and the lively, unpretentious and imaginatively composed work of art in the middle. He may also have been responsive to the firm's ability to convey "both-and" while avoiding "either-or"—asymmetry without imbalance, expansiveness without loss of center, activity without confusion. Mariana Van Rensselaer (*The Century Magazine*, June 1886) commented on this resolution of opposites in the Newcomb design: "A very just medium has been struck, I think, between that dignity which would have been too dignified for the environment and that utter simplicity which would have been out of character with the interior." In *Artistic Country-Seats* (1886–87; reprinted by Dover Publications as *American Country Houses of the Gilded Age*, 24301-X), George Sheldon called it "the pioneer of a new suburban architecture." In the judgment of twentieth-century architectural historian Vincent Scully, the house revealed McKim, Mead and White "at their original best."

The house was also a confident statement of American wealth in 1880–81, of summer wealth casually spread with ordinary materials over ample space in a socially acceptable and exclusive location. Sure

of themselves, the designers and owners dispensed with traditional architectural means of expressing social status, such as formal composition, thick walls, fine materials, proven styles. Yet, without their confidence and skill, this house could have been interpreted differently, as fragile, vulnerable, tentative, insufficiently imposing, poorly controlled. New owners in 1946 were evidently not comfortable with the risks that had been taken. They transformed the Newcomb house into a one-and-a-half-story structure balanced at either end by related projecting gables held together by a long, quiet roof broken only by three symmetrically placed dormers. The brown shingles were replaced by harder and more serious materials.

84. Hall, H. Victor Newcomb house, 1265 Ocean Avenue, Elberon, New Jersey; McKim, Mead and White, architects, 1880–81; standing but altered. This photograph, looking north, catches the spaciousness and easy combination of odd items in this living hall, the hub of the house. The principal entrance on the land side led into the vestibule, seen immediately beyond the bay on the left. Directly ahead was the opening into the stair hall that connected with the back hall and the servants' work area. In the right corner was a reception room overlooking the Atlantic Ocean.

If formality reigned in the Newcombs' New York town house, informality marked their summer residence. Contemporaries remarked on the "freedom and roominess" of this large space, approximately 50′ × 25′, and twentieth-century observers have complained about the Newcombs' inclination to clutter it with varied and often uncomplementary furniture and art. It was a superb spatial exercise of the 1880s carried out with a shrewd mixture of craft and daring. Though the space is the provocative agent here, it is difficult to define. Granted, the objects add a peculiar note, but many of them, particularly the wicker chairs, are not heavy, and their thrown-together look fits with the apparent informality of the planning. This space is elusive more because of projections and cavities, its play of light and dark and the constant suggestions of movement of space and vibrations of surface.

Suspended from the ceiling, White's simple but elegant wooden screens further frustrate our attempts to rationalize the space. While they define a geometric area within the hall, the light and space seen through them raise questions about where this space begins and ends. Furthermore, the movement implied in the ceiling beams and the light entering at the bays and other openings encourage us to look to the hall's edges.

85. Hall, H. Victor Newcomb house. A wide opening on the south side of the hall to the right of the fireplace led to a much more formal sitting room in white and gold, with walls of leather. In the hall the designers contrasted colors, materials and densities. The floor, of brick and marble, was light, the walls and ceiling, of stained American oak, were dark and the screens, unlike the hardness below or the strength above, were delicate. In the *Shingle Style* (1955), Scully claimed these screens were derived from the Japanese *ramma* or transom grille. Clay Lancaster, in *The Japanese Influence in America*, noted this and other Japanese influences in the Newcomb house: "Tangibly Japanese are the *ramma* in the upper part of the openings into the recesses or adjoining rooms, the beams arranged in groups at right angles in various areas of the ceiling, and a key pattern on the floor carried out in brick and marble instead of Japanese mats."

86. Entrance hall, David L. Einstein house, 39 West 57th Street, New York, New York; architect unknown, 1882–83; demolished 1912. This ostentatious entranceway served an expensive mansion on West 57th Street, which had become in the early 1880s a most prestigious residential street. Built for a prominent manufacturer, the residence was a massive brick-and-stone turreted Queen Anne structure that was stretched vertically and constricted horizontally to conform to a narrow New York City lot. The narrowness of the lot required a plan substantially different from what would have been built elsewhere. This long central corridor, sufficiently lavish to convey immediately the wealth of the owners, leads to the dining room at the rear of the house and to the main stairway that provides access to the second-floor parlors. The Einstein house was somewhat informal in its asymmetrical plan, lively exterior and the romantic combination of Classical and Gothic themes that marked the major interior spaces. But the ponderous woodwork and conspicuous effects throughout the interior, lavish even by the standards of this period, suggest a conscious effort to reveal wealth and clarify artistic sophistication.

David Lewis Einstein (May 20, 1839–May 7, 1909) was born in Cincinnati. Involved in textile manufacturing, he became president of the Raritan Woolen Mills and head of the Somerset Manufacturing Company, also in Raritan, New Jersey. He married Caroline Fatman in 1870. Their marriage produced three children: Florence, Amy and Lewis, all of whom were raised in this house. Einstein occupied the house until his death; his wife continued to live there until her death in 1912. Little written information survives on Einstein. Since he was Jewish, it is not surprising that his name is absent from the social registers of the era and from contemporary editions of *Who's Who in New York*. Evidently he was a self-made man who acquired his fortune, estimated at more than $2 million at his death, through a successful business career. The Einsteins traveled to Europe to purchase a number of items suiting their conservative tastes for their new house.

Entering the interior through a pair of stained-glass doors, one was confronted with the view shown here. The woodwork of the entrance hall was striking in its solidity, massiveness and intricacy. The woodwork covering the ceiling and lower half of the walls is all quarter oak which was darkened by the application of ammonia to give the room an aged character. The process of treating wood to change its color was a common practice of the era; some interior designers applied lime to oak to give it a lighter, whitish color. In this case, the darkening was probably an attempt to make the interior more respectable by creating the illusion of age and stability. Complementing the paneled surfaces were immense leather panels, made to order in France, of subdued red embossed with designs.

Each of the major rooms of the house was designed in its own style. As was common in Queen Anne residences, different woods and other decorative materials were used to create a different effect in each space. Here this approach is carried a step further, as each room represents a different style and historic period. The hall was patterned after the Early English Renaissance, the library was in the style of Louis XIII, the dining room was Henry IV and the sitting room was Anglo-Japanese. At the near right is the entrance to the small Chinese reception room, ornamented in dark blue plush fabric accented by red and gold. Located at the end of the hall was the grand stairway, the focal point of this space, which is illustrated effectively in number 88. The floor shown in this illustration is made of intricate pieces of encaustic tile overlaid with a Persian rug in a Tree of Life design. On the right the oak bench is enlivened by a pair of oak griffins serving as armrests.

86

87

88

87. Living hall, David L. Einstein house. Though treated as a living hall at the end of the main hall, this sitting room was too small to accommodate many people. For this purpose the Einsteins used their Louis XVI parlor located at the front of the house and entered from the left side of the hall. The idea of the living hall was based on the large halls of medieval castles which functioned as the principal congregating space. To heighten the room's medieval flavor, the owners hung antique shields and swords on the wall and displayed old drinking mugs on the mantel.

The central feature of this living hall was a substantial fireplace, which Sheldon claimed had "one of the thickest and solidest mantelpieces in New York City." Like most of the major fireplaces in this house, heavily carved woodwork, extending from floor to ceiling, articulated the opening. In this case, the woodwork was particularly robust, highlighted by clustered columns and thick, leafy capitals. The brilliantly polished metal casing that backs the fire opening was so ornate that it is unlikely wood was ever burned here. The absence of pokers and bellows confirm this conclusion. Thus, this fireplace probably functioned ceremonially in a time when central heating was well established. Nevertheless, these owners could afford unused chimneys and flues, and this fireplace, though reduced to a decorative effect, was undoubtedly functional.

Before the fireplace, on the Oriental rug, is teakwood furniture carved in an intricate, weblike fashion. In the foreground the settee, two chairs connected by a common seat, was a shape common in the mid-to late nineteenth century. The walls are finished in embossed leather similar to that of the hallway, and the woodwork repeats the designs a visitor would have seen immediately upon entering the house. Even the paneling of the ceiling is identical to that in the hallway. Suspended from the center of the ceiling is a metal gas lighting fixture with filigree shields.

88. Hall and staircase, David L. Einstein house. This staircase, the final and most spectacular act of the main hall, was a formidable link between the more public spaces of this floor and the more private ones above. Within the jurisdiction of this heavily ornamented enclosure were four separate flights of steps that terminated at the second floor. Walking through and up this massive structure became a ceremonial procession offering unusual vantage points from which to examine the space and decoration. The screen was created by three identical arches; above each were stained-glass panels in an abstract floral pattern. Stained glass was used extensively on this floor, creating, with the darkened oak woodwork and deeply colored leather walls, a dark interior. Striking gas fixtures surmounted each newel post of the stairway, which extended into the hall. In a complicated, if not absurd, lighting system, carved oaken griffins held in their mouths chains supporting a nest of four serpents from whose mouths extended gas burners. When illuminated, the flames looked like flickering tongues. The clustered columns that form the newel posts are medieval in inspiration while the three arched openings above are Renaissance-inspired. The stair rails were heavily carved panels with a free-flowing latticelike pattern.

Though this screen-and-stairway was an impressive achievement, its environment may have been too dark. Furthermore, behind the photographer was a stained-glass bay window illuminated from behind by gas jets, an addition that would have only contributed to the serious mien of this part of the house. Sensing this problem, the Einsteins may have added the brightly colored banner under one of the arches and the scarf on the railing under another to relieve the somberness. The main stairway extended from the first floor to the third floor but did not include the basement or attic. A rear stairway, used by the servants, rose around an elevator shaft, providing access to these floors.

89

90

89. Dining room, David L. Einstein house. The dining room was located in a one-story wing at the rear of the house that had a play area on top of it. In this roof garden, surrounded by a high iron railing, the children of the family played, the family sunbathed in warm weather or sought relief on hot summer evenings. This reference to a children's play space reminds us that the lives of children seldom affected interior planning of these upper-class mansions and almost never the interior decoration.

Because there were no floors above the dining room to interfere, the mahogany beams of the ceiling sloped upward from the sides to the center, creating a sense of height. Despite the dark paneling and heavy floral wall covering, this room was lighter in feeling than the ponderous hall. The woodwork was detailed in a crisp, rectangular manner. Here too, the fireplace was surrounded by floor-to-ceiling woodwork, crowned by a sizable pediment resting on two clusters of peculiar columns. The gasolier, containing metal and stained-glass globes that glowed like jewels at night, was the most elaborate lighting fixture in the house. Not visible in this photograph, a large stained-glass window comprised most of the rear wall.

The Einsteins obtained many of their decorative objects when traveling in Europe. However, most were not antiques, but contemporary copies of museum pieces. Sheldon stated that they owned an excellent copy of a silver goblet for which Baron Rothschild reportedly had paid the astounding sum of $250,000. Their acquisition of copies of European works, as opposed to originals by American artists, reflected the conservative fashion of the time. Many wealthy Americans lacked confidence in American art because most Europeans lacked confidence in it. Dependence on European arbiters of artistic quality may also expose a lack of faith in one's own judgment. The absence of a separate art gallery in this house suggests that Einstein was not a serious collector of paintings, at least by the standards set by the Stewarts (no. 7), the Smiths (no. 51), the Stuarts (no. 99) or the Vanderbilts (no. 119). Nor was the house well designed

to display the objets d'art the couple had collected. Competing with architectural detail for attention, the individual qualities of these pieces were lost in the resulting visual confusion. Paradoxically, then, the greater the number of bric-a-brac attesting to the taste and means of their owners, the more difficulty the admirer had in appreciating the achievement.

90. Library, David L. Einstein house. In this Louis XIII library the usual wainscoting has been replaced by five-and-a-half-foot-high shelves. Although the bindings of the books behind the glass doors may indicate that Einstein purchased sets for display, the fact that this library contained shelves running 50' suggests that he may have been a serious reader. The room was so tall (16') that three registers were required to organize the wall surface, and the overmantel looks as if it has been stretched to fill the void. Mr. Einstein's library—libraries in these days were male preserves—contains comfortable but suitably direct furniture covered with dark leather and velour.

91. Boudoir, David L. Einstein house. Sheldon's comment on this small sitting room deserves to be quoted because it reveals his positive criticism, writing style and attitude toward European pieces:

> We pass now to the second floor, and into the front sitting-room. Its style is Anglo-Japanese. The ceiling is of canvas, hand-painted in greenish blues alternating with tans and reds. The inside panels of the doors recount the story of Orpheus in delicate line-work of gold upon a ground of neutral blue. We see an immense ebony mantel, with cabinets containing *bric-à-brac* of varied and fine interest—an ivory snuffbox of Louis XIV's, a miniature Italian guitar enriched with marquetry, old Nuremburg samplers embroidered with exquisite grace, an old Geneva watch, a French harp-clock—an ebony writing-case, fitted up to be a thing of use as well as of beauty, a corner cabinet laden with specimens of Dresden, Royal Worcester, and enamels, one of the Dresden pieces being curious for its successfully illusive treatment of a woman's gauze veil. Again the visitor is struck with the generous argosies of foreign travel; the host has ransacked the ends of the earth for *objets d'art*.

91

92

92. Reception room, Henry G. Marquand house, 140 Rhode Island Avenue, Newport, Rhode Island; Richard Morris Hunt, architect, 1872–73; destroyed by fire 1973. Marquand (April 11, 1819–February 26, 1902) gave 33 paintings to the Metropolitan Museum in New York in 1889—the first significant collection of old masters the museum received. Marquand deserved much credit for encouraging collectors in the United States to purchase paintings by Renaissance artists when, in 1886, he persuaded the Treasury Department to classify paintings created before 1700 as "antiques" and to exempt them from duty. Active in real estate, banking and railroads, he devoted increasing attention to art during the 1880s and in 1889 succeeded the Metropolitan Museum's J. T. Johnston, becoming its second president.

The Marquands (he married Elizabeth Love Allen on May 20, 1851) chose Hunt to design this summer house at Newport and their new city residence at 8 East 68th Street in New York City (1881–84). The Marquands displayed so many paintings and objects here at "Linden Gate" that their neighbors dubbed it "Bric-a-brac Hall." Although he had a reputation for being unable to say no to a persistent bric-a-brac vendor, the army of authorities that gathered for the week-long Marquand sale in January 1903 agreed "he knew what he was buying when he bought."

This was an unusually formal reception room for a summer house by the shore. Its focal points were the fireplace and overmantel in a wood surround of chestnut that was simple below but not above, where the first register consisted of three panels of tiny figures carved by the Italian sculptor Luigi Frullini (1839–1897). In the center of the next level was *Near Lily Pond, Ocean Drive,* a Newport scene painted expressly for this spot by R. Swain Gifford (1840–1905). Floral designs decorated the five remaining panels of the overmantel. John La Farge had also worked in the reception room, painting on the blue background of the ceiling Oriental-inspired designs, over which a fretwork of mahogany had been laid. This fretwork was then edged by a border of intricately carved mahogany. Below this border was the cornice, hand-painted against a field of gold, and the wall of eighteenth-century tapestry.

93. Dining room, Henry G. Marquand house. The Marquands found places in the dining room for dozens of their objets d'art, particularly their fine pieces of large and petite Chinese ceramics. The overmantel was constructed for display purposes; the Hispano-Moresque chargers at the top look like inlaid discs in a wooden frame. The sideboard held so much that there was little room left over for food and drink. By concentrating on their possessions, the Marquands seem to have deemphasized the function this room served. In competition with the projecting fireplace and sideboard, the table was left with inadequate space. Stretching to the coved frieze, the overmantel may also have been too heavy. On the other hand, we are looking at the windowless corner of the room, in which the woodwork may look more dominant than on the opposite sides. There, light entered through windows with stained-glass depictions of Spenser and Milton.

---

94. Dining room, Henry Belden house, Fifth Avenue, New York, New York; architect unknown, date unknown. Published information about Henry Belden (d. 1902) is scant, and the specific address of this house is unknown. Evidence suggests that he was the son of the Reverend Henry Belden, a fairly prominent abolitionist and the brother of William, a New York broker. He may have been a partner of William in Belden and Company of 80 Broadway, brokers for rapacious investor Jay Gould. Mentally unstable in his later years, Belden died in a sanatorium.

According to Sheldon:

The dining-room is finished in oak, with a mantel-piece of colored marble. Two immense Chinese porcelain vases stand on either side of the fire-opening, above which the design shows niches for other porcelains and for bronzes; but the shelf is not littered with ornaments. This negative feature is in harmony with the general aspect of the surroundings. There is, perhaps, not a beautiful dining-room in the city whose plan of decoration is at once so simple, without baldness, and so solid. The most striking effect in Mr. Belden's dining-room is the immense screen of spindle and perforated work.

95

96

97

95, 96. Library and parlor, Sarah Ives Hurtt house, Yonkers, New York; architect unknown, date unknown. Sheldon wrote that the Hurtt house overlooked the Hudson River at Yonkers, directly opposite the Palisades. However, its precise location remains a mystery. It was evidently owned by Mrs. F. W. Hurtt, who was first listed in the Yonkers Directory of 1885 as living at 117 Glenwood Avenue. She died in New York City on July 31, 1907. Her husband, Francis W. Hurtt, possibly deceased in 1883–84, had owned the company that manufactured and distributed Pond's Extract, an internationally sold panacea for "Piles, Neuralgia, Catarrh, Rheumatism, Diphtheria, Inflamed Eyes, Sore Throat, Toothache, Old Sores, Wounds, Bruises, Scalds, Burns, and all Pain."

Though it was neither expensive nor conventional, Sheldon thought that this house in "a strictly Moresque style" expressed "an artistic atmosphere." His choice of words and his emphasis are revealing:

Every article of furniture, except the frames of the chairs, was selected and bought by Mrs. Hurtt herself in Morocco. The hangings are Moorish embroideries on a ground of yellow silk, or a fabric closely resembling silk, the art of manufacturing which is lost. Along the center and extending the whole length of the black-satin cover of the lounge is a Moorish woman's wedding-sash . . . . The walls offer a choice assortment of Alhambra decorations, and nearly all the designing is in gold on a solid ground. Between the library and the drawing-room rises a triple arch of true Alhambra pattern, colored in red, gold, blue, and black. . . .

It was said that in such a room no book-cases could be put with any pretext of propriety; but, as books are very useful in a library, the hostess solved the difficulty by getting her carpenter to fit into the walls a series of low shelves . . . .

In order that the Moorish feeling of the library might not intrude upon the parlor (whose scheme of decoration is distinctly different), the effect of the triple arch was neutralized, so far as the latter room is concerned, by hangings that conceal the two smaller openings. Here the general tone of the furniture and embroideries is a peacock-blue, the furniture being covered with plush of that hue, except the smaller chairs, which show the delicate tint known as robin's-egg blue. The walls are frescoed in yellow and in pale

blue, and the frieze of solid gold-leaf looks as if several peacock-feathers had been tossed up and stuck there . . . . The ceiling is in gold and silver of Japanese design. All the doors are sliding, and, if we push aside the farthest one, we enter the English dining-room . . . .

Based on this interior and Sheldon's endorsement of it, we can make the following observations. Freedom of movement was not a major consideration. Mrs. Hurtt had a mind of her own. The terms library and parlor could be interpreted freely. Each side of the dividing archway could contribute to separate and different artistic goals. Eclecticism unified the two spaces.

---

97. Smoking room, Frank Furness house, 711 Locust Street, Philadelphia, Pennsylvania; Frank Furness, architect, after 1873; demolished. The only interior from a professional architect's house included in *Artistic Houses,* this den or smoking room was added to the rear of his row house by Furness (November 20, 1839–June 27, 1912). He had spent several summers in the Rockies and had collected the weavings and skins draped on the chairs, sofa and rafter, the stuffed game and ram's head and local souvenirs, such as the snowshoe. Evidently, he wanted a suitable place in which to put these trophies and reminders. Furness constructed his retreat out of unrefined materials, decorating it in a manner that suggests a Colorado trapper's cabin. His fireplace was made of irregular pieces of hard rock and capped by a stone shelf that looked as if it had been found instead of prepared.

He chose cedar for the roof and walls and unbarked cedar saplings for the dado. The "rustic" table and stool, also of cedar, were supported by poles trimmed by hand. On the other hand, there was evidence suggesting this was the outpost of a very cultured trapper. Over the mantel were framed prints and caricatures, and on the right wall unframed Western prints and a row of pewter jugs. How refreshing to see a room that has not been meticulously tidied before the photograph was taken!

98

98. Picture gallery, Joseph G. Chapman house, 1714 Lucas Place, St. Louis, Missouri; Henry G. Isaacs, architect, 1868–69; demolished before 1906. The character of developing cities in nineteenth-century America was often shaped by individuals who were initially successful in business and subsequently used their influence to strengthen local cultural institutions; Chapman did this in St. Louis. He was born in Norwich, New York, on April 27, 1839 and died in St. Louis, October 9, 1897. Following his graduation from Brown University in 1860, he settled in St. Louis, where his father was senior partner of Chapman and Thorp, a prosperous lumber firm with offices in Missouri and Wisconsin. When his father died in 1873, he became vice president and regional head of the newly formed Eau Claire Lumber Co. On October 21, 1868 he married Emma Bridge, whose father headed the hardware firm of Bridge and Beach and was also president of the first line to Kansas City, the Pacific Railroad.

Shortly after their marriage, the Chapmans moved into this house. Isaacs (1840–1895) had studied with Richard Upjohn in New York before moving to St. Louis in 1864. Lucas Place (now Locust Street), an exclusive street requiring a 25′ setback for houses, was blocked from downtown traffic by Missouri Park. The Chapmans' only child, Isabel, was born here.

For 15 years Chapman was a trustee of Washington University, then only a block from his home. A generous benefactor of the St. Louis Museum, he became its second president in 1883. It is not known when he became a serious collector; however, he frequently purchased pictures exhibited at the Royal Academy Exhibitions in London in the 1870s and probably added this one-story gallery to his house shortly after 1880.

In several respects it was unlike many of the well-publicized galleries of New York City, such as the Vanderbilt (nos. 119 & 120), Stewart (nos. 7 & 8) and Martin (nos. 149 & 150). It was smaller and more intimate. Only 35′ long and furnished with a center table on a splendid carpet, it looked more like a living space than an exhibition hall. The polished butternut floor and hand-carved mantel reinforced this feeling of domesticity. Chapman avoided the institutional appearance of the oblong box by including an annex, seen through the wide arches on either side of the fireplace. He also displayed bric-a-brac as well as oil paintings in this gallery. A marquetry clock in the center of the mantel was flanked by a pair of August Rex Bock vases and crystal candelabra. The oak sideboard against the far wall held a service of Dresden china reportedly manufactured in the late eighteenth century. But the major difference between this room and the galleries mentioned was that it was not crammed from floor or wainscot to molding with pictures. Instead, they were hung close together at eye level. Because this exhibition space was not equipped with overhead gas or electric lighting, the objects could be seen effectively only during the day. This suggests that the Chapmans were not inclined to make an issue of their collection during evening social occasions, that the purpose of the collection may have been private enjoyment rather than a public statement.

Though this collection was not one of "great excellence" containing "examples of the highest art," as a partisan local writer tried to argue in March 1882, it was unusual among American collections because it contained works by British artists, not just Continental painters. At the far left is *A Fishing Haven in the Zuyder Zee* by Edward Cooke (1811–1880). In the two pictures to the right, we see a theme popular in nineteenth-century American collections, the struggle for survival in nature. In the center is *A Winter's Tale,* painted by Briton Riviere (1840–1920) about 1880; the collies of a search party have just found an exhausted, lost Highland girl. To the right is an account by Adolf Schreyer of a team of horses chased by wolves, *Winter Travel in Russia.* According to today's market, his most valuable painting was *Dover* by J. M. W. Turner (1775–1851), a portion of which is visible on the easel at the lower right.

99. Picture gallery, Mary Stuart house, 961 Fifth Avenue, New York, New York; William Schickel, architect, 1881–83; demolished 1942. Designed in 1881, this house on the northeast corner of Fifth Avenue and East 68th Street was completed in the spring of 1883, several months after Robert L. Stuart (July 21, 1806–December 12, 1882) had died of septicemia. Robert and his brother Alexander had inherited $25,000 each from their Scottish father in 1826 and two years later formed the R. L. and A. Stuart Co., a firm that continued their father's candy business but also branched into sugar refining. They concentrated on refining exclusively after 1835, becoming the largest sugar processor in New York City. That year Robert married Mary McCrea (1810–1891), daughter of David McCrea, a wealthy New York merchant. In 1862, when the lower part of Fifth Avenue was still fashionable, they built a brownstone residence at the corner of 20th Street. After Stuart retired in 1872, he spent much of his time developing his art collection, adding books to his library and giving assistance and money to cultural, medical and educational institutions. Inheriting between $5 and $6 million at his death, Mrs. Stuart continued to give liberally to charities and institutions.

The *New York Times* predicted the new house would be "one of the most notable of the avenue." It fronted Fifth Avenue for 55' and extended 136' along East 68th Street, was five stories high and cost an estimated $350,000.

At the end of the main hall was the picture gallery, a room that projected from the rear of the house. Compared to the better-known domestic galleries of New York, it was not large; compared to the lesser-known, it was uncluttered and modestly furnished. The chairs were upholstered in carpet fragments. Gas jets on the central rectangular frame augmented natural illumination above. Because of the gallery's size and the relatively narrow band on which the pictures were hung, only 66 canvases were displayed here. According to an 1885 catalogue, the remaining 174 paintings in the collection were hung throughout the house, most in the halls of the first three floors.

This collection was unlike others featured in *Artistic Houses* in two respects. First, Stuart had purchased many works by nineteenth-century American painters. Among the 48 Yankee artists included were Frederick Church, Thomas Cole (1801–1848), J. F. Cropsey (1823–1900), Asher B. Durand (1796–1886), Eastman Johnson (1824–1906), William S. Mount (1807–1868) and A. F. Tait (1819–1905). Granted, this number was less than the 63 European artists represented in the collection, but Stuart was a recognized collector and his endorsement of talent in the United States must have encouraged American painters, who clearly understood that New York millionaires preferred to buy their paintings in Paris. Secondly, the Stuart gallery contained more than fine art. In the ebonized oak cabinets below the picture line were rocks, minerals and archaeological fragments, in addition to prints.

Contemporary critics valued the Stuart collection because of its European paintings. Calling it "one of the finest in the city," the *Times* cited as evidence works by "Schreyer, Gérome, Bouguereau, Merle, Alvarez, Madrazo, Breton, Verboeckhoven, and others." In general, the choice of subjects reflected the subjects that also appealed to other major New York buyers; however, there was a much higher percentage of landscapes because of the higher proportion of American painters. The dominant category was clearly genre, with such canvases as *The Mother's Prayer, The Dispute, The Little Knitter*—most of them painted by French and German artists. On the left, the larger paintings are *Pilgrims Going to Church* by G. H. Boughton (1833–1905) and, below, *The Quarrel* by Ludwig Knaus (1829–1910), *Home Lessons* by Ludwig Bruck-Lajos (1846–1910) and *Tropical Scenery* by Church. In the center of the rear wall are *On the Esopus* by William Hart (1823–1894) and, below, *Grandmother's Birthday* by Wenzel von Broczik (1851–1901). In the right corner is *Luncheon in the Garden* by Munkacsy, below; above, *The Bridal Jewels* by Giuseppe Ferrari (1843–1905). The posthumous portrait of Stuart was commissioned by his wife.

100

101

102

100. Drawing room, Mary Stuart house. The photographs from *Artistic Houses* both reveal and obscure. They are revealing because they record for us the physically rich interiors of the 1880s. Yet they are devoid of human beings—those for whom this artistic effort was intended. Consequently, we may understand the material setting but fail to understand how it was utilized. For example, did the guests at one of Mrs. Stuart's social evenings really sit on these isolated chairs facing various directions?

This space was large enough to absorb, at least partially, the intense decorative attack launched by William Bigelow for Herter Brothers of New York City. The central rectangle of the ceiling contained a painting on canvas of life-size figures representing art. On the frieze, broken into sections by conspicuous brackets, were cherubs playing amid garlands of flowers. Louis XV damask in light cherry covered the walls and also some of the pieces of furniture. An enormous Axminster carpet lay on the floor. On top of this surfeit of dutifully treated surfaces the decorator added focal points: bronze chandeliers with glass crystals attached, two tall Sèvres vases balanced on onyx pedestals and an African onyx mantel capped by the mirror. There were also four paintings on the walls—*Study of Natural History* by A. Gisbert (1835–1901), *The Nine Muses* by P. O. J. Coomans (1816–1889), *May Festival in Spain* by Luis Alvarez (1836–1901) and *The Poet* by Luis Jiménez (1845–?).

101. Dining room, Mary Stuart house. Like the living room, this room was quite spacious for a New York house of the period. Despite the size and the $150,000 spent to furnish the interiors of the first floor, the dining room was relatively informal, its mood affected by the unexpected presence of the piano, sofa and even the bay window. The vast Turkish rug over the parquetry of the oak floor, and the portieres of blue-green plush embroidered with garlands of flowers, also added

warmth to this space. Though the materials differ, the handling of the wall, frieze and ceiling was similar to that of the drawing room. Carefully crafted brackets supported the ceiling of English oak beams. The panels of the ceiling were finished in papier-mâché, those of the frieze in painted plaster and the walls below in stamped leather. Intended to support gas fixtures, the two African marble pedestals of the fireplace look overly precious in this setting impressive for its serious colors and textured surfaces.

---

102. Sitting room, Henry S. Hovey house, 238 Western Avenue, Gloucester, Massachusetts; Hardy and Day, architects, 1879–81; standing but altered. The Hoveys had spent their summers in Gloucester since the 1850s. Their first house on this site, Lookout Hill overlooking Gloucester Bay, burned in 1875, but in 1879 a son, Henry S. Hovey (January 30, 1844–November 19, 1900), commissioned a second, Queen Anne in style, which was completed in May 1881. Hovey owned the Pittsfield Cotton Mills in Pittsfield, New Hampshire, wintered in Boston at 100 Beacon Street and summered in Gloucester with his sister Marion.

The view from the padded window seat of this sitting room was superb and must have pleased Hovey, who was the owner of the sloop *Fortuna* and commodore of the Eastern Yacht Club of Marblehead, Massachusetts. The exterior style and setting probably gave license to the casual mixture of objects in this pleasant space: tall case clock, carved table with spiral legs and stretcher, wicker chair, three-legged side chair, horns above the mantel and Oriental ceramics. Despite the dark ceiling and wall panels of stained quarter oak and the parquetry of the floor, the ample natural light reflected from surfaces and gave this potentially heavy interior a lively appearance.

Samuel M. Nickerson House

This substantial house was designed for Nickerson in 1881 by Edward Burling (1819–1892) of the Chicago firm of Burling and Whitehouse. Later architecture has encroached upon the property, the site originally consisting of the house with a sizable porte cochere and stables behind the rear court. From a ground plan that measured roughly 50′ × 90′, Burling designed a dwelling consisting of 28 rooms on three floors and a basement. Its exterior was spare for a major Chicago mansion of these years. This was due in part to modest use of ornament, which was concentrated in the stringcourses, cornice and lintels and sills of the windows, and also to the heavy but simple blocks of the wall. Contemporaries predicted that the house would last forever; miraculously, new uses have been found to protect it from deterioration and movements to demolish it. In 1919 Chicago citizens contributed money to purchase the house, which was then given to the American College of Surgeons for its national headquarters.

Samuel M. Nickerson (June 14, 1830–July 20, 1914) and his wife, Matilda P. Crosby, who died about two years before her husband, were natives of Chatham, Massachusetts. In 1858 they moved to Chicago, where Samuel started a distilling business, a venture that did not prosper until he received a contract from the Union Army to provide alcohol used in the manufacture of gunpowder. Shortly afterwards, he was able to retire from manufacturing and concentrated on banking and transportation. One of the founders of the First National Bank of Chicago in 1863, he became its president in 1867. In 1865 he was

elected president of the Chicago City Horse Railway, later renamed the Chicago City Railway Company. He was a prominent member of the Chicago Historical Society, was active in the city's musical circles and donated part of his collection to The Art Institute of Chicago. In 1901 the Nickersons sold their house and moved to New York City.

---

103. Hall, Samuel M. Nickerson house, 40 East Erie Street, Chicago, Illinois; Burling and Whitehouse, architects, 1881–83; standing. Like A. T. Stewart's famous house in New York (nos. 1–8), Nickerson's was also called the "Marble Palace," but in Chicago one had to go inside the house to understand why contemporaries had given it this label. The stern, even drab exterior of the mansion did not alert visitors to the glistening surfaces of the palatial main hall. Here the reflections are so dominant that they tend to underscore the plastic properties of lintels, cornice, Corinthian columns and even the ceiling. In this photograph there were no members of the family and no furniture to block one's concentration on these shining planes. The columns were made of marble, as were the wall panels and ceiling slabs, the latter a rare use of the material. The balusters of the stairway were of alabaster. To support all of this weight, Burling required fireproof-brick partition walls from basement to roof and mortared floors laid over brick-arch construction supported by iron joists. Floor strips embedded in the mortar supported wooden floors on which the marble layer was laid. The double staircase leading to the ballroom on the third floor was framed in iron. Durable construction and the expense of the finishing materials contributed heavily to the final bill of $450,000.

On the right of the hall were the reception room, seen through the doorway, and the dining room behind it. Opposite this doorway was the entrance into the drawing room that was connected by sliding doors to the two rooms in the northwest corner of the main floor—the library and the picture gallery.

104. Library and picture gallery, Samuel M. Nickerson house. Bric-a-brac was kept to a minimum in the library, probably because of

the skillful handling of the ebony woodwork in the mantel, the Renaissance-inspired bookcases and the bracketed ceiling. None of the walls of the main part of the house was finished either in wallpaper or in plaster; here the space above the bookcases was covered with gold and green silk. Olive, red and gray accents were painted within the black frames of the ceiling. The windows on the left, overlooking Cass Street, were draped with crimson silk plush embroidered in green and edged with gold cord.

From the rear of the house, the high gallery projected like a nononsense mausoleum. Within, it was the final segment of a long vista that began with the sitting room and continued through the drawing room and library. This final segment was framed by the two marble Doric columns. In the middle of the floor was the *Flight from Pompeii*, a marble group by Italian sculptor Giovanni Maria Benzoni (1809–1873), whose theme combines danger and heroism as the man shields the woman and the woman shields the baby. The largest painting visible in this photograph was *Interior of St. Mark's, Venice* by David Neal (1838–1915). Finished in 1869 and now in the Nickerson Collection of The Art Institute of Chicago, it depicts a wedding party of nobles emerging from the chancel of the cathedral. Above and to the left of this work was Bouguereau's study of a gypsy girl preparing to tell fortunes through the seeds of a pomegranate she holds in her hands. Many of these and other works of art in the house were purchased by the Nickersons on their worldwide trip taken while the house was being built. Their collection of paintings, which included works by Schreyer, Diaz, Mignot, Hubner, Verschnur, Koekkoek, Escosura, Corot and Doré, was regarded as one of the most important in the Midwest.

105. Hall, William H. De Forest house, 12 West 57th Street, New York, New York; Lamb and Wheeler, architects, 1879–82; demolished. W. H. De Forest was born in New York City in 1837. As a youth in the years before the Civil War, he became actively involved in the city's burgeoning silk business. At the time his house was built, he had a reputation as one of the most effective and engaging silk jobbers in New York. Through his contacts with the silk merchants of Paris and Lyons—he served as the American agent of Guanet Brothers, a well-known French firm—he had the opportunity to become acquainted with the latest Second Empire fashions. De Forest was also an investor in local real estate, amassing a considerable amount of property. However, little is known about his family life except that his wife died about 1889, and that they had two sons and a daughter.

In 1882 De Forest was at the height of his business career and able to afford not only this luxurious city residence but also a country estate at Summit, New Jersey. Six years later, suffering financial reverses, he failed in business. A short time later he was committed to an insane asylum at Poughkeepsie, New York. In 1891 De Forest was back in the news after escaping from the asylum and returning to New York. Identifying himself as a wealthy businessman, he aroused suspicion by buying numerous items on credit, by offering a million dollars apiece for certain New York buildings and by boasting of plans to acquire all of New Jersey. De Forest died on July 16, 1896 at his estate at Summit.

De Forest had his hall decorated to recall early English manor houses. Associations with this style were signaled by the dark woodwork, extensive paneling, carved-oak relief in the mantel frieze and the coved frieze above and the vigorous three-dimensional quality of the fireplace. This sculptural strength is particularly noticeable in the caryatids at either side of the opening. But this was a day when consistency in revivalism could look limiting in comparison with creative eclecticism, and Sheldon was a critic who liked the latter. The architect, he claimed, had "introduced into his very eclectic and interesting scheme the salient and most enticing qualities of various schools and epochs, thus avoiding what otherwise might have been some loudly-resounding clashing. In this hall, for instance, the ceiling decoration is Japanese, but, being not of a rabid sort, one experiences no sense of incongruity."

106. Library, William H. De Forest house. After the tightness of the hall, its area partially consumed by the mantel and stairway, the library's modest, right-angled space seemed generous. Here the paneling of antique oak played a commanding role, expressing a sparer and flatter series of planes than the visitor had encountered in the hall. Paintings and objects were really accents that did not upset the room's serious manner. Despite the generous dimensions (50′ × 100′) of this six-story town house, the only source of natural light in the library was a window to the left of the fireplace. Artificial illumination came from the sconces, table lamps, mantel lamps and the chandelier. The fire screen was embossed brass, the table and chair early eighteenth-century.

107. Parlor, William H. De Forest house. The French influence of this room is seen in the lighter colors, the delicate character of the decoration and the floral hangings and coverings brought from Paris. The scheme of this room was based loosely on Louis XVI, a style common in the late nineteenth century and often used in one room as a foil to the darker and heavier character of the other rooms. The parlor was colored in a salmon yellow that served as a relatively neutral background for the floral plush coverings. The ceiling was finished with stucco tiles in variegated designs.

105

108

108. Dining room, William H. De Forest house. This room has a more classic look than the hall and library and was inspired by the English Adam style as reflected in early American Federal architecture. Of course, the aggressive vigor of its surfaces and its relatively graceless space distinguish it from a close interpretation of the style. In contrast to the hall and library, this room was paneled—overpaneled may be more appropriate—in mahogany, which appears quite light in comparison with the wood of the other rooms. The fireplace was huge and overscaled for the classic lines of the room, but its power was underscored by the stained-glass window of the overmantel, which L. C. Tiffany & Associated Artists installed in 1881. The ceiling was also paneled in mahogany. The deep gold plush, embroidered with floral patterns, was not a common material for a frieze. The drapery around the windows was of sapphire-blue plush, embroidered with orange blossoms, and the chairs were covered with alligator skin.

---

109. Entrée room, John H. Shoenberger house, 43 West 57th Street, New York, New York; architect unknown, 1883–84; demolished 1920. Born in 1810 at Juniata Forge, Pennsylvania, Shoenberger received his education at Jefferson College. In 1833 he moved to Pittsburgh to join his father, Dr. Peter Shoenberger, in the emerging iron and steel industry. In addition to owning plants in Pittsburgh and in Huntington County, he was active in banking and was involved with the Pittsburgh, Fort Wayne and Chicago and the Allegheny railroads. After the death of his first wife, the former Margaret Cust, Shoenberger married Alice E. Taylor in 1880, an event that probably influenced his move to New York at the age of 70. He died there on November 12, 1889, leaving an estate of more than $2 million that was dispersed generously to his family and to churches, hospitals and charities in Pittsburgh.

In this small *entrée* room there were three major attractions. Above

was a "Renaissance" ceiling. Opposite the doorway on the left was the elaborate fireplace of oak outfitted with shelves and mirrors and topped by a peculiar window or panel. Directly ahead was the principal attraction, an allegorical painting of Phoebus Apollo after Guido Reni (1575–1642). Rarely do we encounter originals or copies of Baroque paintings in these houses. Despite the fact that the painting was framed in fresco and placed against a neutral ground of silver and gold, implying that that wall had been planned with the painting in mind, the Shoenbergers have disturbed the setting with smaller pictures to either side. D. S. Hess and Company decorated this house.

110. Dining room, John H. Shoenberger house. This well-illuminated dining room had an exceptionally high ceiling, tall enough to contain easily the complex carpentry of the overmantel. There were windows in the niche at the northern end, a recess that could also be used as a smoking nook and could be cut off from the dining room when the portieres of dark olive plush and tapestry were drawn. Opposite the fireplace were two windows and between them a niched and built-in mahogany sideboard with a stained-glass panel above. With the exception of the gasolier, right-angled forms dominated the part of the dining room shown here. If these squares and rectangles suggest the simplicity and flatness that was to mark American interior decoration in the early twentieth century, the dominant mahogany mantelpiece reflected the past. A complex unit, it contained a large mirror and closed and open cupboards that extended to the right and to the left above the wainscoting. The ceiling of the dining room was executed in *al-pasto* work: Gold and other forms of metal leaf are applied directly to plaster to create various patterns and colors. Here the golds and bronzes in a geometric design were surrounded by a floral border. At the top of the walls was a broad frieze of canvas on which was painted scenes of animal life. The lower portion of the walls was covered with embossed leather.

111. Dining room, Samuel J. Tilden house, 15 Gramercy Park South, New York, New York; architect unknown, 1844–45; standing but altered. Though generally considered an effective governor of New York State (1874–76) and popularly regarded as a reformer who stood up to the Tweed Ring in New York City, Tilden (February 9, 1814–August 4, 1886) could also be interpreted as an ambitious politician who lacked the conviction, consistency of position and endurance to fulfill his promise. Troubled throughout his life by poor health and wounded by his loss of the national presidency in the Electoral College in 1876 after he had won the popular vote, he walked slowly and indecisively away from public life.

Purchased in 1863, 15 Gramercy Park South became Tilden's address in 1865. Between 1881 and 1884 Calvert Vaux and George Radford joined this house to an existing one on the west that Tilden had bought in 1874. The ground floor of No. 14 became the Governor's library, containing one of the largest private collections in the city, and the ground floor of No. 15 held the drawing room and dining room.

An avid reader and collector of books, Tilden was not deeply moved by art, music or theater. Nevertheless, the author of *Artistic Houses* wrote of the dining room: "Here is the last word of modern art in this fascinating sphere of effort; or rather, we may say, the first word of this later American Renaissance, which our painters, turned decorators, are creating."

The dining room was distinctive. Its character was inspired by the black-walnut bookcases Tilden had inherited and by the 4'-high black-walnut wainscoting. Black walnut was also chosen for the molding above the relief panels and for the frames of the doors and windows. Ivory-colored panels of satinwood, contrasting with the dark walnut, displayed branches, leaves and birds in a free, asymmetrical, overall pattern. Gold leaf was applied to the background of these panels; alternate blocks in the satinwood diapered frieze above were also gilded.

The ceiling, 31' square, was divided into four sections by satinwood beams that met in the octagonal centerpiece from which hung the heavy gasolier. Smaller satinwood ribs divided the ceiling into squares, each containing a turquoise encaustic tile. The color of the ceiling was picked up by a band of blue tiles that separated the wainscoting from the relief panels of the walls. The firmly built dwelling is now occupied by the National Arts Club. The dining room, now a gallery, has been simplified to meet exhibition needs.

112, 113. Hall, Samuel J. Tilden house, 847 North Broadway, above Lake Avenue, Yonkers, New York; architect unknown, 1868–69; demolished 1948. Following the advice of doctors that he spend more time in the countryside, Tilden found and leased in 1879 the estate "Greystone" at Yonkers, a 63-acre property overlooking the Hudson River. Tilden preferred the spelling "Graystone," but historians have generally used the former spelling.

To avoid contacts, Tilden spent an increasing amount of time in the country, playing the role of intellectual farmer with vigor, and even experienced a moderate improvement in his health. He moved many of his books to "Greystone" and kept all new titles there.

"Greystone" was an asymmetrical and ungainly mass of gneiss rock articulated with Italianate, Gothic and Second Empire detail. From the front door, seen at the end of the hall, the visitor viewed the entrances to the reception room, drawing room and library on the left and the secretary's office, stairhall and dining room on the right. In this traffic hall, the mahogany open armchairs served primarily to fill the long space and soften the atmosphere. The portieres that partially hid the heavy doors to the various first-floor rooms added warmth and color. There were relatively few works of art in the hall: an urn-topped European clock that rested on Corinthian columns, a pair of Chinese urns and several framed pictures. The only identifiable works are two-dimensional reproductions of a Roman copy of the *Discus Thrower* by Myron and *Moses* by Michelangelo. Reproductions in the main hall of a proper New York town house would have been a rarity. The moosehead, somewhat incongruous in the side hall, would have been considered more discordant in the main hall.

111

112

113

WILLIAM H. VANDERBILT HOUSE

Not since the building of Stewart's "Marble Palace" in the late 1860s had New Yorkers paid as much attention to a house as they did to this one. After all, one of the richest men, if not the richest man, in the world had decided he wanted a house that reflected his worth. In 1877 William H. Vanderbilt (May 8, 1821–December 8, 1885) inherited about $90 million from his father Cornelius, became president of the New York Central Railroad immediately and by 1883 had won control of the Chicago and Northwestern, the Nickel Plate Road and other systems that extended his network westward to St. Louis and Minneapolis–St. Paul. At the time of his death his fortune had increased to an estimated $200 million, a figure so incomprehensible that one Wall Streeter in 1884 translated its value into more meaningful terms: On interest and dividends alone Vanderbilt earned "$28,000 a day, $1200 an hour, and $19.75 a minute." New York newspapers realized they had good copy—the construction and decoration of a huge mansion for a man of inordinate means who wanted nothing but the best—and they watched its rise and subsequent alterations closely.

Mrs. Vanderbilt, Maria Louisa Kissam (d. 1896), daughter of a Brooklyn minister, did not want to leave their comfortable home at 450 Fifth Avenue. Furthermore, most of their eight children were no longer living with them. She urged her husband to add a wing to the old house to provide the space he needed for his growing collection of paintings. But in 1879 Vanderbilt paid $700,000 for property that stretched from West 51st Street to West 52nd Street on Fifth Avenue. Then, with adequate land in a currently fashionable location, he asked the decorating firm of Herter Brothers to design and furnish the house.

Charles B. Atwood (1849–1895), an architect working for Herter Brothers, was probably the designer of the Vanderbilt house. However, the firm wanted the credit and wrote to the *American Architect and Building News* (May 2, 1885) claiming responsibility and characterizing Atwood as a mere employee. Historians, however, have had difficulty attributing this house to a decorating firm. To complicate the matter, the building permit was taken out in August 1879 in the names of Atwood and John B. Snook (1815–1907). Snook was a contractor hired by Vanderbilt to be general superintendent of the construction process. He added to the confusion by introducing himself as the architect when showing members of the press through the partially completed building.

The house was completed in two and a half years, a short period considering the profuse and costly interior decorations, and the Vanderbilts moved in at the end of January 1882. The photograph on this page shows their section at 640 Fifth Avenue; at the right is a portion of the northern half of the double house containing the residences for two of their daughters, Margaret Louisa (Mrs. Elliot F. Shepard) and Emily (Mrs. William D. Sloane). To speed construction, the marble initially planned for the exterior was rejected in favor of sandstone from Connecticut. From the street the house looked like a three-story dwelling but actually contained four interior floors. The first two floors were 16½′ high and the third 15′ high while the width was approximately 80′ and the depth 115′. Vanderbilt wanted a mansion large enough to express his position but also one that was removed from the common life of the sidewalk and street. Here his objectives clashed. Because the house was too large for its site, only a symbolic moat of grass and a sandstone wall provided defensible space. Newspapers hinted that Vanderbilt would purchase and then destroy

The Fifth Avenue facade.

the block-long building directly opposite, a Roman Catholic orphanage, in order to obtain a garden forecourt.

As an architectural statement, the Fifth Avenue facade was not memorable. It contained the beginnings of messages that were not finished. Were the owners and designers short on courage? Were they too self-conscious? The plastic promises were ironed flat, the strength of supports compromised by meticulous enunciation, the bands of decoration hygienically isolated. Inspired by the rationalized classicism of earlier French architects, the design was restrained and dignified but lacked a topic sentence.

Architectural critics of the day were not pleased with the results. "If these Vanderbilt houses are the result of intrusting architectural design to decorators, it is hoped the experiment may not be repeated," was an expected response from the *American Architect and Building News* (May 21, 1881), a journal that called repeatedly for a stronger profession. Clarence Cook (*North American Review*, September 1882) called the twin houses a "gigantic knee-hole table." Montgomery Schuyler (*Harper's New Monthly Magazine*, September 1883) thought its decoration unrelated to its structure, and Mariana Van Rensselaer (*The Century*, February 1886) agreed with Schuyler but added that without their carved bands the two would look like "brown-stone packing-boxes." Initial reactions to the interior were quite different. Stunned by the magnificence of the rooms of No. 640, critics expressed their amazement rather than their opinions.

During the last year of work on the interior, Vanderbilt visited Herter Brothers almost every day. He was an ideal customer—enthusiastic, generous, trusting. He made no contracts with them; they simply carried out the work and sent him the bills. To celebrate the completion of the interior, he invited 2000 friends to a reception on March 7, 1882. "Nothing could equal its magnificence in a decorative sense," reported the *Times*. Announced as a house, it became New York's newest and most discussed museum, its contents familiar to a public unable to visit it.

Vanderbilt died there 47 months after he moved in. He willed it to his wife, who died in 1896, and through her to successive Vanderbilt males. It was occupied until 1944 and demolished in 1947 to make room for the Crowell-Collier Publishing Co. The northern half of the block was razed in 1927.

114. Hall, William H. Vanderbilt house, 640 Fifth Avenue, New York, New York; Charles B. Atwood and John B. Snook, architects, 1879–82; demolished 1947. The main entrance led into a vestibule that linked the two halves of the building. At the south end of this space was an inner vestibule, roughly 12′ square, through which one reached the main hall with its superimposed galleries. In this photograph the entrance to the picture gallery on the west is directly ahead, the stairs on the north side are to the right, the door to the dining room on West 51st Street to the left and the opening to the drawing room overlooking Fifth Avenue behind the photographer. With its opulent, eclectic furnishings, this hall was more demonstrative than inviting. It contained a seventeenth-century Lille tapestry, a German bronze of a female falconer, a Japanese sculpture of a sea god and a Chinese screen. The boxy chairs were carved from English oak. Turkish

rugs covered the hardwood parquetry, and the walls were divided into a high oak wainscoting and a Celtic frieze inlaid with small panels of marble. Twelve piers of dark red African marble with bronze capitals supported the gallery on this level.

115. Hall, William H. Vanderbilt house. A bas-relief frieze of festoons separated by female masks, interrupted near the corners by double cupids, completed the decoration of the first level. In a matching register a floor higher were reclining figures, symbolizing the seasons, painted by an unidentified French artist. Six tapestries executed in 1624 at Fontainebleau covered the wall of this level. This court rose through four stories and was illuminated primarily by nine stained-glass windows in the roof by day and at night by the sconces attached to the piers of the second level.

116

116. Drawing room, William H. Vanderbilt house. A sumptuously illustrated four-volume study entitled *Mr. Vanderbilt's House and Collection*, by Earl Shinn [Edward Strahan], was published in 1883–84. It was paid for by William H. and probably written with the unacknowledged assistance of Samuel Avery, his art adviser. Historians consider this publication the best record of any millionaire's house erected in this period. Vanderbilt undoubtedly thought such an achievement should be documented for contemporaries and posterity, and he may have wanted immediate confirmation in print that he was not just a successful businessman but also a friend, if not a student, of art.

In 1911 Gustavus Myers (*History of the Great American Fortunes*) ridiculed Vanderbilt: "With the expenditure of a few hundred thousand dollars he instantly transformed himself from a heavy witted, uncultured money hoarder into the character of a surpassing 'judge and patron of art.' " Today, we may conclude that Vanderbilt was self-indulgent and not well informed about art, and while some contemporaries in 1883 would have agreed, a large majority would also have regarded his house as a gift to his city, and its contents as proof and promise of national artistic growth. Paradoxically, this private museum was promoted as evidence of cultural progress about which the public, banned from its doors, could feel proud.

Overlooking Fifth Avenue, the drawing room (31' × 25') was located between the library on the north and the Japanese parlor, seen through the parted portieres, on the south. Herter Brothers lavished such attention on this room that even Sheldon sounded mildly critical: "almost every surface is covered, one might say weighted, with ornament. . . ." Within the coved ceiling Pierre-Victor Galland of Paris painted on canvas a procession of knights, ladies and their entourage bringing in the first grapes. Below, the surfaces sparkled. Light was reflected from the mother-of-pearl butterflies and cut crystal sewn on the red velvet walls, from the beveled mirrors in each corner and from the stained-glass vases containing the gas jets. There were additional gas jets in each corner, shielded by a silver figure of a young woman.

Mother-of-pearl was everywhere—in the frieze, on the backs of chairs, on the cabinets and casings of doors and windows. The central table, by R. M. Lancelot, was inlaid with gold in addition to mother-of-pearl. On top of this table was an ivory statue encased in glass, *Fortune* by A. Moreau-Vauthier (1831–1893). The carpet was woven in Europe.

117. Dining room, William H. Vanderbilt house. Located to the west of the Japanese parlor, the dining room (37' × 28') was unlike the glittering drawing room. Here the expressive element—the dark stained English oak—was seen in the arched ribs of the ceiling, the wainscoting (12' high) and the heavy cabinets and shelves surrounding the room. Carved from the same wood were the chairs, which were covered with a dull red stamped leather, a color that suggested age and decorum and matched the hue of the velvet hangings. Solid, rich and Renaissance, this room, more than the drawing room, was closer to Vanderbilt's self-image, once expressed in a startling phrase, "We are plain, quiet, unostentatious people . . . ." Counteracting the heaviness of the woodwork were the red figures, white, gray and brown horses and the pale blue sky of the scenes painted by E. V. Luminais (1822–1896) of Paris at either end of the dining room and in the central panel of the ceiling.

118. Japanese parlor, William H. Vanderbilt house. According to Sheldon, whose criticism was compromised by his relentlessly positive verdicts, this parlor was "in perfect harmony with the surrounding rooms." This judgment makes no sense because the Japanese parlor was distinctly and intentionally different. Here Vanderbilt was simply putting on the style—and simultaneously fearing a vacuum—to convince diners on their way back to the drawing room that if he was familiar with the Renaissance he was also aware of the Far East. Sheldon took pains to point out that its setting was invented, not copied. The split bamboo nailed to the plastered ceiling was natural in color, the rafters were lacquered red and the dark red of the wall brocade was fronted by the blues, browns and yellows of the porcelains.

117

118

119

120

121

119. Picture gallery, William H. Vanderbilt house.
According to a catalog of 1884, Vanderbilt's collection consisted of 207 oils and watercolors, the majority of which were French. Only two were American. Art historians and critics have been hard on Vanderbilt, depicting him as an aesthetic dunderhead who, with little knowledge and even less feeling, sent Samuel P. Avery to Europe with a fistful of dollars to assemble a collection simply because owning art had become fashionable. Avery denied this in print.

Vanderbilt did rely heavily on his adviser and gave Avery authority to act in his behalf. However, to argue that he was incapable of being moved by art is insulting. Because subject matter was important to him—more important than style—he liked paintings with clear themes, clearly presented. At the left of the archway connecting the gallery and the main hall are two examples of subject matter he enjoyed, the animal picture (*After the Chase* by Edwin Landseer, 1802–1873) and below it the North African or Turkish scene (Gérome's *Sword Dance*, purchased in London in 1880).

The picture gallery (32′ × 48′ and at least 30′ high) was directly west of the hall. A gigantic rug hid the fine parquetry floor. When the Vanderbilts needed a ballroom, the rug and furniture were removed. When the doors between the hall court and the musicians' loft above the archway were opened, music could be heard throughout the house. The pictures were hung above the ebonized oak paneling and against dull red tapestry. Mahogany was used for the architectural and sculptural highlights and in the ceiling. A skylight containing opalescent and tinted glass illuminated the space during the day. At night, the gallery was lighted by 169 gas jets attached to pipes that crossed it and by naked light bulbs projecting from the walls at the base of the second level. In addition to the musicians' loft, there were balconies on the north and the south that opened to the halls of the second floor.

120. Picture gallery, William H. Vanderbilt house.
William H. also liked sentimental genre, exemplified by Munkacsy's *Two Families* on the left above the wainscoting in this photograph. Another favorite category was military paintings, specifically, the depictions of French heroism in the recent Franco-Prussian War. On the huge easel near the

center of the left wall was the largest painting in the gallery, *The Defense of Bourget*, which Alphonse De Neuville (1836–1885) painted in 1878 to honor those who had gallantly defended the village of Bourget against a division of Prussian troops.

In these years when private collection rivaled public museums in quality of material, effectiveness of display and even in documentation—the Metropolitan Museum in New York had published nothing comparable to *Mr. Vanderbilt's House and Collection*—collectors frequently set aside times for artists and the interested public to study their holdings. Initially, Vanderbilt followed this practice. By cards of invitation art lovers were admitted at a special entrance on 51st Street on Thursdays from 11:00 A.M. until 4:00 P.M. A year after Vanderbilt moved in he concluded the gallery was inadequate to display his growing collection and commissioned Snook to make major changes that created a vista of almost 140′ from the windows of the drawing room through hall and gallery to the walls of a new, glassed-in garden. On December 20, 1883 Vanderbilt invited 3000 men from the worlds of business and art to inspect the galleries and tour the house. They wandered at will, looked at books, handled costly bric-a-brac and even trimmed some plants as souvenirs. In 1884 Vanderbilt discontinued the Thursday openings.

121. Library, William H. Vanderbilt house.
The library was the same size as the Japanese parlor. The most conspicuous feature of this relatively intimate space (17′ × 26′) was its ceiling of small beveled mirrors set in molded plaster. Mahogany and rosewood were the principal woods, the latter visible on the jambs, inlaid with mother-of-pearl and bronze, of the opening directly ahead. The room contained several prized objects. On the left the large painting, done on order by Gérome in 1878, celebrates *The Reception of the Great Condé by Louis XIV* on the grand staircase of Versailles in 1674. Below this painting is a vase, *Science*, attributed to M. L. E. Solon (1835–1913) and to its right a fan said to have been owned by Marie-Antoinette. The inlaid rosewood table, decorated with a globe surrounded by stars, was attributed to Charles Goutzwiller (1810–1900).

122

122. Stairs, William H. Vanderbilt house. This photograph of the main stairway was taken from the first landing. Like most of the spaces on the first level, this section of the stairs was overdecorated. The newel post with its bronze figure of the slave girl illuminating the way, designed by Tony Noël (1845–1909) and cast by Ferdinand Barbedienne in 1881, cost a reported $2000. English oak was used for the stairs, paneling and soffit. Between the hand-carved posts of the railing were open panels of bronze strapwork. Red plush cushioned the top of the railing. Amid such surroundings, the picture at the bottom, *Dance in a Roman Tavern* by Francesco Vinea (1846–1902), depicting dancers and barnyard fowl in a crude interior, was a curious choice. On this landing was one of John La Farge's most important stained-glass windows, which allegorized in three lights the ships and railroads that had secured the Vanderbilt fortune. A floor above was an equally large window, *Hospitality.*

Solidly constructed, the Vanderbilt house rested on bedrock and was supported by exterior walls that varied in thickness from 36″ to 8″ and by solid-brick interior walls that were a minimum of 16″ thick. Instead of conventional wood laths, these interior walls were faced with iron wire to which the finished surface was applied or attached. To support such a heavy structure, the designers called for iron columns and beams with brick-arch construction between the beams to insure against fire.

123. Mr. Vanderbilt's bedroom, William H. Vanderbilt house. The Vanderbilts found repose in the private quarters of the family on the second floor, where he enjoyed his library rocking chair and she could relax in her boudoir. His bedroom was located in the southeast corner of the house near the library. Its walls were decorated with golden-yellow tapestry paper and pale blue draperies, and its ceiling

was stenciled with tiny cupids. This room was connected to a dressing room paneled 8′ high with glass tiles and containing a tub and basin of silver set in frames of mahogany.

124. Mrs. Vanderbilt's boudoir, William H. Vanderbilt house. Searching through the rooms of the Vanderbilt house for signs of human habitation, a writer for the *Times* wondered if clothes were ever mended there or whether in the midst of such splendors William H. ever needed a button sewn on. In effect, this writer was asking if mere mortals could function in such a rarified domestic environment. In contrast to the main-floor rooms, the boudoir contained clues to the private life of Mrs. Vanderbilt. On the shelf under the foreground table is her sewing basket and above are recently examined books, one of them containing a slip of paper to mark the place. On the rear table is an envelope that has escaped the tidying process that inevitably preceded these photographs.

Compared to the other rooms of the house we have seen, this one was more inviting and also more flexibly arranged. Despite its high ceiling and relatively tall overmantel, its center of gravity was also lower. The boudoir's most distinctive fixed feature was the mantel hood, carved below and painted above. The frieze, probably designed by Christian Herter (1840–1883) of the New York firm of Herter Brothers, described a *Triumph of Cupid* in which a maiden, a soldier and even a monk bring gifts. Another mural, depicting cupids singing and dancing, can be seen in the oblong panel of the ceiling. Against the far wall was a cabinet of ebony inlaid with ivory. Among the choice smaller objects, concentrated above the fire opening, was a mantel clock and flanking vases attributed to M. L. E. Solon. The portieres were made of light blue silk; the carpet was predominantly of gold and blue.

125

125. Hall, George F. Baker house, 258 Madison Avenue, New York, New York; architect unknown, 1880–81; demolished.
Today corporations rather than powerful individuals influence the course of American capitalism. This was less true at the end of the nineteenth century and during the years before World War I. George F. Baker (March 27, 1840–May 2, 1931), the "Dean of Wall Street," "the last of the old guard in the world of American finance" and, at his death, probably the wealthiest person in the United States after Henry Ford and J. D. Rockefeller, once admitted his enormous power before a Congressional committee investigating the Money Trust in 1913. The financial power of the country, he testified, was under his control and that of J. P. Morgan and associates to such a degree that "no great enterprise could be carried forward successfully unless it had their confidence."

From his base at the First National Bank of New York, he became, at the height of his power, director of 43 corporations and companies. Estimates of his fortune ranged up to half a billion dollars. Yet his home on Madison Avenue, where he lived with his wife, Florence Tucker Baker, whom he married on November 18, 1869, his son and two daughters, was surprisingly modest. On the other hand, the Bakers also owned houses at Tuxedo Park and on Long Island. In 1917 he moved uptown to the corner of East 93rd Street and Park Avenue, and in his later years he spent more time at his retreat on Jekyll Island, Georgia.

The Bakers moved to this address in 1881. Their hall, one of the least cluttered of this series, was, like his reported public style, functional and unpretentious, but not ordinary. The walls of the hall were divided into two parts, a high wainscoting of American oak below and a brocade of jute above. The landing was faced by a screen of spindles and leaded crown glass. Through the door at the right can be seen the mantel of the music room, which connected the dining room at the rear of the house with the drawing room in front.

126. Dining room, George F. Baker house. Sheldon responded positively to the modesty of the Baker dining room:

> No guest can sit at its generous board unmoved by the pleasantness of the deep and significant message of the artistic surroundings. A wainscot of antique oak, about ten feet high, extends around the room, terminating at the top in a series of pretty cabinets of the same material, behind whose glass doors appear porcelains and earthenware of excellent pedigree and color. . . . The ceiling, of paneled antique oak, is connected with the walls by a deep and beautiful frieze of painted canvas, and it is difficult to say which elicits the more admiration, the unconventional interpretative design of leaf and fruit ornamentation, or the bold and decisive touches that have wrought the subdued beauty of tones. . . . The concord of the various decorations in these rooms does, indeed, constitute an exquisite harmony, but the dexterity of the painter's brush shines with peculiar effulgence.

127. Drawing room, 55th Street, New York, New York. This was the final plate of volume II of *Artistic Houses*. No additional information accompanied the photograph.

126

127

128

129

128. Dining room, Jacob Ruppert house, 1451 Fifth Avenue, New York, New York; William Schickel, architect, 1881–83; demolished. Jacob Ruppert (March 4, 1842–May 25, 1915) was one of the wealthier individuals featured in this publication. Upon his death he left an estate valued at $20 million in trust to his widow, the former Anna Gillig, whom he had married in 1864. Ruppert, a brewer, learned the trade from his father, who came to America from Bavaria in the early 1830s. With profits from the brewery, which he established in 1867 on Third Avenue, Jacob formed a successful real-estate company. A patron of the arts and especially of music, Ruppert owned the Central Opera House in New York. He also raised trotters on his estate near Poughkeepsie.

This house was large (50′ × 100′) and freestanding and cost $90,000. The dining room was richly paneled in antique oak by Schickel and Herter Brothers. Its ceiling was finished in elaborately paneled antique oak and supported at the edges by broad wall brackets. At left, the fireplace was recessed within a broad opening and flanked by built-in seats. The small musicians' gallery above, with a railing carved from solid oak, was supported at either side by atlantes in the form of satyrs. The walls were covered by a heavily embossed leather paper with designs of grapes and leaves accented in gold against a dull-red background. Along the top of the wall was a frieze showing a Bacchanalian procession of children, leopards and other creatures. This room had a heavy, intricate, Germanic character reflecting Ruppert's background and social style.

129. Drawing room, Jacob Ruppert house. In its light tones and relatively subdued decoration, this room contrasted sharply with the character of the dining room and hallway. Like the dining room, it featured a frieze, depicting children involved in various sports, painted on canvas with a gold background. The room had a modified Louis XVI treatment with woodwork that was painted ivory with trim accented in gold leaf. A soft red amplified the papier-mâché ornaments of the wainscoting. Divided into square patterns with intricately painted fresco work, the ceiling received the most elaborate handling. The

furniture, graceful and delicate in form, was made of enameled wood. The numerous lights of the bronze chandelier would be reflected by the pier mirror above the mantel.

---

130. Hall, O. D. Munn house, Mountain Avenue, Llewellyn Park, West Orange, New Jersey; Alexander Jackson Davis, architect, 1858–61; standing but altered. This residence was one of three owned by Orson Desaix Munn (June 11, 1824–February 28, 1907) and his wife, the former Julia Augusta Allen (d. October 26, 1894), whom he married in 1849. Their Manhattan residence was located on East 22nd Street, and their large farm was not far from this Llewellyn Park retreat. This was one of a number of fine houses built in Llewellyn Park, a private community for which the celebrated Romantic architect A. J. Davis laid out the picturesque grounds and designed the impressive gatehouse. Many of the residences survive today in what continues as a well-maintained, exclusive residential community. Called the "Terraces" today, the house was designed for stone by Davis but executed in wood. The Munns purchased the Italianate villa in 1869 and commissioned Lamb and Rich to enlarge it in the early 1880s.

At the age of 22 Munn, with Alfred E. Beach, purchased the *Scientific American*. In addition to publishing this increasingly influential journal, Munn and Company also worked with inventors to obtain patents and to market new inventions.

The walls and ceiling of this hall were paneled in quarter-sawn oak that had been specially treated to give an aged appearance. Above the wainscoting and carved-oak furniture the walls were covered in leather in intricate patterns. This hall is an eclectic space, combining medieval features, such as the wrought-iron lanterns, with Moorish features, such as the stairway screens with their carved diagonal baluster work. The inner hallway was illuminated by stained-glass windows, making it appear somewhat dark, probably to create a contrast with the spacious, airy living hall, which took advantage of the fine vistas Llewellyn Park afforded.

131. Drawing room, William A. Hammond house, 27 West 54th Street, New York, New York; architect unknown, 1873; demolished. *The Art Amateur,* commenting on Dr. Hammond's house in June 1879, concluded that "the doctor uses his own ideas and selects his designs, and himself gives instructions to the artisans he employs." Sheldon also saw a connection between Hammond's strong personality and cultural breadth and the individualistic manner in which the house was decorated.

Hammond (August 28, 1828–January 5, 1900) was a remarkable person. At 21 he graduated from the medical school of the City University of New York. During the Civil War he served as Surgeon General of the Army but was court-martialed and dismissed from service for criticizing superiors, an act nullified by Congress in 1878. He held several professorships at medical schools in New York City, founded or edited five journals of medicine, authored 280 articles, published 30 books and wrote seven novels. His library of more than 1300 items contained early editions of Ariosto, Boccaccio and Dante. He married Helen Nisbet on July 4, 1849 and Esther Chapin in 1886. Two of his five children from the first marriage survived him, and one of them, Clara, became the Marchioness of Lanza.

Mrs. M. E. W. Sherwood (*Harper's New Monthly Magazine,* October 1882) regarded these rooms as possibly the first "artistic interiors in New York." In retrospect, they are good examples of the personalized interiors that appeared between the proper settings of the pre-Centennial period and the self-consciously refined rooms of the later 1880s. In reflecting the American discovery of both Western and Eastern styles and objects, they verify that this new internationalization of taste welcomed simultaneously the Gobelin tapestry, the Caterina Cornaro chests, the Japanese cups and the Spanish faience.

Hammond hired Engel and Reynolds to paint the Celtic cross pattern of turquoise blue on the ceiling of the drawing room and to reproduce on the frieze scenes from the Bayeux Tapestry. The walls were covered with raw silk; below the wainscoting was satinwood inlaid with ebony. Most of the furniture was also of ebony. Unfortunately, the wainscoting was obscured by cabinets and tables, and the walls were weighted with Persian, Moorish, Egyptian, Chinese and Japanese plaques. In the center of the room was a small table on which was a cloisonné chessboard, and directly behind it in the corner stood a miniature version of the Medici *Venus.* Natural light for this dark room came from stained-glass windows that portrayed two Saxon princesses. To the next generation, this unabashedly worldwide eclecticism looked naive; to Mrs. Sherwood, it represented a learned and courageous step "which will be difficult for artists to surpass for some time to come."

132. Japanese bedroom, William A. Hammond house. Clay Lancaster (*The Japanese Influence in America*) is probably correct in claiming that this bedroom, redone somewhat inconsistently to look Japanese, was not original with the house. Nevertheless, it was one of the earliest examples of Japanese influence in American interior design. *The Art Amateur* (June 1879) described it enthusiastically:

> The ceiling is frescoed in bold work of black and gold of unsymmetrical design. The walls are paneled with Japanese painted stuffs framed in gilt bamboo, and the frieze is a continuous band of brilliant figures on paper crêpe. Over the doors, and in the spaces where the tint of wall is flat, fans of brilliant colors have been tastefully displayed. A table in blue and white, and red lacquer saucers inserted in the dull black wood of the furniture, help the effect; while on the mantel, formed like a lacquer cabinet, is a clock made out of an exquisite Chinese lantern in blue and white.

Though Japanese in materials, the room was not Japanese in feeling or function. Did the Japanese shade their gas jets with parasols? Hammond has collected and exhibited Oriental creativity but has disregarded, probably intentionally, the restraint and coolness of the typical Japanese room.

131

133. Bedroom, William A. Hammond house. The pictorial friezes, ceilings of flat surfaces and relatively quiet wall decoration, particularly in the Japanese bedroom and this room in which Mr. Hammond slept, implied that the rooms of this house were bounded by thin panels incapable of serious support. In this bedroom the responsibility for structural reassurance has been transferred from the walls and ceiling, where it was often expressed in the early 1880s, to the fireplace of oak articulated with Gothic ribbing. Similar ribbing appeared on the dressing table at the far left, behind the leather dressing screen, and in an 8' × 10' cabinet, also of oak, directly opposite. Near the corner was a Spanish washstand, no longer used, with a storage cabinet for shaving equipment above. The debate over the advisability of movable washstands or fixed stands with running water was still alive around 1880, but here running water was probably available nearby.

Compared to the fireplace and solid pieces of furniture, the finely detailed brass bed looked delicate, if not flimsy, and insufficient for the task of supporting the 6'2", 250-pound Hammond. The fabrics of the framework of the canopy have been removed; perhaps they had never been fitted. The right side of this photograph is unusually bare, even for a bedroom. Several small fine rugs have been placed over the plain carpet. The fire opening had a brass-turned fender flanked by two Chinese porcelain vases. Divided into two parts, the wall was composed of heavy composition paper stamped and painted in India-red impasto below and a dark band of raw silk above. Scenes from medieval life were displayed in the frieze. The simple ceiling in black, crimson and gold may have been unfinished when the photograph was taken.

---

134. Hall, Herman O. Armour house, Fifth Avenue and East 67th Street, New York, New York; Lamb and Rich, architects, 1882–83; demolished. Born near Syracuse, N.Y., Armour (March 2,

1837–September 7, 1901) initially settled in Chicago, where he worked as a grain-commission merchant. In 1865 he went to New York City as the Eastern representative of Plankington, Armour and Co. In 1870 he became a partner in Armour and Co. and was its vice president at the time of his death. On February 4, 1887, at the age of 50, he surprised his friends by quietly marrying Jane P. Livingston of New York.

The hallway in this house was one of the more peculiar illustrated in *Artistic Houses.* Despite the fine materials—white mahogany used in the front door (seen at the far left), the wainscoting, the band that continues the horizontal lines of the balcony, and the strongly beamed ceiling, and despite the skilled workmanship evident in the woodwork of the balcony, the stained glass above and the Lincrusta Walton wall surfaces—the hallway looked pinched, dark and uninviting. (Lincrusta was an imitation leather derived from solidified linseed oil, introduced by Frederick Walton in 1877.) The two chairs and the plant, obviously included to make this entranceway more attractive, only obstruct a route intended primarily for traffic. The fireplace was probably never used, but its polished reliefs were seen as soon as a visitor crossed the threshold. The stained-glass window illuminated the toilet under the balcony. The focal point of the hall was the mezzanine balcony, which was reached after a series of decisive turns. From it one could view the front door.

135. Dining room, Herman O. Armour house. The first floor must have been at least 18' high. In the dining room this height enabled Lamb and Rich to insert stained-glass windows between the lower section marked by the lintels of the doors, windows and the cornice of the sideboard and, above, by the paneled frieze of Santo Domingo mahogany. In contrast to the simplicity and calm of the extension table and its matching set of chairs, the semioctagonal section is confused by disparate forms and levels.

133

136

137

138

136. Hall, William S. Hoyt house, Pelham, New York; William S. Hoyt, architect, date unknown; demolished. Many of the New York families of wealth and prestige maintained a primary residence in the city and a summer or weekend retreat at the shore or in the mountains. Usually, the city house was a self-contained structure finished in stone, brick and sometimes marble, while the resort or country house, of wood or rough stone and wood, tended to engage its environment informally. Despite his Wall Street business address, Hoyt (January 1, 1847–April 27, 1905) lived in this rural area considerably north of Manhattan. His wife was the former Janet Ralston Chase, daughter of former Chief Justice of the Supreme Court Salmon P. Chase. Not trained as an architect, Hoyt claimed to have designed and built the house using stones from the area for the first story and shingles for the walls above.

The interior reflected the vernacular quality of the exterior. The hall of the Hoyt house was expansive, particularly in the 50′ × 15′ section to the left of the fireplace. Instead of the Japanese vases and tufted ottomans we might expect in the city, this space was decorated with products of the wilderness and medieval weapons. Despite the refinement momentarily asserted by the foreground table and tea set, the character of this part of the hall was shaped by the simple, strong and engulfing fireplace and its inviting but hard seats. The weapon collection was assembled during European trips.

137. Hall, Swits Condé house, West Fifth Street and Seneca Street, Oswego, New York; Oscar S. Teale, architect, 1882–83; demolished 1912. Condé (April 24, 1844–January 21, 1902) and his wife, the former Apama Tucker (June 1845–October 20, 1911), invited 300 guests to celebrate the opening of this $150,000 house, "Mon Repos," on June 7, 1883. The presence of the Utica Symphony Orchestra at this event reminds us of the wealth and influence of this upstate textile baron.

Edouard Leissner of New York City was responsible for the interior decoration. The woodwork was Santo Domingo mahogany, the ceiling was composed of flocked panels held by mahogany beams and the chimney hood and chandelier were made of antique brass. The outer

panels of the overmantel symbolized Night and Morning, a clock standing between them. To the right of the fireplace was a marble-top table on which we here see a cane, a karakul hat and a card plate. To the left were Chinese porcelains and a corner bench covered with Spanish leather. The relieving vistas to the library at the left, the stairway in the center and the rear hall to the right compensate somewhat for the narrowness of this entrance hall.

In the last years of his life Condé was embroiled in numerous legal actions. In 1898 he tried to have the Navy court-martial an ensign who was seeing one of his daughters. He was fined six cents in 1900 for slandering his butler and a year later he brought suit against his son-in-law to recover $5700.

138. Hall, John L. Gardner house, 152 Beacon Street, Boston, Massachusetts; architect unknown, 1860–62; demolished. David Stewart purchased this Back Bay property for his daughter Isabella (April 14, 1840–July 17, 1924) in 1859, a year before her marriage to John L. Gardner (November 26, 1837–December 10, 1898). Because their house at 152 Beacon Street had become too small, in 1880 the Gardners commissioned John Sturgis to combine it with the single residence next door, No. 150. Though the house is no longer standing, a plaque on the site explains that Mrs. Gardner requested that the number never be used again; currently there is no 152 Beacon Street.

This photograph of the hall of the "Queen of the Back Bay" was taken when her interest in European art was growing but before she had developed, with the assistance of connoisseur Bernard Berenson, her remarkable collection of old masters now in the Gardner Museum in the Fenway. Despite the Renaissance details of the mantelpiece and the paired cathedral candlesticks and cloisonné ducks to the sides and below the inlaid painting, this hall was unusually puritanical and clean for the early 1880s. Its energy came primarily from the lathework of the balusters; its focal points, the painting and the French regimental banner, were limited in number and controlled in expression. To a greater extent than in most of these halls, the light coming from behind the balcony conservatory (John's hobby was horticulture) and the plants themselves shaped the character of this space.

139

139. Hall, George Kemp house, 720 Fifth Avenue, New York, New York; architect unknown, 1879–80; demolished. Described by the *Times* as "one of the most widely-known men in business and social circles in this city," Kemp (1826–November 23, 1893) was not active politically and, unlike many of the millionaires whose houses were featured in *Artistic Houses*, was neither a serious art collector nor a philanthropist. His wealth came through his firm of Lanman and Kemp, one of the largest dealers in drugs and chemicals in the country. His wife, the former Juliet Augusta Tryon, died four years after he did.

This broad corridor hall connected the front door with the main stairs, seen beyond the wooden archway. At the right were the doorways to the main rooms of this floor. Characterized by simplicity and elegance, the space held few pieces of furniture or artistic treasures. On the left wall was a Persian rug from the early eighteenth century and on the floor a wide Oriental runner. Neither the built-in double seat at the base of the dividing screen nor the inlaid table that held the card plate and bust was conspicuous, but they were finely crafted. Slightly offbeat though modest, this passageway probably did not prepare visitors for Tiffany's spirited handling of the adjacent salon.

140. Salon, George Kemp house. In the early 1880s, numerous comments were published about the Kemp house, and particularly about this salon. The most exhaustive description was written for *Harper's New Monthly Magazine* by A. F. Oakey in April 1882:

In this room Messrs. Louis C. Tiffany and Co. have made an elaborate attempt to assimilate the moresque idea to modern requirements, and no expense has been spared to attain the most perfect result in every respect, even the grand piano being made to assume a moresque garb . . . . The fireplace is lined with old Persian tile in blue, blue-greens, and dark purplish-red on a white ground, making a valuable sensation in the surrounding opal tile, of which the hearth is also composed. . . . The dado and the floor would not be described by the word "parquet," being much more than this term implies—

an intricate system of inlaid-work of all manner of native and foreign woods, highly polished, and forming gradations and contrasts of browns, buffs, yellows, reds, and black. All the wood-work above is executed in white holly, the panels in which are filled with various incrustations of stucco in delicate moresque patterns re-enforced with pale tints, gold, and silver. Such portions of the walls as are not otherwise occupied are covered with stamped cut and uncut velvet on a satin ground, in tones of pale buff, red, and blue, receiving the light in various ways, so that no two portions appear the same from any stand-point.

The frieze between the bands of silver and red mosaic and moulded lines of turquoise blue is brought out in bold disks at varying intervals on a buff ground, filled in with an infinite detail of silver, gold, pale purple, and white. The cornice is formed by a procession of carved silver corbels appearing against a brilliant chrome background, and on these rests the ceiling of galvano-frosted iron overlaid with geometric tracery in relief, forming hundreds of small panels of various forms, in which enrichments of gold and silver appear against the frosted background.

The panels of the bevelled mirrors above the mantel serve to reflect the white enamelled shafts in the large bay-window opposite, and the mother-of-pearl effects of the double stained glass windows draped in rich folds of olive and gold embroideries.

The furniture is all of white holly, carved, turned, and inlaid with mother-of-pearl, making rich effects with the olive plush coverings embroidered in cream and gold-colored floss.

The room is lighted by five lanterns, not including the three small ones over the mantel, which, though dimly lighted, are only intended to complete the decoration in brass and turquoise. . . .

The only fault we think it fair to find is one for which the decorator is only indirectly responsible: the room is too small for such a treatment, and refuses in other ways to lend itself absolutely to the scheme. However, the result is a fair example of consistency throughout, as far as it is possible to be consistent in transplanting an exotic to a Northern clime, and it is to this faithful preservation of style, as well as the delicate distribution of color, that the apartment owes most of its charm.

141

142

141. Dining room, George Kemp house. According to biographer Robert Koch, this was the first house decorated extensively by L. C. Tiffany & Associated Artists. Kemp had been a friend of Tiffany's father. The grand sideboard of the room was carved oak, the same material used for the 10'-high paneling. Above the wainscoting was a scene painted on gilded canvas of fruits, plants and vegetables, including Tiffany's beloved pumpkins. Above two of the doors were transoms of opalescent leaded glass, similar to the frieze in theme and continuing the decoration in this register. One panel represented gourds, the other featured eggplants. In these transoms the leading was also employed decoratively as the stems of plants.

Tiffany may have utilized the glass left over from the Kemp commission in two windows for his own apartment on East 26th Street in New York. Over the four windows of the dining room were double transoms that filtered light through thin colored glass. In order to soften the relatively hard surfaces, he chose heavy hangings and portieres of embroidered plush.

As was true of his later dining room for Dr. William T. Lusk (no. 18), this one contained a simple table surrounded by studded leather chairs. Reflecting the design tendencies of the firm, but atypical of the majority of decorators in the early 1880s, these two dining rooms were defined by walls subdivided nervously into right-angled sections.

142. Library, George Kemp house. Although there are several Tiffany effects in this library, the room looked less fashionable and more traditional than either the salon or the dining room. The decorator's hand is visible in the interlaced tracery of the transoms above the two front windows and in the iridescent shells of the coved ceiling. But the sturdy upholstered chairs, the solid bookcase and the ponderous entablature of the mantelpiece produced, comparatively, a heavier and slower-paced interior. Colors also contributed to this room's restraint—the mahogany of the table, bookcase and entablature, the bronze plush of the hangings and the chairs and the relatively dark walls of silk topped by an even darker border of embroidered plush. Neither the bric-a-brac in the library nor the few paintings were exceptional.

143. Library, Franklin H. Tinker house, 39 Knollwood Road, Short Hills, New Jersey; architect unknown, 1878; standing. We know little about the Tinker family. Franklin H. Tinker (1853/54–May 14, 1890), the head of one of the largest trade-journal publishers in the country, Root and Tinker, was also the editor of *The American Exporter* from 1883 until 1887. He died at 36 of spinal meningitis, leaving a wife and one child. When *Artistic Houses* was published, there were approximately 35 houses in the picturesque suburb of Short Hills, a thoroughly residential planned community near Millburn, New Jersey, founded in the mid-1870s by Stewart Hartshorn. Initially, there were not even stores or a bar to disrupt this suburban fairy tale.

The original owners of "Sunnyside" were the Russells, who had moved into "Redstone" (no. 74) by Lamb and Rich in April 1882. In the same year Lamb and Rich remodeled and expanded this library to create more space for Tinker's impressive collection of rare and autographed books. (He owned signed copies of works by Hugo, Tennyson, Ruskin, Bancroft, Whittier, Holmes, Aldrich and Strickland.) For the new walls the firm used bronzed Lincrusta (see no. 134). Although these walls and ceiling were enlivened by an allover pattern, they looked qualitatively different from the allover patterning created by L. C. Tiffany & Associated Artists. Lacking the disciplined fragmentation and abstraction of Tiffany's work, it was, for all of its heavy energy, an inventive, vernacular summary rather than a preview of interiors to come. Mahogany was chosen for all woodwork and furniture. Above the low cases of the alcove were three stained-glass windows that symbolized, from left to right, art, science and history. The fabric casually draped over the plate on the left wall partially obscures the picture wires; below it, the large bow or butterfly of white lace is used as an antimacassar.

143

NICHOLAS L. ANDERSON HOUSE

Designed by Henry Hobson Richardson for its site on the southeast corner of K and 16th Streets, N.W., Washington, the house of General Anderson was singled out for commentary and illustration by critics of the period. Even Matthew Arnold, the English critic and poet, wanted to see the house on his trip through the United States in 1883–84. E. W. Lightner discussed it in *Harper's New Monthly Magazine* (March 1885) and Mariana Van Rensselaer in *The Century* (March 1886). Among the reasons for focusing on this house was the fact that it had been designed by Richardson, the architect considered not only by Americans, but also by Europeans, as the foremost architect of the country in the first half of the 1880s. Anderson may have chosen Richardson because they had been classmates at Harvard in the late 1850s. During the planning and building process, Anderson complained frequently about Richardson's habits and demands. In a letter to his son Larz (January 1883) he wrote:

> Mr. Richardson is with us, but as his valet broke his arm and did not accompany him, our Edward has had to act as nurse. He bullies and nags everybody; makes great demands upon our time and service; must ride, even if he has to go but a square; gets up at noon; and has to have his meals sent to his room. He is a mournful object for size, but he never ought to stay in a private house because he requires so much attention.

On the other hand, Richardson had reason to be unhappy with Anderson. Evidently, the General was insensitive to his architect's deteriorating health (he died of nephritis in 1886). Furthermore, Anderson, concerned about the threefold increase from the original estimate of $33,000, complained to his friends that the cause was Richardson's propensity to change his mind.

The house also attracted critics because it was erected in Washington, a city not previously noted for outstanding domestic architecture. According to the Washington *Evening Star* (August 18, 1883), quoted in the magnificently researched and clearly written *Sixteenth Street Architecture* (vol. 1) by Sue Kohler and Jeffrey Carson, the Anderson house "has drawn more general attention to it than is usually the case in this city, where handsome, costly residences are springing up on all sides . . . ."

Because Richardson's design was not picturesque, inviting or gracious, and because Washingtonians were unaccustomed to houses expressed with such power and decisiveness, not all local reactions were positive. Defending it in another letter to Larz, Anderson wrote: "It is so essentially different from any other that the public taste must be educated up to it, and it requires a severe and well educated taste to see in its grand lines and simple beauty all that we claim for it." Although its ground dimensions were not exceptionally large (approximately 57′ on K Street and 69′ on 16th Street), the building looked massive because of its battered foundation, its relatively plain red-brick walls and its vast roof that protected, but also appeared to exert enormous pressure on, the interior. Some thought the restrained ornament made

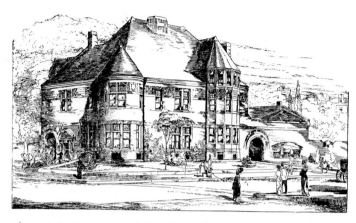

the exterior too reserved. Van Rensselaer essentially seconded local reservations: "And Mr. Richardson has built a great brick house which is impressive because very simple and very strong, but looks a trifle eccentric—perhaps because the latter good quality is somewhat over-emphasized. Mr. Richardson's manner is, in truth, almost too monumental to lend itself gracefully to domestic work." Today, critics tend to agree with a statement Van Rensselaer made at a later date. In her 1888 monograph on Richardson she wrote: "Yet in spite of these faults the building is a fine one—grand in mass, harmonious in proportions, coherent in design, and dignified in its severe simplicity."

Finally, the house attracted attention because of its owners and their friends. The grandson of millionaire Nicholas Longworth of Cincinnati, Anderson (April 22, 1838–September 18, 1892) went to Harvard, studied at Heidelberg University and returned to fight for the Union in 1861. At 26 he became the Union's youngest major general. In 1865 he married Elizabeth Kilgour, of a well-established Cincinnati family; Larz was born in 1866 and their daughter Elsie in 1874. Anderson studied law and moved to Washington in 1881. In the nation's capital he became reacquainted with Henry Adams, whom he had met in Magdeburg in 1858. The Adamses and John Hay and his wife commissioned Richardson in 1884 to design adjoining town houses for them at the corner of 16th Street and H Street, N.W., a story systematically told by Marc Friedlaender in the *Journal of Architectural Historians* (October 1970).

Commissioned and designed in 1881, the Anderson house was completed two years later. The Andersons moved in during the middle of October 1883 and the following month entertained Marian and Henry Adams—the first of many bright occasions Washington society enjoyed in the house. Mrs. Anderson resided there until her death in 1917 at the age of 75. Sold by her children the following year, the house was razed in 1925 to clear space for the Carlton Hotel.

---

144. Hall, Nicholas L. Anderson house, 16th Street and K Street, N.W., Washington, D.C.; Henry H. Richardson, architect, 1881–83; demolished 1925. When he described this house as "easily the most interesting private residence in the capital of the nation," Sheldon probably was thinking of its interior. From the porte-cochere or the modest main door, one entered a rectangular vestibule, paneled in oak with a tiled floor, that led to the main hall. Approximately 25′ long and 19′ from fireplace to stairway, the hall was also finished in oak. Some of the artistic highlights of this space were concentrated in the stairwell: the hand-turned balusters, the fine Egyptian screen and four stained-glass windows designed by Treadwell of Boston. Although competently handled, the remaining woodwork, including the ceiling beams and paneling, was less impressive. Opposite the windows was the fireplace with a mantel of yellow Italian marble. The first four steps of the main stairway, to the left of the clock, led to the door of the study. The door to the rear hall was concealed in the paneling at the right of the clock, and in the right-hand corner was the door to the dining room.

The plan of the first floor was excellent. The hall was impressive, implying generous-sized rooms beyond, and provided efficient access to adjacent spaces without permitting the doorways to weaken its unity or alter its character. For highlights, the Andersons depended on

plants, fans and a parasol carefully placed to insure asymmetrical balance.

145. Dining room, Nicholas L. Anderson house. In this photograph the Anderson dining room appears to be one of the few illustrated in *Artistic Houses* in which space dominated the materials within it, although, with the table fully extended and all of its chairs in place, we might conclude otherwise. The owners did not add more furniture than necessary, tried to keep the lower paneling visible and concentrated bric-a-brac in disadvantaged places, for example, in front of the two stained-glass windows by John La Farge and below the inlaid portrait of Anderson's father attributed to Gilbert Stuart (1755–1828). Similarly, the vases and pots were imprisoned rather than presented in the unusual recessed shelf of the mantel. On the other hand, this enabled the Andersons to show the thickness of their slab of Siena marble. Another reason the space seemed uncluttered was the size of the room, approximately 22′ square. Furthermore, the interior seemed to expand toward the concave wall of light. From the built-in seat under these six windows one could look sharply left to see the White House three blocks away. The room was also impressive because its wood surfaces were simple but not dull, for they were polished Santo Domingo mahogany. In summary, this was a dining room that was large, strong, warm, bright and uncrowded.

146

146. Study, Nicholas L. Anderson house. The room behind the fireplace in the hall was identified on the plan as a "library," and this one off the main stairway as a "study." The first room was a showcase library that also served as a reception room and possibly as an after-dinner smoking room for the men; the latter was a working library, the General's den. The room was about 17' deep and 16' wide with a bay (7' × 10') at the right overlooking the stable, servant's room and clothes yard. Beside the bay was a small lavatory. The color scheme was rather dark, some of the woodwork an olive green, and the Japanese paper of the upper walls and ceiling red and gold. With the exception of the mantel area, the study was an underdecorated interior in which shades on rollers replaced the usual curtains or drapes. However, most of the objects on the shelves were not works of art but photographs, keepsakes or lighting devices. The sword hanging on the overmantel was probably Anderson's own from the Civil War. The wicker and side chair, like the two matching window seats, were comfortable and functional. On the table are several books, an album, a tea service and a student lamp that could be raised or lowered.

---

147. Hall, Walter Hunnewell house, 261 Commonwealth Avenue, Boston, Massachusetts; Shaw and Shaw, architects, 1880–82; standing. The process of filling in the Back Bay area of the Charles River with gravel and dirt from pits at Needham, Massachusetts, began in 1857 and continued until the eve of the First World War. As the filling process moved westward, fine residences sprang up. Today this district and, particularly, Commonwealth Avenue offer in quantity and quality a collection of late nineteenth-century urban houses unmatched by other cities of the Northeast.

Designed in the "Academic Brick Style," to quote Bainbridge Bunting, this row house, sparely ornamented with light stone facing below and brick on the upper walls, was finished between 1880 and 1882. Slightly left of center and running through four floors was a prominent bay that was the principal feature of the facade. The hall, approximately 36' long and paralleling Commonwealth Avenue, occupied the entire front of the house. Visitors walked from the vestibule, seen in the center of this photograph, under the stairway and were immediately blocked by the landing and balustrade. Shunted to the

right, they discovered the spacious and empty main hall ahead of them. Though minimally furnished, this space was handled with aristocratic simplicity. The figures and designs of the stained-glass windows did not curtail the natural lighting needed for such a deep space. This grand space became the prologue to the equally grand stairway, which made ritualistic changes of direction as it rose gradually to the next level.

This house was completed less than ten years after Walter Hunnewell (January 28, 1844–September 30, 1921) married Jane A. Peele (December 8, 1848–September 15, 1893), during the years they were raising their six children. Unfortunately, there is little evidence to suggest that children affected the design and planning of these houses, so hospitable to art and so sensitive to society approval.

Unlike many of his friends and many of the home owners included in *Artistic Houses*, Walter Hunnewell performed philanthropic acts and services that were not token, his primary concern being with the needy. Like his better-known brother Hollis Hunnewell (nos. 11 & 12), he was a wealthy banker and broker associated with H. H. Hunnewell and Sons.

148. Drawing room, Walter Hunnewell house. This drawing room also stretched across the front of the house, its bay and supporting Corinthian columns directly above those in the hall. The opening at the right led to a central corridor and the dining room opposite. If the main hall encouraged formal behavior, this room encouraged informal loitering. The Hunnewells chose unmatched chairs that were deeply tufted and inviting. Judging from its accessibility, good lighting, adequate space, pleasant atmosphere and books tossed randomly on the tables, this room was probably used by the family as its gathering place. Because it is so informal, open and comfortable in appearance, we may overlook the effort and expense behind some of the decoration and pieces. The ceiling, for example, was frescoed in gold, and the walls were covered with light red silk and old gold linen. On the Renaissance Revival mantel complex were glassed-in sections for choice porcelains and faience. Below, the fire opening was actually used. The dark cabinets to either side were atypically curtained. Note the combination of the wicker armchair and the highly ornate French dressing screen on the right.

147

148

149

150

151

149. **Picture gallery, John T. Martin house, 28 Pierrepont Street, Brooklyn, New York; architect unknown, ca. 1851; demolished ca. 1897–1901.** Sheldon wrote enthusiastically about Martin's well-known collection and gallery in Brooklyn Heights:

> Through the glass panels of two doors in the drawing-room the visitor receives the most pressing of invitations to enter, and, when the door has slidden aside to admit him, finds himself in a commodious and beautiful apartment, whose wainscoting of ebonized cherry is inlaid with mahogany and plain cherry and ornamented with gilt lines, and whose walls are hung with a dark, neutral-blue brocade of worsted and silk, shot through with a delicate thread of gold. One of Christopher Dresser's papers, of a pattern probably not to be seen elsewhere in this country, covers the cove of the ceiling to the borders of the immense, oblong, octo-paneled skylight, whose wood-work again is of ebonized cherry, smoother than polished ebony itself.

The prize work was *Going to Work, Dawn of Day* by Jean-François Millet, seen directly behind the sofa at the near left. Sheldon was also pleased to see *La Charrette* by Corot and two paintings by Narcisse-Virgile Diaz because they proved that American collectors were beginning to discover the Barbizon school of French painting.

Despite these recent purchases, most of the 80 paintings in the Martin house either recounted history or doted on life's messages. Immediately above the Millet was *A Charge of Dragoons at Gravelotte*, which Alphonse de Neuville painted to order in 1879. Directly above the folio cabinet was a painting that illustrated the virtues of life, *Reapers' Rest* (1873) by Jules Breton. Above and to the right of this painting was another moral poem, *The Spirit Hand* by Gabriel Max (1840–1915), which the Martins ordered in 1879.

150. **Picture gallery, John T. Martin house.** Martin (October 2, 1816–April 10, 1897) had made his fortune from the clothing contract he had with the Union Army and from his even more lucrative banking and real-estate ventures after the Civil War. He lived in a Greek Revival house on Pierrepont Street with his wife, the former Priscilla Spence, until 1895, when they moved to 20 West 57th Street in Manhattan. The

major pieces of this collection were purchased after the Centennial in Philadelphia and the gallery, built as an addition on the east, was probably constructed in the last half of the 1870s. Comfortably furnished, it looked more like a living room than most private New York galleries of the day, but it was also functional with its drawers and cabinets and with its gas jets and raised skylight to provide illumination.

Despite his late interest in the Barbizon school and his acknowledgment of the Japanese influence after the Centennial (evident here in the prizewinning vase by Tiffany from the Parisian Exposition of 1878, seen between *A Charge* and *Reapers' Rest*), Martin's paintings were becoming old-fashioned in the 1880s. Auctioned on April 15 and 16, 1909 in New York, these canvases brought only $281,000. Although bidders competed for the Barbizon landscapes and peasant pictures, Martin's anecdotal and sentimental paintings had fallen from grace. The Millet went for $50,000 and the Corot for $30,000, but *A Charge* was sold for only $10,200, *Reapers' Rest* for $6000 and *The Spirit Hand* for $1600.

151. **Dining room, John T. Martin house.** Because of the limited floor area and high ceiling that marked this house as a product of the 1850s, this interior did not resemble the spacious, professionally designed dining environments popular in New York in these years among families of means. Its size, however, did not discourage the Martins from displaying numerous choice objects and china; nor did they stint on the quality of the materials. The chairs, based on a Louis XIII model as the table probably was as well, were made of carved mahogany, which was also used around the closed fireplace and for the buffet to the right. Stamped leather covered the walls and hand-painted canvas was used to finish the ceiling. The hangings were made of bronze plush. The unidentified scene above the mantel of two dogs contemplating a hanging fowl may have been a fragment from a tapestry.

152. Dining room, Joseph S. Decker house, 18 West 49th Street, New York, New York; architect unknown, 1881–82; demolished. At the age of 20 Decker (ca. 1836–January 28, 1911) began his career, probably with the help of his banker father, in the banking house of Turner Brothers in New York City. Eventually he formed his own firm, Decker, Howell and Company, which in the early 1880s helped the Northern Pacific Railroad secure a $40 million loan to complete its road to the West. Decker retired about 1901; his wife and only child died before he did.

Cottier and Company, New York decorators, was responsible for the expensive front parlor, but it is not known to whom the decoration of the dining room was entrusted. Falling between success and failure, the room looks like a representative outcome of abundant money in search of artistic and social approval, producing a strong interior dominated by the dark mahogany of the wainscoting, mantelpiece and ceiling beams. Despite a few unusual features, such as the mural of the coved frieze above the mantel, the leaded window and the birdcage in the corner, decorative risks did not dominate this interior. Though proper, the Decker dining room looks eclectic or somewhat hollow, as if its expression was superimposed rather than revealed.

---

153. Hall, Henry J. Willing house, 110 Rush Street, Chicago, Illinois; Palmer and Spinning, architects, 1880–81; demolished before 1909. After spending his working life in dry-goods businesses in Chicago, Henry Willing (July 10, 1836–September 29, 1903) retired in 1883 as a junior partner of Field, Leiter and Company (renamed Marshall Field & Co. in 1881). He retired early to spend more time with his wife Frances Skinner, whom he married in 1879, and his two children.

Willing took the responsibilities of wealth seriously. He worked hard to strengthen public institutions and support causes that he thought would improve the quality of life in Chicago—the Y.M.C.A., Chicago Home for Incurables, Newberry Library, The Art Institute of Chicago and Chicago Historical Society. Though deprived of much formal education, he was actively curious about the past. In this distinctive hall, he expressed his fascination for history earnestly though perhaps naïvely.

Frederick Almenralder (1832–?) of Wiesbaden and Chicago took 14 months to carve the mantelpiece. Inspired by illustrations by Gustave Doré (1832–1883), the nine scenes were (left to right): Rebecca, a corner statuette of Oliver Cromwell, Moses, Solomon, in the center Michelangelo's seated Moses, Abraham and Isaac, Daniel among the lions, a corner statuette of Richard Cœur-de-Lion, and Ruth gleaning. The frieze below these figures contained the coats of arms of leading nations: Germany, the United States and Great Britain in the middle. The portieres from India and rugs woven in Paris contributed color to the hall finished in white oak.

154. Library, Henry J. Willing house. The house contained some unusual copies of Western masterpieces. Resting on engaged Doric columns, the frieze that divided the library into two sections was a diminutive version in mahogany of the north frieze of the Parthenon. Another distinctive reproduction in the library was that of the Cumean Sibyl, the central figure carved on the mantelpiece in the second room. Carved in Iowa stone, the figure had been adapted from Michelangelo's painting in the Sistine Chapel. Above the mantel are more common reproductions. From the right, the first framed picture is a Raphael self-portrait and the fifth the *Four Apostles* by Albrecht Dürer. An enthusiastic innocence characterizes Willing's peculiar assemblage of great works.

The portieres that divided the rooms were reportedly from a private apartment of the Empress of China, and the table in the foreground, of cedar of Lebanon, was once owned by Maximilian of Mexico. For all of its ingenuous effects, this library looked surprisingly comfortable, its feeling of informality being conveyed through the tacked carpet, slanting stacks of books and modest furniture.

152

153

154

J. PIERPONT MORGAN HOUSE

When Morgan died on March 31, 1913, his worth was estimated to be more than $68 million. He had made his fortune by timely, forceful acts, among them the control he and his senior partner Anthony Drexel exerted over the federal securities market in the early 1870s, his effective reorganization of several railroads in the 1880s and his banking investments and the consolidation of major corporations (General Electric, American Telephone and Telegraph, International Harvester and U.S. Steel) in the 1890s and the early years of the twentieth century. Born on April 17, 1837, he began life with a solid silver spoon in his mouth. His father, Junius Spencer Morgan, was also a banker, based in London after 1854. J. P. went to a private school in Vevey, Switzerland, and later studied for two years at the University of Göttingen.

Although $68 million amounted to a personal treasury that could be equaled or surpassed by a number of his contemporaries, the power Morgan could exert could be matched only by a few. He was asked by President Grover Cleveland in 1895 to protect federal gold reserves from a run on their resources and in 1907 he was instrumental in setting the course to stabilize the stock market in a time of panic. As pervasive as his influence in national finance was his influence on the international art market. Under the heading "Art Dealers Alarmed," the *New York Times* reported the nervous reaction to his death in Rome: "J. Pierpont Morgan's death has caused something akin to consternation among art dealing circles in London, not so much because he himself was for so many years the greatest buyer, but because his example stirred the ambition of others, and the threat of his competition stimulated other wealthy collectors."

With his strong family credentials, Morgan did not have to scramble or act slyly in his business ventures; he was known in the world of finance as a trustworthy hard worker and hard driver. Furthermore, he did not manifest a nouveau-riche weakness for a trendy address or a fashionably designed street front. In fact, the Morgans were one of the rare New York families of means to move south rather than north in the early 1880s. Formerly at 6 East 40th Street, in 1880 they purchased a larger house, a brownstone at the northeast corner of Madison Avenue and East 36th Street, for $215,000. Built in 1853–56, the house was one of three brownstones erected by members of the copper firm of Phelps, Dodge and Company between East 36th and East 37th Streets. Morgan hired Christian Herter of the respected Herter Brothers company to make the necessary structural alterations and to redecorate the interior. Herter moved the principal entrance from Madison to East 36th Street and replaced the void with the great bay window of the drawing room, maintaining in the process the basic character of the original facades. The family moved in during the summer of 1882. In addition to this city house, the Morgans owned "Cragston," a 700-acre estate at Highland Falls on the west side of the Hudson River. Morgan's house at Prince's Gate, London, and "Dover House," a country retreat near the Thames outside of London, had formerly been owned by his father.

Of Morgan's two marriages, the first ended tragically and the second, apparently, faded into a relationship of accommodation. Amelia Sturges was not well when Morgan proposed and then insisted, despite

her deteriorating condition, that they marry. The wedding took place in 1861; a few months later she died of consumption. In 1865 he married Frances Louise Tracy, who, with her four children, survived him. Fanny did not share his addiction to art and traveled with him less frequently as their partnership aged. Although they did entertain, the Morgans did not try to compete with the Astors, Vanderbilts or Martins socially. Stories of the increasingly taciturn J. P. playing solitaire at his own parties contributed to his national reputation as a dark, brooding sphinx. Yet he was a dedicated Episcopalian who supported his church through gifts and even by participating in diocesan meetings. The *Times* classified him as a generous millionaire who had not hoarded his wealth but had distributed it "quietly and spontaneously."

At the time these photographs were taken, Morgan was not known for astute or bold art purchases. Granted, Earl Shinn included the Morgan paintings in *The Art Treasures of America* (1879–82), but he regarded the collection, rightly, as one of the minor ones of the country. Morgan owned about 35 paintings which included numerous subject categories from the leading national schools of Europe but also included American artists—Church, S. R. Gifford, Kensett, Vedder. Morgan did not begin to collect manuscripts until the late 1880s. From then on he spent more than $60 million acquiring whole art and manuscript collections to obtain choice pieces and paying high prices for the single works he wanted—for example, $500,000 for Raphael's *Madonna with Saints* of 1503–05 and an equal amount for a Gothic tapestry from Aygalades near Marseilles. Because Morgan had served as president of the board of the Metropolitan Museum from 1904 until 1913, New Yorkers expected him to will his collection to the museum; however, only 40 percent of his works were given, in part because a Morgan wing in the museum was never approved.

In 1906 McKim, Mead and White completed the Morgan Library, 29 East 36th Street, to house Morgan's remarkable collection of rare books, manuscripts and letters. In 1928 an annex to the library was erected on the site of this brownstone.

155, 156. Staircase, J. Pierpont Morgan house, 219 Madison Avenue, New York, New York; architect unknown, 1853–56; demolished 1927. The front doors of Circassian walnut on the East 36th Street side admitted visitors to a vestibule that had a mosaic floor and ceiling. On one side was a coat room; a dressing room was on the other. Two stained-glass sliding doors, visible in number 155, separated the vestibule from the stair hall, the floor of which was also finished in mosaic. Three stories above was a stained-glass dome designed in the studio of John La Farge.

On the right, a short stairway led to the main level of the house. On this level and directly opposite the front door was a recessed mantelpiece of oak that held *The Bird Song* by the German painter Wilhelm von Kaulbach (1805–1874). The top of this painting can be seen under the second-story railing in number 156. Immediately to the left of the fireplace was a door to the reception room and farther to the left was the entrance to the drawing room along Madison Avenue. To the right were the morning room of Mrs. Morgan and the library.

American white oak was used for the staircase. While its wainscoting was simple and beat a steady rhythm for ascent and descent, the panels under the railing were meticulously packed with spindles. In the spandrels of the triple arch of the first landing, small pieces of stained glass were set between gilt wires within squares of oak. Standing in front of the fireplace, one could enjoy the effects of light coming from the small conservatory over the vestibule.

The most innovative feature of the house was its electrical system, one of the first, if not the first, installed in a New York City house. Morgan had met Thomas Alva Edison in 1881, at the time that Christian Herter was remodeling and redecorating the interior of 219 Madison Avenue. We see several naked bulbs hanging in the stair hall. To provide power for these lights, a steam generator was installed in the basement of the stable behind the house. However, short circuits occurred when maintenance personnel forgot their required daily check of the equipment. Once the system short-circuited at 11:00 P.M., while the Morgans were entertaining a crowd of friends. On another occasion, hot wires burned Morgan's library desk and carpet. According to Herbert Satterlee (*J. Pierpont Morgan*, 1939), Everitt H. Johnson, Edison's assistant, was examining the damage when Morgan appeared in the library and asked, "What are you going to do about it?"

Johnson answered, "Mr. Morgan, the trouble is not inherent in the thing itself. It is my own fault, and I will put it in good working order so that it will be perfectly safe."

Pierpont asked, "How long will it take to fix it?"

Johnson answered, "I will do it right away."

"All right," said Pierpont, "see that you do." And he turned and went down the hall and so on out.

The result of the new installation was so satisfactory that Pierpont gave a reception, and about four hundred guests came to the house and marveled at the convenience and simplicity of the lighting system.

157

158

157. Drawing room, J. Pierpont Morgan house. Sheldon thought this drawing room emitted an "aroma of perfect taste." Though "Pompeian" in inspiration, he admitted it was "no slavish copy." And if it was not a plagiarism of another epoch's taste, neither was it a blunt or egotistical declaration of contemporary preferences. Sheldon liked the reminder of Pompeii and, for that matter, the flavor of Japan and Persia, all delicately combined with restraint and coolness in this spacious setting. Christian Herter understood that the distinguishing feature of this drawing room was its length; the opening to the central bay, which once had been the entranceway from Madison Avenue, was 17' feet wide. He reinforced this impression of length by the simple ceiling, the continuous cove and frieze and the low center of gravity.

Herter's ability to coordinate eclectic elements was impressive. He painted the lower woodwork in ivory sprinkled with flecks of gold, the wooden frieze and pilasters in Pompeian red, and kept the coved ceiling a light tone. The hangings of silk and gold thread elaborated with Persian embroidery were made in Japan. The chair coverings were black accented with gold thread. For the divans and cushions, Herter chose cherry plush, also highlighted with Persian embroidery. The rugs were Persian.

There were four focal points in this room: the elliptical mantelpiece projecting from the north wall; the alcove; the entrance to the hall opposite it; and the window (here unseen) on the south. Remaining wall surfaces were accented with works from the Morgan collection.

158. Library, J. Pierpont Morgan house. Unshaded bulbs hang from the ceiling of the drawing room and on the fireplace side of Morgan's library. Perhaps in these early years of domestic electric lighting the miracle deserved to be exhibited rather than partially obscured by shades. In addition to the lights hanging from the ceiling, Herter included wall sconces and shaded desk lamps in this room. The absence of sconces and table lighting from the drawing room was one of the reasons for the neat appearance of that large space.

The finish of this room, including its high wainscoting and comfortable inglenook, was fine Santo Domingo mahogany. To separate this fireplace recess from the rest of the room, Herter elevated its floor and tiled both floor and fire front with squares of blue and ochre. The soft furniture was covered with plush of peacock green. The ceiling was divided into octagonal panels, six of which were larger and contained painted allegorical figures representing History and Poetry. Morgan prized this work of Herter: "He painted for me in my library six panels for the ceiling—painted them *himself*, with his *own hands.*" When the house was refurbished in 1893, he reportedly said, "Renew, by all means, but retain the original designs of Herter. You cannot improve upon them." Designed by John La Farge, the stained-glass partitions at the right separated the library from the conservatory.

The library was Morgan's favorite room—a dark, strong environment in which he held meetings, relaxed with his friends and enjoyed his books. After the library became too small to hold his purchases, he stored his rare books and manuscripts in a basement room. When the Morgan Library was completed in 1906, his manuscript collection was moved next door.

159. Dining room, J. Pierpont Morgan house. In contrast to the restrained elegance of the drawing room, the dining room was impressive because it looked so solid and established. This impression was conveyed largely through the wainscoting of English oak 8' high, the heavy built-in sideboard to the right and the broad mantel with deep niches below and above to the left. The mantel area, 12' wide and 10' high, was faced with Siena marble. Surrounded by oak and leather chairs, the table appeared to be underscaled and unequal to the challenge of its environment. Above it was a skylight, 12' square. The painting over the sideboard is *Near Damascus* by Frederick Church, and below it, reflected in the mirror, is a miniature statue of the Primaporta Augustus, a work of art popular in the homes chosen for *Artistic Houses.*

160

160. Dining room, Joseph H. White house, 535 Boylston Street, Brookline, Massachusetts; Peabody and Stearns, architects, 1880–81; standing but altered. "Elmhurst" was a rambling house designed in the Queen Anne style but remodeled in 1924 to look more stately and less picturesque. When the house was completed in 1881, White, 57, had been married twice—to Mary E. Stantan on January 13, 1853, and to Ellen Tewksbury on November 13, 1855—had four children from the second marriage and was a prosperous partner in the firm of White, Payson and Company of Boston. The company marketed products of the Manchester Mill of Manchester, N.H.

The dining room, on the south side of the house, was connected to the hall through double doors. Four linked windows brightened a room in which the furnishings were dark and the furniture and fixed pieces heavy: The room expressed New England's respect for strong woodwork. The thick table stretchers, heavy sideboard, 15'-wide arch over the mantel and emphatic geometric design of the ceiling produced an impression that was solid, old and comfortable. Leather paper in old gold covered the walls above the wainscoting of stained oak. Most of the chairs were finished in leather except those near the arch, which were covered by French embroideries. These textiles and the unidentified paintings and hand-painted ceramics were relieving accents in this heavily finished room.

161. Library, William Goddard house, 38 Brown Street, Providence, Rhode Island; architect unknown, date unknown; standing but altered. William Giles Goddard (1794–1846) commissioned a three-story, foursquare brick house with hip roof at the southwest corner of Brown and George Streets in Providence. It was inherited by his son William Goddard (December 25, 1825–September 29, 1907) in the 1870s. He hired the firm of Stone and Carpenter to double the size of the house and to move the original entrance from George Street to Brown Street. Remodeled in 1880–81, this house was one of the earliest examples of the Colonial Revival. Acquired by Brown University in 1940 and carefully rehabilitated in the mid-1970s, it now serves as the alumni office.

From the center of the library one could see the ponderous fireplace of the dining room through the equally massive doorway separating the two rooms. These two strong forms defined space and determined the artistic roles of supporting pieces. Though part of the interior decoration, the doorway and fireplace were really architectural entities conceived by an architect inclined to miniaturize monumental structures. Even Sheldon, who normally did not dwell on the integration of architecture and interior decoration, hinted that the doorway might be overscaled. "In any ordinary scheme this treatment would seem almost obtrusive. . . ." Pieces such as the Elizabethan Revival lamp and table in the foreground seem dwarfed by the scale of the portal, though the giant Chinese cloisonné urn on a teakwood pedestal certainly held its own. The floor treatment was unusual in two respects: A hardwood floor divided into large geometric patterns by strips of darker wood was not common, and the rugs, surprisingly small for a room of this size, were not arranged to repeat the rectilinear orientation of the frescoed ceiling.

162. Dining room, William Goddard house. There were few overmantels of the early 1880s that expressed the Renaissance Revival in interior decoration as well as this one. At either side of the mirror were plinths that rested on the mantel shelf. These supported columns with molded bases, partially fluted shafts and volutes at the top. Then came the architrave divided into two faciae, a decorated frieze, a register of dentils and a register of projecting blocks supporting the cornice. Note the quiet way in which details of the sideboard repeated details on the built-in woodwork. The rectangles reappeared beside the fixed mirror above, the arches restated those over the entrance from the library, and the tapered pilasters were similar to those at either side of the fire opening. Sheldon predicted approval for this room.

William Goddard married Mary Edith Jenckes on February 19, 1867; their only child, Hope, married C. Oliver Iselin (no. 182) on June 10, 1894. Goddard was a principal in the firms of Brown and Ives and Goddard Brothers, companies that between them owned nine cotton mills. In 1888 he was elected Chancellor of Brown University.

161

162

The Phillips family purchased a lot at the corner of Berkeley and Marlborough Streets in Boston in 1877 and commissioned Peabody and Stearns to design a house for it, one of only two freestanding houses in the Back Bay district. The house, according to Peabody biographer Wheaton Holden, was French Renaissance with château-esque features. Though not one of the first ten, this was the only house in Boston cited in *American Architect and Building News*'s celebrated poll of 1885 to determine the most beautiful buildings in the United States. Nevertheless, it was not one of the most successful designs of Peabody and Stearns.

Phillips (October 21, 1838–March 1, 1885) was a socially respected and philanthropic Bostonian whose ancestors had founded Watertown, Massachusetts in the 1630s. An inheritance from a distant cousin in 1873 influenced the rest of his life. That year he formed John C. Phillips and Company, an import firm concentrating on trade with China and the Philippines. He spent most of 1874 traveling in Europe, and the following year married Anna Tucker of Boston. They had five children, the best known being ornithologist Charles Phillips.

163. Hall, John Charles Phillips house, 299 Berkeley Street, Boston, Massachusetts; Peabody and Stearns, architects, 1877–79; demolished 1939. The shape and placement of this hall and stairway were somewhat unusual. The hall was shallow, in part because of the deep entranceway and in part because of the advancing, centrally placed stairs. The stairway probably was featured because of its carved frieze of garlands, formidable newel posts and distinctive balusters and panels. The effect of its projection into the hall was to invite visitors to move ahead rather than horizontally into the reception room to the right or the drawing room to the left. The rear hall, off-center at the left, led to the parlor behind the drawing room but did not service equally well the two rooms behind the reception room on the right: the library and dining room. Nevertheless, this space illustrates the local preference for beautifully shaped and finished wood, and though the scale of the architectural decoration may have been too large for the setting, the oak, red-painted walls and portieres of embroidery on olive-green plush probably added sufficient warmth to make this a pleasant central area of family movements.

164. Drawing room, John Charles Phillips house. This room leaves the impression of relaxed and durable wealth confident enough to combine favorite items with disconnected objects in a setting that was usable and comfortable. The shelves contain pieces that Phillips probably acquired in 1860–62 while in India and the Far East. These are displayed unself-consciously alongside Western objects such as the bronze and marble French mantel clock and the porcelain vase on the table. Above the mantel is a painting by the German artist Adolf Schreyer, and in the passageway separating the drawing room and parlor stands Thomas Crawford's statue *Cupid in Contemplation* of the early 1840s. In these two rooms were paintings by Bouguereau, Daubigny, Ziem, Corot and Alfred Stevens (1823–1906) indicating the interest of Mr. and Mrs. Phillips in Barbizon work as well as the more conservative nineteenth-century schools. Above the fireplace is a Middle Eastern scene by Eugène Fromentin (1820–1876).

165. Dining room, John Charles Phillips house. This dark, strong interior implies that eating here was a very serious, if not primarily male, affair. The ceiling was painted in oil to represent growing pomegranates and the walls hung in jute in variations of green. Evidently the men retired after dinner to the large chimney nook to smoke and converse. Rarely in these photographs do we see logs burning. Although this dining room was too weighty both in color and in its woodwork and furniture to be modish, it offered, like the drawing room, a pleasant and reassuring domestic atmosphere.

163

THE OPULENT INTERIORS OF THE GILDED AGE 151

166

167

168

166. Hall, James W. Alexander house, 50 West 54th Street, New York, New York; Robert H. Robertson, architect, 1881–82; demolished 1906. The halls on these two pages represent three versions of the "living hall," in which the woodwork played a significant decorative role and the setting was relatively informal. This kind of hall would have been more common in the suburbs (Hinckley) or the country (Wadsworth) than it would have been on West 54th Street in New York City. Warm, comfortable and unpretentious, the central space in the Alexander house seems modest for an expensive brick house of four floors. Alexander (July 19, 1839–September 21, 1915) joined the Equitable Life Assurance Society in 1866, was first vice president of the firm when his house was built and served as its president from 1899 to 1905. He married Elizabeth B. Williamson (November 24, 1862); they had three children.

After crossing the threshold, one immediately sensed the invitation to relax offered by the fire and the warm glazed tiles of the fireplace, open-arm Windsor chair with plank seat, built-in cushioned chimney seat, warm stained-oak paneling and red and gold portieres pushed aside to reveal the stair hall. Because it was physically connected with the main stairs, this section of the hall, paradoxically, offered protection and freedom, stillness and movement, reassurance and adventure. The architect, responsible for designing the carved mantel face, paneling, cupboards, brackets and stair railing was the real decorator of this part of the house.

167. Hall, Samuel P. Hinckley house, Central Avenue and Hicks Avenue, Lawrence, New York; Lamb and Rich, architects, 1883; demolished. Unlike the dark, semienclosed Alexander hall, this was a light, porous space. The hall was not intended to be seen as an isolated compartment, but as a spatial link fluidly connected with the dining room, through the wide double doors on the left, and with the parlor, entered at the base of the stairs. Uncluttered by city standards, this summer-house hall contained several distinctive pieces and features: the Brewster and Carver armchairs on the left, the eighteenth-century grandfather clock, the Dutch door, the transomed English casement

windows and the rampant lions in relief between the brackets of the mantel hood. The leopard skin and animal rug were casual touches considered appropriate in a semirural setting.

"Sunset Hall" was one of five houses designed for Hinckley's estate (see *Building*, September 1888) by Lamb and Rich, among the least inhibited and most sensuously playful architects of the early 1880s. Initially a builder in Lawrence and by the mid-1890s successful in real estate, Hinckley (1850–October 20, 1935) and his wife, formerly Rosalie Neilson, were peripheral figures of New York society. They separated in 1910.

---

168. Hall, James W. Wadsworth house, Avon Road, Geneseo, New York; architect unknown, 1835–38; standing. James Samuel Wadsworth, the father of James W., had married Mary Craig Wharton of Philadelphia in 1834, and while touring Europe the couple met Lord Hartford in London, were impressed by his Regent's Park mansion and asked him for its plans in order to erect a similar house in Geneseo. "Hartford House" was occupied in 1838. James W. (October 12, 1846–December 24, 1926) inherited the house and 8000 acres of valley land in 1872 and on September 14, 1876 married Marie Louisa Travers of New York City. They had a daughter and a son, James W., Jr., who served in the United States Congress for 35 years. James W., Sr., served in Congress for 16 years before his retirement in 1907. Known as "The Boss," he ran an extensive farming and cattle-raising operation in Livingston and adjoining counties.

Europeans in the 1880s often interpreted the absence of a separate vestibule in American houses as a sign of Yankee confidence in the surrounding community. Here one walked directly into a sitting hall that was attractively supported by a stair hall containing columns, screen, paneling, balustrade, landing and stained-glass window. The low couch, Windsor and Bar Harbor wicker chairs, steerhorns and bison head, and functionally placed hat rack conveyed an immediate impression that the Wadsworths, not a New York decorator, determined the artistic tone of their house.

CHARLES A. WHITTIER HOUSE

Two adjacent houses were completed on Beacon Street in Boston in 1883, one designed by Henry Hobson Richardson for Francis L. Higginson and the other by McKim, Mead and White for General Charles A. Whittier and his wife Elizabeth. Both houses attracted considerable attention because they had been designed by major firms in American architecture and because they were major additions to the resplendent section the Back Bay had become. Mariana Van Rensselaer compared them in her series on recent American architecture in *The Century Magazine* (March 1886):

> They differ greatly in style and treatment, but each has considered the other in its own growth, and consequently is helped, not hurt, by the presence of its neighbor. Mr. Richardson's [on the left] is the more striking of the two, and there is always a fervor about his work that seduces the would-be critic. But it has been called a trifle too "mediaeval" in its massiveness and in the element of grotesqueness introduced into its ornamentation. Perhaps it is true that the expression of the other is better suited to a modern home—to the voicing of that modern life whose ideal is elegance rather than physical force. So charming a house is it, indeed, that one longs to give it unstinted praise. And one might if only the porch worked in better with the general design—looked more as though it had taken its place and shape by virtue of an unmistakable impulse of artistic *growth*.

Richard G. Wilson also compared the two elevations in his dissertation, "Charles F. McKim and the Development of the American Renaissance" (University of Michigan, 1972):

> Both houses were built of the same red brick and Longmeadow stone, they had the same high pitched roofs, and continuous string courses and cornices, but in feeling and style they were different. Richardson's house was by far the heavier mass, and in contrast to the upward lift of McKim's tower, the Higginson tower appeared shrunk in on itself. The stone of the base in the Richardson design was continued up into the tower which created the feeling of a solid mass in contrast to the lighter brick wall behind. The houses had equal frontages of 52 feet apiece, and both adopted a scheme of three unequal bays. While both houses were symmetrical, Richardson's was only awkwardly balanced, but McKim was able to balance the house and also create a homogeneous interrelationship of the different elements. McKim's fenestration had a constant scale that was lacking in Richardson's design. Richardson used a variant of his normal Romanesque-Gothic detailing, with perhaps traces of the Queen Anne in the bay window. Richardson's detailing, when it did appear as in the bay window or the dormer, was clumsy and unrelated. In contrast to the spareness of Richardson, McKim's ornament was freely applied with a lushness and continuity to all three bays that tended to unite the house both vertically and horizontally. The porch and spandrels of McKim's Whittier House were François I, but there was a Queen Anne air to the dormer. The dissenting note was the awkward porch, that was merely an added appendage.

The Higginson house (left) and the Whittier house (right).

McKim had designed the house for one of the partners of the investment firm of Lee, Higginson & Company, the same Higginson who now lived next door. Charles A. Whittier (August 6, 1840–May 14, 1908) had graduated from Harvard in 1860, joined the Union forces during the Civil War and was a brevetted brigadier general by 1865. He returned to the military after the fall of Manila in the Spanish-American War, again serving as brigadier general. His wife was the former Elizabeth J. Chadwick; they had two daughters, Pauline and Susie. He died on the *Mauretania* during one of his many crossings of the Atlantic.

Commissioned in 1880 and completed in 1883, the Whittier house stood until 1929, the same year in which the Higginson house was demolished. Despite the fact that the owners had spent approximately $80,000 on the structure and almost as much for their interior decoration, the house appealed to Sheldon because it combined quality and moderation. For him it symbolized sophisticated and restrained wealth, and expressed ownership that knew the difference between size that was demonstrative and size that was useful, between effects that were conspicuous and effects that were fitting.

---

169. Hall, Charles A. Whittier house, 270 Beacon Street, Boston, Massachusetts; McKim, Mead and White, architects, 1880–83; demolished 1929. Fortunately, the new houses of the Back Bay district in Boston were not constrained in width as were town houses erected on New York's narrow lots. Architects in this section of Boston could plan generously in width as well as in depth and create halls that were larger, better illuminated by natural light and looked like hubs of family activity rather than lengthy corridors. This hall, designed by a firm that often placed spacious living halls at the center of its contemporary country houses, was one of the most attractive of this series.

Although this photograph reveals the size of the Whittier hall and provides a view into the reception room, it does not emphasize its principal feature—a triple archway opposite the fireplace that divided that side of the room into the base of the stairway, a large inglenook in the center and a vestibule that led to the entrance porch. McKim, Mead and White contrasted one side of this space with the other. On the right the wall was composed of carved panels arranged symmetrically around the fireplace. This wall, well-crafted and tightly controlled, was a handsome backdrop for Chinese porcelain urns and mounted, hand-painted chargers. The left side, however, was open, light and articulated by fluted shafts, nervous spindles and graceful broad arches. If the one side expressed order and solidity, the other celebrated movement and lightness. The flutes and the spindles of both the balustrade and the screen between the inglenook and vestibule represented another cadence. One climbed the stairs around three sides of the nook and from different locations could look into it as well as into the hall. The framing wood, dark oak, was used for the columns

and arches, the strips of the ceiling and the architrave that determined the top of the overmantel, the height of entrances and the height of the capitals.

170. Library, Charles A. Whittier house. The author of *Artistic Houses* wanted very much to prove that American architecture and interior decoration had come of age and to argue that their achievements were natural outgrowths of a maturing national sensibility. He realized that this was impossible without wealth but also was aware that money in the hands of the tasteless rich could be counterproductive. Thus, when he encountered wealth seemingly untempted by ostentatious effects, he was especially pleased. The Whittiers were models:

> The owner's good taste has been not only active and pervasive, but authoritative; and one may imagine him to have constantly enjoined upon the man who had contracted with him to be the spender of his money: "Spend what you like, but keep your effects down. If you must have a great deal of cash in order to produce what I want, remember, please, that what I don't want is meaningless and ostentatious show."

Compared to other libraries in this collection, this one was above average in size and number of volumes and below average in clutter. Furniture was modest and not coordinated; bric-a-brac was kept to a minimum. In this photograph the library appears to be divided into two parts, a relatively simple and open main section on the right and a more complex chimney nook on the left. In the latter, surfaces of marble contrasted with the quieter woodwork in walnut. The area around the fire opening was faced with marble tiles and the corner niche, containing book shelves, with dark, grained marble slabs. At either end was an unusually high window and chimney seat below.

171

172

173

171. Dining room, Charles A. Whittier house. Like the hall and the library, the dining room gives the impression of spaciousness that is intentional and unhurried, as if space were an architectural ingredient to be used or exhibited for its own sake. The result is an emptiness uncharacteristic of the period. With the exception of the wall opposite the only windows of the room, the wall dominated by the large painting by de Neuville, the mahogany woodwork looked extremely dark. In order to catch the details of these tenebrous surfaces, the photographer exposed the film for 20 minutes. The fireplace side of the room would have been less gloomy and just as dignified if the ponderous cupboards at the corners had been deleted.

The painting *Un Porteur de Dépêches*, painted in 1880, was a curious choice for this room. Dining-room paintings usually referred to food or eating, and while this scene depicts a meal during the Franco-Prussian War, the attention of the French officers is fixed on a recently captured German. Too large for the dining room, the painting would have appeared less dominant had it been hung lower, but this was impossible because of the height of the room's paneling. On the other hand, paintings were hung at a higher level in these houses than they would be in late twentieth-century American houses. Furthermore, the Whittiers may have reasoned that this relatively dark and spare room needed a commanding focal point.

172. Boudoir, Charles A. Whittier house. If formal solemnity characterized the dining room, here we sense a personalized space. This boudoir was a private retreat that met needs not addressed by the reception room, the drawing room or even the library. A boudoir in the 1880s would be a small sitting room on the first floor used by the mistress of the house, often the control center from which the house was run or, as in this case, part of a bedroom suite. Beyond the portieres we see a brass bed and a Chippendale mahogany chest on chest.

The woodwork of the boudoir was in flat relief and painted a yellow-brown. The wallpaper, also light in color, was floral in pattern, as was

the pattern of the portieres and the Turkish frame chaise longue. Distributed through the room were small vases, statuettes of lovers or amorous putti, family photographs and prints and reproductions. Another feature not evident in the proper rooms of the main level was the signs of habitation. There is a sewing basket under the table and gloves and a letter opener on top.

---

173. Dining room, Gilbert R. Payson house, 456 Belmont Street, Watertown, Massachusetts; Van Brunt and Howe, architects, ca. 1882; standing but altered. On the highest point in Watertown, which provided a fine view of the Boston skyline, the Payson house on Oakley Hill was certainly one of the most impressively situated residences in Sheldon's collection. Located today on the grounds of the Oakley Country Club, a section of the original elevation (see *American Architect and Building News*, February 2, 1882) is still visible in the heart of a large, recently opened condominium complex.

Payson (ca. 1840–June 9, 1891) graduated from Harvard in 1862. He was a partner in White, Payson and Company, which became one of the major dry-goods commission merchants in Boston in the 1880s. He was survived by his wife, the former Althea Train of Framingham, and three sons and a daughter.

Ash, not commonly found in either city or country houses of this decade, was used throughout this dining room. The sideboard in the niche to the right was stained ash, as were the china cabinets above and the paneled cupboards below. Ash was cut into narrow strips and pieced together in a tongue-and-groove fashion, as if it were a hardwood floor, to form the herringbone design of the ceiling and the surface of the coved frieze over the mantel. The wood was also shaped into curves to form the arches within the overmantel, the larger arches above and to either side of it and the supporting brackets. Complementing the warm color of the wood were the yellow-brown tiles of the fireplace, dark green wallpaper and golden flowers in sections of the frieze.

174

174. Ladies' parlor, R. H. White and Company Warehouse Store, 30 Bedford Street, Boston, Massachusetts; Peabody and Stearns, architects, 1882–84; demolished. The dry-goods firm of R. H. White and Company erected a store on Washington Street in Boston in 1877 and built additions to it until its ground area was approximately 55,000 square feet. Wheaton Holden claimed that the Warehouse Store addition at the corner of Bedford Street and Harrison Avenue by Peabody and Stearns was "the most important of all the firm's commercial buildings of the 1870s, '80s, and '90s" because of its influence on other noted architects, among them John Root, Louis Sullivan and Henry Hobson Richardson.

What a sensible, appealing idea—a respectable parlor offering women shoppers a quiet alternative to the noisy floors and a central place to meet friends! Yet this women's oasis had a distinctly masculine flavor. Its great arch was massive and heavily textured, its furniture strong, its high ceiling dark and deeply coffered. The plaster panels of the upper walls were also dark, red and gold against a deeper red ground, and the oak paneling below was stained blue-green. Even the poem below the clock celebrates the rugged life: "Blow high, blow low, not all the winds that ever blow can quench our hearth fires ruddy." There were counterbalancing accents—delicate tiles above the arch, intricate carving around the fireplace and a diminutive musicians' gallery in the right wall.

175. Dining room, William G. Dominick house, 35 East 57th Street, New York, New York; architect unknown, 1881–82; demolished 1928. Dominick (January 14, 1845–August 31, 1895) was a descendant of a Huguenot named Dominique who arrived in New York in 1742. In 1874 he married Anne De Witt Marshall, whose ancestors had arrived in Virginia in 1624. Not surprisingly, they belonged to societies created for those with lineage. Though active with several New York social clubs and riding and hunting organizations near their summer home at Quogue, Long Island, the Dominicks also worked steadily for the city's poor. When he died suddenly at the age of 50, he was the senior partner of the brokerage firm of Dominick and Dickerman.

The dining room was not large for a new house erected on 57th Street in the early 1880s. Consequently, the architect and decorator concentrated three-dimensional effects, weight and dark hues at the base, and created a three-part wall composed of a mahogany dado slightly higher than the backs of the leather-covered mahogany chairs, a flat plane of wallpaper that was brighter in tone in a neutralizing floral pattern and, finally, a light frieze closely related to the design of the ceiling. From this viewpoint, the clarity of this three-part system was weakened by the sideboard and by the fireplace and its overmantel. However, by facing the upper part of the sideboard with transparent glass cabinets and a central mirror and by inserting a stained-glass window above the mantel, the decorator tried to keep the middle section as light and as flat as possible. Though mirrors were common in overmantels, stained-glass windows were not because they required background lighting and split chimney flues. The range of decorative objects was mixed in theme and international in origin.

176. Dining room, John Wolfe house, 8 East 68th Street, New York, New York; Detlef Lienau, architect, 1881–82; demolished. Wolfe (December 18, 1821–January 17, 1894) was recognized as an influential figure in the New York art world from 1850 until the early 1880s. He began collecting works by German artists, sold them in 1863 for $114,000 and then concentrated on French paintings, for which he received $132,000 at auction in April 1882. The two paintings visible in this room were holdovers from his first collection. Directly ahead was a self-portrait by J. P. Hasenclever (1810–1853) showing the artist, in front of his famous *Wine Tasters*, toasting his patron, Wolfe. To the left was a depiction of a La Fontaine fable, *The Stork Invites the Fox to Dinner* by Paul Friedrich Meyerheim (1842–1915).

This interior was designed by Lienau (1818–1887), who was born in Schleswig-Holstein and came to the United States in 1848. It was filled with European paintings, furniture and objets d'art, including the two suits of armor seen through the doorway. This Renaissance Revival dining room was finished entirely in black walnut; the built-in pieces as well as the embossed-leather–covered chairs were of carved walnut. The chandelier was ordered from Paris.

177

177. Hall, Elizabeth E. Spooner house, 196 Commonwealth Avenue, Boston, Massachusetts; Peabody and Stearns, architects, 1881; standing. Boston, steeped in the Colonial tradition and possessing many buildings from the late eighteenth and early nineteenth centuries, led in the revival of early American architectural forms during the last quarter of the nineteenth century. An example is the home of Mrs. Daniel Nicholson Spooner at the corner of Commonwealth Avenue and Exeter Street. Very little is known about Daniel N. Spooner, who was born about 1825. He married Elizabeth Elliot Torrey; they had one child, Elizabeth Elliot. Mrs. Spooner had lived at one time in China, but it is not known if her husband, who had died when this house was completed, also had some association with the Orient.

The hallway reflects the Federal style in its light woodwork, delicate classical detailing and massive fireplace, which resembles an old cooking fireplace with its small decorative hanging kettles. These historicizing elements are woven together with other decorative statements more typical of the period to create an interior materially more demanding than any historic American prototypes. Still, compared to many contemporary town houses of the affluent, the Spooner hall expressed restraint and refinement. The plates, vases and medallions displayed in the hall were collected by Mrs. Spooner while in China. The bronze maiden on the newel post attracts attention to the main stairway on the right, which rises to the second-floor railing seen at the top of the photograph. Colored textiles were often conspicuously displayed on banisters and railings to add both color and a touch of informality.

178. Drawing room, Elizabeth E. Spooner house. Mrs. Spooner paid close attention to the importance of color in a decorative

arrangement. This relatively serene and comfortable living space had walls of crimson and gold, upholstery of more subdued tones of the same hues, portieres of satin panels of light blue against old gold plush and a ceiling that was a cool, neutral area. The room was accented by exquisitely carved teakwood, specifically around the fire opening and in the overmantel and, opposite this, in the frame of the large mirror accented on either side by extravagant wall sconces. To either side of the mantel were teakwood cabinets on ebony tables. The large painting to the left is a *Madonna and Child* by an unidentified student of Rubens. The room was unified above by the continuous broad frieze with a raised floral pattern.

179. Dining room, Elizabeth E. Spooner house. This room, with its elliptical shape and strikingly articulated ceiling with sunburst pattern, received its inspiration from the Federal style. Its plan is identical to that of the Blue Room in the White House in Washington and is similar in form to elliptical parlors designed by Boston architect Charles Bulfinch. In this instance the ornamentation is much richer and deeper than in earlier buildings. The curved walls provide space for four closets, the first of which was used as a silver safe, the second as a refrigerator, the third for glassware, and the fourth for china. The wood in the room is darkened oak, the paneled ceiling gold and silver. The leather-covered walls had embossed patterns slightly lighter than the woodwork. The strong fireplace at the left was balanced on the other side of the dining room by a substantial sideboard of old oak. Above this was an oblong piece of Venetian tapestry in creams. Despite Mrs. Spooner's interest in Oriental objets d'art and their presence in all of her rooms, these rooms architecturally followed the general directions of American interior planning and decoration of the early 1880s.

180

181

182

180. Entrance hall, John W. Doane house, 1827 Prairie Avenue, Chicago, Illinois; T. V. Wadskier, architect, 1883; demolished.
The Doane house by Wadskier, a Danish immigrant who had first practiced in Philadelphia before arriving in Chicago in the 1850s, was, according to Sheldon, already regarded as one of the most elaborately finished residences in the city. From Prairie Avenue a grand flight of steps led to the heavy oak doors that admitted visitors to the vestibule illuminated by stained-glass windows from the workshop of John La Farge. Then one stepped into this entry hall with a conveniently located reception room on the right, a hall so spacious and magnificently furnished that it may have seemed like the primary hall of the house. Its ceiling was approximately 15′ high, and its openings to the reception room and stairhall were unusually wide. However, the room was probably too small for the overinflated system of plinths, carved columns and capitals, and deep lintels. Color effects came from the oak woodwork, the heavy portieres, Persian rugs and a stained-glass window. In the foreground is an ebony table on which visitors placed their calling cards and, in the distance against the side of the stairway, a fountain surrounded by ferns and rare plants.

181. Hall, John W. Doane house. At the fountain one turned right to walk into the grand hall, a space approximately 30′ square that looked larger than it was because of the oval opening above. On the north side were four identical arches supported by columns, two of which were also the newel posts of the main stairway. The stained-glass windows of the landing can be seen under these arches. The reception room, visible through the tied portieres, was in the northwest corner of the house. Like the entrance hall, this space was finished entirely in oak. Other rooms on the main floor were completed in cherry, Santo Domingo mahogany and bird's-eye maple. One of the larger halls of this collection, it was also one of the more emphatically furnished, the

result of an odd combination of contemporary open space and old-fashioned tactile overstatement.

In addition to his Chicago town house, Doane (March 23, 1833–March 23, 1901) and his wife, the former Julia Moulton, maintained a hotel apartment in New York and a summer home in Thompson, Connecticut, where he had been born. He first arrived in Chicago about 1855. After the Great Fire of 1871 he entered importing, circumventing Eastern markets to bring teas and coffee directly to Chicago. To this shrewd venture he added directorships in four railroads and, from 1884 to 1898, the presidency of the Merchants' Loan and Trust Company. Doane was neither a dedicated philanthropist nor an art collector.

182. Hall, C. Oliver Iselin house, Hunter's Island, New York; McKim, Mead and White, architects, 1882–83; demolished. Iselin (June 8, 1854–January 1, 1932), head of the banking firm of Iselin and Company, was a sportsman's sportsman who was active in 15 social and athletic clubs in and around New York City. He is best remembered as the canny yachtsman who sailed in several America's Cup victories between 1893 and 1903. He married Frances Garner in 1880, but she died a decade later. In 1894 he married Hope Goddard, daughter of the influential William Goddards of Providence (nos. 161 & 162).

This country house was located in picturesque and unpopulated surroundings. According to Leland Roth, it was designed by McKim, Mead and White in collaboration with Sidney Straton and cost only $6522, exclusive of furnishings. This photograph suggests that the Iselins could be both formal and informal. The arch acted as the frame of this scene and the stairway, oddly planned with an extensive but low landing yet exquisitely finished, was its main protagonist. Within this relatively uncluttered though spatially active area, the Iselins placed objects discreetly.

HENRY VILLARD HOUSE

Although his rapid rise and dramatic fall were not uncommon in the 1870s and 1880s, the early years of Villard (April 10, 1835–November 12, 1900) were atypical of the beginnings of most late-nineteenth-century American millionaires. Born in Bavaria, he studied briefly at the Universities of Munich and Würzburg prior to his emigration in 1853 and began his life in the United States as a sophisticated European, not a pragmatic Yankee. He had little to do with business initially, and his friends were not the "prosaic moneymen" whose reputations were already known in Europe. Villard became a journalist and war correspondent for several newspapers, among them the *New York Herald*, *New York Tribune* and *Chicago Daily Tribune*, and his sympathies for the Northern cause led to friendship with abolitionist William Lloyd Garrison and to marriage with his daughter Fanny on January 3, 1866. At the height of Villard's journalistic career, he owned the *New York Evening Post* and *The Nation*, the latter one of the leading liberal journals of the day.

Villard became publicly involved in railroad speculation in 1873 when he represented the interests of German bondholders in the Oregon & California Railroad. Eight years later, with the aid of the so-called "Blind Pool"—investors did not know the ultimate destination of their money—he purchased a controlling interest in the Northern Pacific Railroad. His reputation as a wunderkind soiled through overspending, Villard resigned the presidency of the railroad early in 1884. Although he was later reaccepted by the New York business community as well as by the directors of the Northern Pacific, he never again equaled his startling successes of 1881–83.

Villard did not follow the millionaire crowd when he purchased this site on Madison Avenue, behind St. Patrick's Cathedral, for $260,000 in 1881. Fifth Avenue, not Madison, was then the desired address. Furthermore, he rejected the common relationship between a New York City residence and the street in preference for one reflecting European planning. The U-shaped plan of the house was built around an almost square courtyard that was separated from the public space of the sidewalk by a metal fence. Larger than the William H. Vanderbilt house on Fifth Avenue, it was designed to accommodate several families—another European approach. Villard planned to occupy the south wing (451 Madison Avenue) at the corner of Madison and East 50th Street. Behind the building on this 200′-deep lot, he envisioned a garden shared by those who purchased the remaining sections.

The brother of Mrs. Villard was married to McKim's sister. In all probability, Villard and the firm agreed upon the shape and stylistic character of the house though its details were worked out by Stanford White's assistant, Joseph Wells. Evidently Villard overrode the firm's preference for light stone. In *The Century Magazine* (February 1886), Mariana Van Rensselaer, noting the choice of brownstone for this modern Renaissance palace, expressed a common reaction by calling the effect "very quiet, a little cold, perhaps a little tame." However, she also stressed the "refined" character of the house and its contrast to surrounding "vernacular" designs inspired by similar sources. Referring to it as more grand than beautiful, *The Architect* of London (January 12, 1884) thought it was the "first attempt made to reproduce an Italian palace in America."

The Madison Avenue facade, the hotel tower rising at the rear.

Construction began on May 4, 1882. When his Northern Pacific operation collapsed a year and a half later, Villard moved his family from an expensive hotel to the unfinished mansion to save money. Hounded by citizens and the press, who thought that by this act Villard was mocking those who had lost money in the crash, the family moved out the following spring, bravely declaring it was doing so "without regret." Two years later their quarters were purchased by Mrs. Whitelaw Reid.

In the mid-1970s the Catholic Archdiocese of New York, which had used the Villard-Reid mansion since the 1940s, leased the site to hotel developer Harry B. Helmsley. He and architect Richard Roth, Jr., of Emery Roth and Sons, proposed the demolition of parts of the rear of the mansion to join it to a new hotel–office tower behind. Many groups and individuals in New York objected to the original plans because they would have eliminated some of the celebrated spaces, including the music room (no. 188), later called the Gold Room when it was remodeled by McKim, Mead and White for the Reids in the 1890s. After several years of spirited discussions about the future of the houses, construction of a 51-story hotel—the Helmsley Palace—began on March 14, 1978. The hotel opened in March 1981. Breakfast, tea and cocktails are now served in the Gold Room. According to William Shopsin and Mosette Broderick, who have recently published a solid history entitled *The Villard Houses: Life Story of a Landmark:* "the long debate about the fate of the Villard houses resulted at last in a creative marriage between preservation and development, an encouraging conclusion to a difficult chapter in their history, and a promising beginning for their second century."

183. Reception room and hall, Henry Villard house, 451 Madison Avenue, New York, New York; McKim, Mead and White, architects, 1882–85; standing but altered. The main entrance to the Villard section of the building was in the middle of the south side of the court on East 50th Street. In this photograph the entrance to the hall is on the left just beyond the square opening; the reception room is in the foreground. This vista, looking east, revealed a long, impressive corridor illuminated by the light coming from the stairway on the left and the music room at the end. The fireplace on the right had a marble mantelpiece with an overmantel by Augustus Saint-Gaudens (1848–1907) depicting peace as a female figure flanked by two children. Mexican marble and inlays of marble covered the walls, and the floor and groin-vaulted ceiling were finished in mosaic. Although the seats in the hall indicated it could be a lounging area, it is difficult to imagine this hard, shiny environment used except for traffic. By contrast, the reception room, the central section of a three-part drawing room, though proper and intentionally balanced, was much less formidable. The pilasters on either side of the doorway were inlaid with mother-of-

pearl. Like some of the wall spaces of the drawing room, the Turkish frame furniture was covered with terra-cotta silk embroidered in orange-yellow.

184. Stair hall, Henry Villard house. The shimmering marble stairway to the second floor has been freed of its grime and polished to its original luster, making it one of the most exquisite spaces of the new Helmsley Palace Hotel. The reflections from the finished panels of Siena marble transform the area into a visual experience. This dark photograph shows the upper landing of the stairway, the triple arcade and the hall of the second floor—a hall that was less splendid but warmer than the one immediately below. The transition from the semipublic space below to the private space above was marked here by the shift from marble to leather-covered walls. On the second floor there were three bedrooms, three bathrooms, a library and a boudoir; on the third, five bedrooms, four bathrooms and a boudoir; on the fourth, 12 bedrooms and three bathrooms; and on the fifth, at least a dozen bedrooms.

183

184

185

185. Hall, Henry Villard house. The round-arch construction of the sturdy ceiling is divided into bays by unribbed, mosaic-decorated groin vaults. Despite the cost, craftsmanship and quality of materials, the effect of the Villard hall is authoritative but not encouraging, leaving the visitor with unanswered questions about what lies beyond the closed drawing-room doors of this architecturally orchestrated ritual of passage.

186. Drawing room, Henry Villard house. This room, part of the triple drawing room that could be treated as a single social space, was located in the southwest corner of the mansion. Although the stained cherry woodwork was dark, the space was adequately lighted by the East 50th Street windows at the right and the Madison Avenue window, behind the photographer. At the left is one of the four freestanding segmentally fluted columns at the entrance to the hall, and beyond the opening are several stained-glass panels of the front door. The wall surface of the drawing room, composed primarily of panels separated by pilasters, was inlaid with white mahogany, satinwood and holly, in addition to mother-of-pearl. Built to call attention to selected bric-a-brac, the two fluted niches at the sides of the mantel complemented similar forms at the opposite side of the drawing room. When the Whitelaw Reids remodeled the drawing room in 1891, they removed some of the paneling but left the plaster ceiling, the mantel of onyx and the parquet floor. In transforming the drawing room into the Madison Room, a chandeliered cocktail lounge of the Helmsley Palace, the mantelpiece was discovered behind built-in office cabinets.

Sheldon made an odd observation about the Villard house: "No attempt at ostentation appears in any part of the architectural outline or the decorative scheme. Not only good taste prevails, but good taste as understood by persons of refinement and education and experience."

Perhaps he was moved to write this because serious demeanor triumphed over the bizarre in every square inch of this house. Perhaps his reaction was affected by the absence of portieres and other drapery or the fact that the house was not completely furnished when these photographs were taken. When he used "ostentation," he was evidently not thinking of size, for this was the largest building of its kind in the city, or of cost, for it amounted almost to a million dollars.

187. Dining room, Henry Villard house. Located between the fireplace of the hall and the doors to the music room were sliding doors leading to the dining room (20′ × 60′). The west third could be closed off by a movable screen and used as a breakfast or informal dining room. The focal point of the dining room was the vast fireplace complex with two recessed basins and busts symbolizing joy, moderation and hospitality carved by Saint-Gaudens. The unit has been moved in its entirety to the center of the lobby of the new hotel. The walls were profusely carved and the panels between the ceiling beams finished in Lincrusta, indicating the decorator's determination to avoid a vacuum. If the eye tired of these visual delights, it could read old sayings about the joys of good friends and good food worked into the frieze and other registers in white mahogany.

Channing Blake (*Antiques*, December 1972) commented perceptively about the role of the black English oak furniture:

The furniture was laid out in dogmatic Renaissance patterns. There was a heavy table in the center with a chair at each end, while all the rest of the chairs, and a chest or credenza or two, were backed stiffly up to the wall. White used furniture as the Italians and French had done for centuries; as rhythmic punctuations along the long expanse of a wall. The furniture thus became part of the walls rather than elements in the room's space.

188. Music room, Henry Villard house. The music room, now the Gold Room of the Helmsley Palace, was bathed in light from stained-glass east windows. The Gold Room today looks much more inviting than the cavernous and unfinished space in this photograph. Some surfaces of the room have changed little—the carved paneling at the base, the relatively neutral middle section and the frieze. This photograph makes the music room look barnlike and bare, in part because the barrel-vaulted ceiling had not yet been decorated by Stanford White and the lunette above the cornice had not yet been painted by John La Farge. The musicians' gallery, reached by the door in the far-right corner, remains, as do five well-preserved plaster casts of a work by Luca della Robbia (ca. 1400–1482), the *Cantoria*, originally in the Cathedral of Florence. Five additional panels from the *Cantoria* were installed on the opposite wall, above the doors to the dining room. Shopsin and Broderick point out that Villard, in Rome in 1874, studied fifteenth-century Italian sculpture and returned with casts of work by della Robbia, Donatello, Ghiberti and Verrocchio.

189. Guest room, Henry Villard house. Despite the rich carving of the canopied bed, a bureau, the corner of which is seen at the left, and the fireplace, this guest room, like many of the Villard rooms, seems unexpectedly barren. The bare hardwood floor accentuated this appearance of spareness. Crimson-and-gold brocade covered the walls. The ceiling was divided into rectangular panels by beams. The woodwork was oak.

Judging from the absence of chandeliers in most of the Villard interiors, these rooms were probably not well lighted after dark. Although gas was the principal source of artificial light, the Edison Electric Lighting Company had installed wiring for later use. Impressed with the formidable interior decoration, critics have tended to overlook the modern conveniences of the Villard house. Its central-heating system consumed almost a ton of coal each day. There was also a hydraulic elevator off the vestibule. In Villard's section of the mansion there were 13 flush toilets.

---

190. Dining room, Richard T. Wilson house, 511 Fifth Avenue, New York, New York; architect unknown, date unknown; demolished 1915. Once known as the "Old Tweed Mansion," the home of "Boss" Tweed, the Wilson house was a four-story brownstone on the southeast corner of Fifth Avenue and East 43rd Street. Built in the 1860s, its principal rooms were small and dark measured by the standards of the affluent in 1882, the year the Wilsons moved in. The Renaissance Revival redecoration, probably done by the New York firm of Duncan, Johnston and Fenton, was heavy for the room's size. The wall was divided into two basic parts: Below were the dado and woodwork of oak and above were disparate sections of nineteenth-century French tapestries. The built-in oil painting and fringed drapery over the fire opening, as well as the shiny andirons and absence of a screen and tending equipment, suggest that the fireplace produced more conversation than heat. When extended, the table probably accommodated ten.

Like their dining room, the Wilsons were more determined than casual and more calculating than graceful. They settled in New York City after the Civil War, during which Wilson (1829–November 26, 1910) had been a commissary general in the Confederate Army and also sold the South's cotton in Europe. With a modest fortune of $500,000 from the cotton transactions, he founded the banking firm of R. T. Wilson and Company and by the mid-1870s was regarded as a minor millionaire on the fringes of New York society. Mrs. Wilson, the former Melissa Clementine Johnson (ca. 1831–May 29, 1908) of Macon, Georgia, was a shrewd matchmaker for her children—so shrewd that the family became known as the "marrying Wilsons" or the "devouring Wilsons."

190

191. Dining room, Edward E. Chase house, 14 West 49th Street, New York, New York; architect unknown, 1882–83; demolished. This dining room was decorated by John C. Bancroft of Boston, who used inlaid woods extensively and contrasted heavily patterned sections. The ceiling, for example, was an intricately pieced mosaic of mahogany, sumac and walnut. Around the mantelpiece and at the side of the large buffet, Bancroft used strips of brass and silver to divide the inlaid wood into a checkerboard design. The most extravagant display of pieced work was his handling of the jambs and lintel of the wide opening that separated the two rooms. Above the wainscoting, the wall was covered with golden "Japanese cloth" that was partially covered by prints of landscape and peasant themes in frames that were also designed by Bancroft. Despite the apparent attempt to define this environment through planes of abstract energy, the results are more overbearing and relentless than the designer may have intended.

Chase (ca. 1841–April 23, 1900) was a minor New York broker closely associated with the Iowa Central Railroad. Mrs. Chase died childless in the early 1890s; he retired in 1898.

---

192. Library, George P. Wetmore house, Bellevue Avenue, Newport, Rhode Island; Seth Bradford and Richard Morris Hunt, architects, 1851–52 and 1869–73; standing. The original house on this site was erected in 1851–52 for William Shepard Wetmore, a merchant who traded with China. It was designed by local builder Seth Bradford. Despite its reputation as the finest house in Newport, George Peabody Wetmore (August 2, 1846–September 11, 1921), who had inherited the property from his father, asked Richard Morris Hunt to remodel and enlarge it. Hunt transformed "Château-sur-Mer" by adding a vast billiard room and splendid staircase on the north and a dining room on the east and by replacing the old dining room with a new library on the west. Hunt's work was begun in 1869, the same year that Wetmore married Edith Keteltas. Governor of Rhode Island for two terms, Wetmore also served as a United States Senator from 1895 until 1913. Further changes were made in the house in the 1880s.

The walnut surfaces of the library were the work of noted Florentine carver Luigi Frullini. According to Winslow Ames (*Journal of the Society of Architectural Historians*, December 1970), the Wetmores may have met Frullini while on their wedding trip. He was responsible for the competently designed and carved arabesques of the frieze and at either side of the fire opening, the frequent pilasters that emphasized the height of the ceiling and an elaborate built-in writing desk. The walls of stamped and painted leather were partially obscured by paintings and Chinese chargers. Other souvenirs of the family's China contacts were displayed on the tops of the bookcases and at the sides of the desk. By the fireplace a Chinese ceramic pug stands guard by a doghouse.

193. Dining room, George P. Wetmore house. Winslow Ames explained that in the dining room Frullini was responsible for the twin sideboards, serving tables and overmantel. The sideboards, heavily ornamented with small relief busts and bunches of grapes and supporting Bohemian wine sets, were pressed so tightly against the ornate mantelpiece, festooned with drunken putti above and painted with an Italian majolica hunting scene below, that the whole became a single decorative unit that upstaged the fireplace's function. Opposite, according to Ames, the majolica was repeated in a plaque inserted in the woodcarving over the sideboard, its ceramic blue and yellows joining the walnut of the wood and the polychrome of the wall "in an extraordinary florid celebration of the hunt and of food." Despite this outburst, which continued around the room in the painted leaves, this dining room also expressed soberer thoughts. Exceptionally large (23′ × 33′ and 17′ high), it did not look crowded. The respectable family portraits matched the American Empire dining table.

191

194. Hall, William Clark house, 346 Mount Prospect Avenue, Newark, New Jersey; Halsey Wood, architect, 1879–80; standing. Trained in his father's cotton-thread business in Paisley, Scotland, Clark (1841–July 7, 1902) arrived in the United States with his brother George in 1860 and settled in Newark four years later. There the two brothers began to manufacture spool thread in a small factory on the banks of the Passaic River. By the 1880s the factory had expanded to both sides of the Passaic and employed several thousand workers. The management was praised at that time for its concern for its employees.

Clark was survived by his second wife, the former Jennie Waters, and four children, two from each of his marriages. A yachting enthusiast, he died aboard his yacht at Portland, England. During the last five years of his life, his primary address was Largs, Scotland.

Renovated after a destructive fire in 1976, the house is now known as the North Ward Educational and Cultural Center. One entered the original vestibule through brass-mounted doors of ebonized oak and proceeded from the vestibule into the main hall (22′ × 26′). On the left was the staircase; directly ahead, the dining room. Though large, the hall was relatively simple—too simple for the ornate, lumbering stairway that demands our attention. The architect and decorator seem to have consciously minimized the oak wainscoting, neutral wallpaper and simple frieze to prevent competition with the overstated stairway. The broad stairs rose slowly and heavily to a landing 8′ above the floor and from there continued around an open shaft to the top floor. Conspicuously placed on the carpet is an armchair made from the horns of Western animals and cattle, a type that was popular in the last quarter of the nineteenth century.

195. Dining room, William Clark house. Apparently, the objective of the Clarks and Wood here was a dining room that looked modern, one free of high-relief ornament, grave walls, oppressive hangings and cumbersome furniture. Although they avoided these features, they did not replace them with a coherent program. To counteract the height of the ceiling, they divided the walls into registers that were too numerous and too strongly differentiated. These attempts to minimize the impression of height resulted in a complicated wall plane that served as a poor backdrop for featured pieces. For example, the two side tables looked dwarfed and the paintings as if they had been "skied" by a revengeful exhibition hanger. Furthermore, the setting lacked consistency; the wall opposite the one illustrated contained windows of stained glass held in place by robust stone mullions. Yet the room was neither pedantic nor pretentious; it was a product of goodwill and innocence and, consequently, had a charm of its own.

196. Drawing room, William Clark house. Unlike the dining room, the drawing room was pretentious. Its dominant central feature was the ottoman, upholstered in damask and supporting a Chinese porcelain bowl on its column. The ottoman, with the complicated gasolier above, became, in effect, a static carousel that obstructed traffic and devoured space. But at least this piece of furniture was given sufficient space for its richness to be appreciated. Unfortunately, this was not true elsewhere. Fabrics competed with the mantel shelf of Mexican onyx and columns of white marble. The heavy flowered drapes to the right, selected to complement the stained-glass windows, actually weakened their effect. The glass and drapes formed a screen two feet from a heavily mullioned bay window. If this wealth of fine stuffs is too strong for twentieth-century tastes, it was acceptable to Sheldon: "The walls of the drawing-room, finished in satin-wood, and decorated in ebony and gold, are upholstered in a rich, tufted silk damask, with a dark-red border at the angles, giving a prevailing effect of a golden glow of color, to which the quiet, rich tone of the carpet is auxiliary."

194

197. Library, J. Coleman Drayton house, 374 Fifth Avenue, New York, New York; McKim, Mead and White, architects, 1882–83; demolished. Historians have not been kind to J. Coleman Drayton, focusing almost exclusively on his divorce, one of the most publicized scandals of the 1890s. In 1879 he had married Charlotte Astor. On March 18, 1892 he read in the *New York Sun* that she had run off with their next-door neighbor in Bernardsville, New Jersey. Before their divorce was settled in December 1896, New York gossips had a field day.

The Draytons moved into this house, one of the earliest urban projects of McKim, Mead and White, in 1883 but relocated in Bernardsville in 1886. Despite Sheldon's report that the library contained shelves loaded with books two and three deep, this photograph implies the room was an obligatory gesture seldom put to use. Certainly, the room was distinctively furnished. There were Beauvais tapestries of hunting scenes on all the walls, printers' marks of the sixteenth century painted within the ceiling frames of ebony, a musicians' gallery at the right fronted with a screen of Chinese latticework and a hand-carved Renaissance-style table in the center. But the suggestion of emptiness persists. Perhaps the Draytons had moved in only shortly before this photograph was taken.

198. Drawing room, John Taylor Johnston house, 8 Fifth Avenue, New York, New York; architect unknown, 1856–57; demolished. Johnston (April 8, 1820–March 24, 1893) is primarily remembered as the first president (1870–89) of New York's Metropolitan Museum of Art. Although he passed his bar examination in 1843, he acquired his wealth through the Central Railroad of New Jersey. He married Frances Colles (d. July 20, 1888) on April 15, 1850; they had four daughters and one son.

Before it was dispersed at auction in December 1876, the Johnston collection of approximately 200 oils was probably the finest in the United States. It consisted of outstanding American painters (West, Allston, Stuart, Sully, Trumbull, Cole, Homer, Church) as well as works by the popular, conservative artists of contemporary France and Germany. Johnston realized $300,000 from the auction, evidently held to meet his debts caused by the depression of 1873–77.

Johnston's drawing room had recently been redecorated by L. C. Tiffany & Associated Artists. They had created a warm environment using salmons, red, yellows and browns. Above the double doors they inserted a latticework transom that contained pieces of colored glass. Most of their effort, however, was concentrated on the mantel area where they surrounded the bevel plate mirror with smaller mirrors held by frames of leaded glass. The fire front was faced with panels of East India teakwood and tiles of Siena and colored glass. The pattern of the ceiling was applied by a palette knife while that of the wall was brushed on.

---

199. Library, Rectory, Trinity Church, 233 Clarendon Street, Boston, Massachusetts; Henry Hobson Richardson, architect, 1879–80; standing. The first rector to occupy the residence was The Right Reverend Phillips Brooks (December 13, 1835–January 23, 1893), who had been called by the parish in 1869 and under whose charge the new Trinity Church on Copley Square was built and finally consecrated in February 1877. A brilliant preacher whose liberal social and religious views were well publicized, Brooks was probably the best-known Episcopal rector in the United States.

The archway of this cozy inglenook off the first-floor library contained matching sunburst panels and was decorated above with incised hexagons. Dominating this intimate space was a simple, if not crude, fireplace composed of brick sides and slabs of brownstones that formed its shelves. On these shelves Brooks put objects and souvenirs he had received from friends or collected on his travels. This setting, then, was determined by experiences and personal choice rather than artistic rules. This was one of the rare private spaces illustrated in *Artistic Houses* on which contemporary decorative etiquette exerted little influence.

197

200

200. Drawing room, George W. Childs house, 2128 Walnut Street, Philadelphia, Pennsylvania; John McArthur, Jr., architect, 1869; destroyed by fire 1970. Though not well remembered today, Childs (May 12, 1829–February 3, 1894) was respected in the late nineteenth century as a responsible and benevolent millionaire. His story was one of the true fairy tales of American capitalism. He left school at 13, was an errand boy in a bookstore at 15 and the owner of a bookstore three years later. During the 1850s he became a partner in the publishing firm of Childs and Peterson and married his partner's daughter, Emma Bouvier Peterson. In 1864 Childs purchased the ailing *Public Ledger,* made the necessary managerial and editorial changes and confirmed the newspaper's recovery by erecting the magnificent Ledger Building in Philadelphia in 1867. Financially secure, he gave increasing attention to collecting rare books and letters, to hosting international dignitaries and to philanthropy.

In several respects this house was a modest version of A. T. Stewart's palace (nos. 1–8), completed the same year in New York. Both had a marble exterior and were studiously detailed within. When completed, both were considered foremost examples of expensive interior decoration in their respective cities. This photograph shows the drawing room from the adjoining music room. The drawing-room floor was covered with an Aubusson carpet, the wainscoting was made of amaranth wood (not a commonly used material), the walls were covered with panels of crimson satin and the ceiling was decorated in fresco with papier-mâché relief. The mantel mirror, framed in satinwood, was placed to reflect the lights of the chandelier and its Florentine glass pendants. At the end of the room was one of the world's most expensive parlor clocks (Childs owned more than 50), a medal winner at the 1867 Parisian Exposition for which Childs had paid $6000, outbidding A. T. Stewart. Nine feet high and weighing ap-

proximately two tons, the clock consisted of a 4'-high base on which stood a silver figure of a woman holding a gold pendulum in her raised hand.

201. Dining room, George W. Childs house, 401 South Bryn Mawr Avenue, Bryn Mawr, Pennsylvania; John McArthur, Jr., architect, date unknown; standing but altered. Emma and George Childs owned two additional houses. Their summer home at Long Branch, New Jersey, was next to the summer house of Ulysses S. Grant. Their summer and weekend house at Bryn Mawr was a Queen Anne design called "Wootton." Today this house serves St. Aloysius Academy. The dining room was comforting in scale, playful in its wallpaper frieze and table covering and warm in its mahogany paneling and beams—in effect, an interior suitable for the relatively relaxed summer life at a country seat.

202. Drawing room, George W. Childs house, Bryn Mawr. Compare this drawing room with the same family's city drawing room. Here the ceiling is flat and quiet, encouraging the eye to look below. Even the pale wallpaper is relatively unobtrusive and emphasizes the stronger colors of the portieres. The room has been divided into three basic registers. The first includes the carpet, throw rug, chairs and divans (of blue and crimson plush), piano, table and fire opening, and extends to the top of the butternut wainscoting. Here the colors and textures are the strongest. Above this is a less demanding though more formal register that ends at the top of the rods over the doorways and the top of the mantelpiece. Finally, there are the flat, paler upper walls and frieze. This system has been reinforced by the small size and subdued themes of the paintings. On the far wall is a watercolor of a standing dragoon and his horse by Detaille.

203

203. Office, William M. Singerly, *Philadelphia Record* Building, 917–919 Chestnut Street, Philadelphia, Pennsylvania; Willis G. Hale, architect, 1880; demolished 1932. Singerly (December 27, 1832–February 27, 1898) was publisher of the *Philadelphia Record* and owner of the Record Publishing Company on Chestnut Street. He was twice married: to Pamelia Jones in 1854 and to Mary Ryan in 1872. In addition to his publishing activities, he served as president of the Chestnut Street National Bank, the Chestnut Savings Fund and Trust Company and the Singerly Pulp and Paper Mill.

With its fine furnishings and odd assortment of "authentic" works of art, this office suite looked more like a domestic than a commercial setting, and was probably included in *Artistic Houses* for this reason. This room of the suite was approximately 20′ from side to side and also from floor to ceiling. The sides visible in this photograph were filled with cabinets lined with sea-green plush and fronted with doors and

mirrors of beveled glass. Below the cabinet on the left was a fireplace faced with Formosa marble and lined inside with Minton tiles. Opposite was a sink, also of Formosa marble. Clusters of turned columns accented the cabinets and framed the entranceway. The furniture was of wicker or black walnut with maroon leather. The simplified gasolier with two globes held an awkwardly attached electric wire that ran from the floor through the table lamp to bare bulbs. Silver, gold and turquoise blue were the colors chosen for this space. The frieze near the top of the room showed birds of paradise in ornate panels.

In this man's world of late nineteenth-century American capitalism, most of the fine art glorified women. Right of center is a small marble, *The Diver*, by Odoardo Tabbacchi (1831–1905); the bronze statuette of a woman dancing with bells next to the entranceway is unidentified.

SELECTED BIBLIOGRAPHY

This bibliography is primarily concerned with the categories of wealth and art. Though essential to our research, we have not included references to the following: biographical dictionaries; obituaries; genealogies; city, county and regional histories; city directories and newspaper articles.

BOOKS, PAMPHLETS AND DISSERTATIONS

Amory, Cleveland, *The Proper Bostonians*, New York, 1947.

Andrews, Wayne, *The Vanderbilt Legend*, New York, 1941.

Avery, Samuel P., *The Diaries, Eighteen Hundred and Seventy-One to Eighteen Hundred and Eighty-Two, of Samuel P. Avery, Art Dealer*, New York, 1979.

Baker, Paul R., *Richard Morris Hunt*, Cambridge, 1980.

Baltzell, Edward Digby, *Philadelphia Gentlemen*, Glencoe, Illinois, 1958.

Banham, Reyner, *The Architecture of the Well-Tempered Environment*, Chicago, 1969.

Benjamin, S. G. W., *Art in America*, New York, 1880.

Bigelow, John, *The Life of Samuel J. Tilden* (2 vols.), New York, 1895.

Bishop, Robert, and Coblentz, Patricia, *The World of Antiques, Art, and Architecture in Victorian America*, New York, 1979.

Brunner, Arnold, and Tyron, Thomas, *Interior Decoration*, New York, 1887.

Bunting, Bainbridge, *Houses of Boston's Back Bay*, Cambridge, 1967.

Burt, Nathaniel, *Palaces for the People*, Boston, 1977.

Calhoun, Arthur W., *A Social History of the American Family*, New York, 1945.

Canfield, Cass, *The Incredible Pierpont Morgan*, New York, 1974.

Carter, Morris, *Isabella Stewart Gardner and Fenway Court*, Boston, 1925.

Churchill, Allen, *The Splendor Seekers*, New York, 1974.

Clark, Robert Judson (ed.), *The Arts and Crafts Movement in America: 1876–1916*, Princeton, 1972.

Clews, Henry, *Twenty-Eight Years in Wall Street*, New York, 1888.

Coleman, Oliver, *Successful Houses*, Chicago, 1899.

Cook, Clarence, *Art and Artists of Our Time* (3 vols.), New York, 1888.

——, *The House Beautiful*, New York, 1878.

——, *What Shall We Do with Our Walls?*, New York, 1881.

Cowles, Virginia, *The Astors*, New York, 1979.

Craven, Wayne, *Sculpture in America*, New York, 1968.

Crawford, Mary Caroline, *Famous Families of Massachusetts* (2 vols.), Boston, 1930.

Croffut, W. A., *The Vanderbilts and the Story of Their Fortune*, Chicago, 1886.

Davidson, Marshall B., *Three Centuries of American Antiques*, New York, 1979.

De Kay, Charles, *The Art Work of Louis C. Tiffany*, Garden City, 1914.

Drury, John, *Old Chicago Houses*, Chicago, 1941.

Eliot, Elizabeth, *Heiresses and Coronets*, New York, 1959.

Exman, Eugene, *The Brothers Harper*, New York, 1965.

Garmey, Stephen, *Gramercy Park*, New York, 1984.

Gibson, Louis Henry, *Convenient Houses*, New York, 1889.

Goode, James M., *Capital Losses*, Washington, D.C., 1979.

Green, Harvey, and Perry, Mary E., *The Light of the Home*, New York, 1983.

Hall, Henry (ed.), *America's Successful Men of Affairs* (2 vols.), New York, 1895–96.

Harrison, Constance Cary, *Woman's Handiwork in Modern Homes*, New York, 1881.

Hatch, Alden, *The Wadsworths of the Genesee*, New York, 1959.

Henderson, Helen W., *The Pennsylvania Academy of the Fine Arts*, Boston, 1911.

Holden, Wheaton Arnold, "Robert Swain Peabody of Peabody and Stearns in Boston: The Early Years (1870–1886)," Ph.D. dissertation, Boston University, Boston, 1969.

Holly, H. Hudson, *Modern Dwellings in Town and Country*, New York, 1878.

Howe, Winifred E., *A History of the Metropolitan Museum of Art*, Vol. 1, New York, 1913.

Key, Jack D., *William Alexander Hammond, M.D.*, Rochester, Minnesota, 1979.

Koch, Robert, *Louis C. Tiffany's Art Glass*, New York, 1977.

——, *Louis Comfort Tiffany: Rebel in Glass*, New York, 1964.

Koehler, S. R., *The United States Art Directory and Year-Book* (2 vols.), New York, 1882–84.

Kohler, Sue, and Carson, Jeffrey R., *Sixteenth Street Architecture*, Vol. 1, Washington, D.C., 1978.

Lancaster, Clay, *The Japanese Influence in America*, New York, 1963.

Langford, Laura Holloway, *Famous American Fortunes and the Men Who Have Made Them*, Philadelphia, 1885.

Lewis, Arnold, *American Country Houses of the Gilded Age: Sheldon's "Artistic Country-Seats,"* New York, 1982.

Lowe, David, *Chicago Interiors*, Chicago, 1979.

Lucas, George A., *The Diary of George A. Lucas: An American Art Agent in Paris, 1857–1909*, Princeton, 1979.

Lynes, Russell, *The Domesticated Americans*, New York, 1963.

Maass, John, *The Victorian Home in America*, New York, 1972.

Martin, Sidney Walter, *Florida's Flagler*, Athens, Georgia, 1949.

Miller, Edgar G., Jr., *American Antique Furniture* (2 vols.), New York, 1966.

Montgomery, Walter (ed.), *American Art and American Art Collections* (2 vols.), New York, 1978.

Myers, Gustavus, *History of the Great American Fortunes* (3 vols.), Chicago, 1911.

Ochsner, Jeffrey Karl, *H. H. Richardson: Complete Architectural Works*, Cambridge, 1982.

Phillips, David Graham, *The Reign of Gilt*, New York, 1905.

Roth, Leland M., *The Architecture of McKim, Mead & White, 1870–1920: A Building List*, New York, 1978.

——, *McKim, Mead & White, Architects*, New York, 1983.

Russell, William Ingraham, *The Romance and Tragedy of a Widely Known Business Man of New York*, Baltimore, 1922.

Saisselin, Rémy G., *The Bourgeois and the Bibelot*, New Brunswick, New Jersey, 1984.

Satterlee, Herbert L., *J. Pierpont Morgan*, New York, 1939.

Schlesinger, Arthur M., *Learning How to Behave*, New York, 1946.

Seale, William, *Recreating the Historic House Interior*, Nashville, 1979.

——, *The Tasteful Interlude: American Interiors Through the Camera's Eye, 1860 to 1917*, New York, 1975.

Sherwood, Mary Elizabeth Wilson, *Manners and Social Usages*, New York, 1884.

Shinn, Earl [Edward Strahan] (ed.), *The Art Treasures of America* (3 vols.), Philadelphia, 1879–82.

Shinn, Earl [Edward Strahan], *Mr. Vanderbilt's House and Collection* (4 vols.), Boston, 1883–84.

Shopsin, William C., and Broderick, Mosette Glaser, *The Villard Houses*, New York, 1980.

Short Hills Club: A Centennial History, 1875–1975, Short Hills, New Jersey, 1975.

Simon, John Y. (ed.), *The Personal Memoirs of Julia Dent Grant*, New York, 1975.

Smith, Eugenia Brandenburger, "Rhode Island Resort Architecture by McKim, Mead & White," M.A. thesis, University of Wisconsin, Madison, 1964.

Spofford, Harriet Prescott, *Art Decoration Applied to Furniture*, New York, 1878.

Sterling, Charles, and Salinger, Margaretta M., *French Paintings: A Catalogue of the Collections of the Metropolitan Museum of Art*, Vol. 2, Greenwich, 1966.

Tharp, Louise Hall, *Mrs. Jack*, Boston, 1965.

Titled Americans, New York, 1890.

Van Rensselaer, Mariana Griswold, *Henry Hobson Richardson and His Works*, New York, 1969.

Weinberg, H. Barbara, *The Decorative Work of John La Farge*, New York, 1977.

Weisberg, Gabriel P., *The Realist Tradition: French Painting and Drawing, 1830–1900*, Bloomington, Indiana, 1980.

Wharton, Edith, and Codman, Ogden, Jr., *The Decoration of Houses*, New York, 1902.

Whitehill, Walter Muir, *Museum of Fine Arts, Boston* (2 vols.), Cambridge, 1970.

Wilson, Richard Guy, "Charles F. McKim and the Development of the American Renaissance," Ph.D. dissertation, University of Michigan, Ann Arbor, 1972.

——; Pilgrim, Dianne H; and Murray, Richard N., *The American Renaissance*, New York, 1979.

Young, John H., *Our Deportment*, Detroit, 1881.

ARTICLES

"American Interiors," *American Architect and Building News*, 16 (Aug. 9, 1884), 64–66.

Ames, Winslow, "The Transformation of Château-sur-Mer," *Journal of the Society of Architectural Historians*, 29 (Dec. 1970), 291–306.

"Art and Art-Life in New York," *Lippincott's Magazine*, 29 (June 1882), 597–605.

"The Art of Furnishing," *Art Amateur*, 3 (June 1880), 12–14.

"Beauty Versus Bric-À-Brac," *Lippincott's Magazine*, 31 (Feb. 1883), 202–206.

Bell, A. N., and Trowbridge, W. P., "Rival Systems of Heating," *North American Review*, 138 (Feb. 1884), 191–203.

Blake, Channing, "Stanford White's New York City Interiors," *Antiques*, 102 (Dec. 1972), 1060–1067.

Boime, Albert, "America's Purchasing Power and the Evolution of European Art in the Late Nineteenth Century," in *International Congress of Art History Proceedings*, Bologna, 1978, 123–139.

——, "Les magnats américains à la conquête de l'art français," *L'histoire*, 44 (Apr. 1982), 38–48.

Broderick, Mosette Glaser, "Nineteenth Century Decorating Studios in New York City," *Oculus*, 45 (Feb. 1984), 4–5, 12–13.

Bronner, Simon J., "Manner Books and Suburban Houses," *Winterthur Portfolio*, 18 (Spring 1983), 61–68.

Cantor, Jay, "A Monument of Trade: A. T. Stewart and the Rise of the Millionaire's Mansion in New York," *Winterthur Portfolio*, 10 (1975), 165–197.

"Ceiling and Wall Paper," *Art Amateur*, 3 (Sept. 1880), 84–85.

Cicerone, "Private Galleries: Collection of the Estate of Alexander Turney Stewart," *Art Amateur*, 1 (July 1879), 29–30; (Nov. 1879), 116–118.

Cleveland, Paul R., "The Millionaires of New York," *Cosmopolitan*, 5 (Sept. 1888), 385–398; (Oct. 1888), 521–528.

"The Colman and Tiffany Wall-Papers," *Art Amateur*, 3 (June 1880), 12.

Cook, Clarence, "Architecture in America," *North American Review*, 135 (Sept. 1882), 243–252.

Croly, Herbert, "Rich Men and Their Houses," *Architectural Record*, 12 (May 1902), 27–32.

The Editor, "The Progress of Painting in America," *North American Review*, 124 (May 1877), 451–464.

Faude, Wilson H., "Associated Artists and the American Renaissance in the Decorative Arts," *Winterthur Portfolio*, 10 (1975), 101–130.

Godkin, E. L. "The Expenditure of Rich Men," *Scribner's Magazine*, 20 (Oct. 1896), 495–501.

Harris, Neil, "The Gilded Age Revisited: Boston and the Museum Movement," *American Quarterly*, 14 (Fall 1962), 545–566.

Harrison, Constance Cary, "Some Works of the 'Associated Artists,'" *Harper's New Monthly Magazine*, 69 (Aug. 1884), 343–351.

Hart, Charles Henry, "The Public and Private Collections of the United States," *American Art Review*, I (Apr. 1880), 231–235.

Jones, Shirley, "The Condé Family and 'Mon Repos,'" *Journal of the Oswego County Historical Society*, (1974–75), 55–66.

June, Jenny, "The Art of Dinner-Giving," *Cosmopolitan*, 3 (Mar. 1887), 63–66.

Landy, Jacob, "The Domestic Architecture of the Robber Barons in New York City," *Marsyas*, 5 (1947–49), 63–85.

Lockwood, Belva A., "The Present Phase of the Woman Question," *Cosmopolitan*, 5 (Oct. 1888), 467–470.

McClaugherty, Martha Crabill, "Household Art," *Winterthur Portfolio*, 18 (Spring 1983), 1–26.

Mitchell, Donald G., "From-Lobby-to-Peak," *Our Continent*, I (Feb. 15, 1882), 5; (Feb. 22), 21; (March 1), 37; (March 15), 69; (March 22), 85; (March 29), 101; (Apr. 5), 117–118; (Apr. 12), 132; (Apr. 19), 148; (May 3), 185.

Oakey, A. F., "A Trial Balance of Decoration," *Harper's New Monthly Magazine*, 64 (Apr. 1882), 734–740.

Oswald, Felix L., "Healthy Homes," *Lippincott's Magazine*, 33 (March 1884), 283–289; 34 (July 1884), 97–103.

"Our Local Art Treasures," *Art and Music*, 1 (March 1882), 189–197; (Apr. 1882), 221–228.

"Private Galleries: Collection of Ex-Judge Henry Hilton," *Art Amateur*, 2 (Jan. 1880), 31 and 32.

Schuyler, Montgomery, "Recent Building in New York," *Harper's New Monthly Magazine*, 67 (Sept. 1883), 557–578.

Sherwood, M. E. W., "Certain New York Houses," *Harper's New Monthly Magazine*, 65 (Oct. 1882), 680–690.

Smith-Rosenberg, Carroll, "The Female World of Love and Ritual: Relations between Women in Nineteenth-Century America," *Signs*, 1 (Autumn 1975), 1–29.

Stone, May N., "The Plumbing Paradox," *Winterthur Portfolio*, 14 (Autumn 1979), 283–309.

Van Rensselaer, Mariana Griswold, "Client and Architect," *North American Review*, 151 (Sept. 1890), 319–328.

——, "Decorative Art and Its Dogmas," *Lippincott's Magazine*, 25 (Feb. 1880), 213–20; (March 1880), 342–351.

——, "The Development of American Homes," *Forum*, 12 (Jan. 1892), 667–676.

——, "The New York Art Season," *Atlantic Monthly*, 48 (Aug. 1881), 193–202.

——, "Recent Architecture in America: V, VI, City Dwellings," *Century Magazine*, 31 (Feb. 1886), 548–558; (March 1886), 677–687.

"The Villard Houses," *Architectural Record*, 169 (Feb. 1981), 65–68.

P. B. W., "A Millionaire's Architectural Investment," *American Architect and Building News*, 1 (May 6, 1876), 147–149.

Waring, George E., Jr., "The Principles and Practice of House-Drainage," *Century Magazine*, 29 (Nov. 1884), 45–51; (Dec. 1884), 255–267.

Wingate, Charles F., "The Unsanitary Homes of the Rich," *North American Review*, 137 (Aug. 1883), 172–184.